A CALL TO
REMEMBER

Follow Your Heart,
Change the World

First published by O Books, 2008
O Books is an imprint of John Hunt Publishing Ltd., The Bothy, Deershot Lodge, Park Lane, Ropley,
Hants, SO24 0BE, UK
office1@o-books.net
www.o-books.net

Distribution in:

UK and Europe
Orca Book Services
orders@orcabookservices.co.uk
Tel: 01202 665432 Fax: 01202 666219
Int. code (44)

USA and Canada
NBN
custserv@nbnbooks.com
Tel: 1 800 462 6420 Fax: 1 800 338 4550

Australia and New Zealand
Brumby Books
sales@brumbybooks.com.au
Tel: 61 3 9761 5535 Fax: 61 3 9761 7095

Far East (offices in Singapore, Thailand,
Hong Kong, Taiwan)
Pansing Distribution Pte Ltd
kemal@pansing.com
Tel: 65 6319 9939 Fax: 65 6462 5761

South Africa
Alternative Books
altbook@peterhyde.co.za
Tel: 021 555 4027 Fax: 021 447 1430

Text copyright Carol Fitzpatrick 2008

Design: Stuart Davies
Cover photograph: Duncan Walker

ISBN: 978 1 84694 140 5

A CIP catalogue record for this book is available
from the British Library.

Printed in the US by Maple Vail

For information on promotions, bulk purchases, premiums,
educational use, please contact the relevant distributor.
More about the author:
www.carolfitzpatrick.com & www.planetaryawakening.org

O Books operates a distinctive and ethical publishing philosophy in all areas
of its business, from its global network of authors to production and
worldwide distribution.
No trees were cut down to print this particular book. The paper is 100%
recycled, with 50% of that being post-consumer. It's processed chlorine-
free, and has no fibre from ancient or endangered forests. This production
method on this print run saved approximately thirteen trees, 4,000 gallons
of water, 600 pounds of solid waste, 990 pounds of greenhouse gases and 8
million BTU of energy. On its publication a donation for planting a tree was
sent to The Woodland Trust

A CALL TO REMEMBER

Follow Your Heart,
Change the World

*A sacred call to wake-up and
reclaim your power*

Carol Fitzpatrick

BOOKS

Winchester, UK
Washington, USA

CONTENTS

5. Changing the Way Souls Learn

6. The Quickening of Light Draws Near

Part 3: The Big Shift
7. Humanity's Probable Future

8. Transforming Duality

ABOUT THE WORK

"A Call to Remember provides the reader with a fabulous guide to this magical period that we have entered into as well as explanations and analogies of how, through personal responsibility and the power of intention, each one of us contributes to creating a favorable and preferred outcome on this planet that we call home. Carol Fitzpatrick provides a very enlightened and guided tour of our global shift in consciousness...a must read."

Malia Scanlan, Global Designs, LLC

"A Call to Remember is for everyone who wants to live an authentic life and manifest in every moment. Carol Fitzpatrick has laid it out for us step-by-step with a simple and inspirational message. Her words remind us of the connections we sensed in our hearts."

Martha Randolph Carr, author of *A Place to Call Home*

"Carol Fitzpatrick is at the cutting edge of human consciousness evolution. She offers clear, positive, and useful information and insights of practical relevance both for individual development and societal change."

Mary Jane Banks, editor, Washington, DC

"I have felt unbelievably blessed to have Carol in my life. She is a wholly seer, capable of guiding and uplifting us into our highest expression of joy, helping us to maintain deep connection to Source. In a world that often looks to be doing otherwise, she speaks for the Real at the heart of All. My own capacity for joy and for spiritual seeing has opened significantly since working with Carol- she is a national treasure!"

Maureen Riley, Chicago, Illinois

"Carol has tremendous gifts, as a psychic, seer, healer, and teacher. Lots of people claim to be spiritual masters of one sort or another, but few have achieved her level. Her path to understand and cultivate her gifts was not an easy one, which is even more impressive. What makes Carol truly special is her dedication to use her gifts to help others achieve their highest self-expression. With Carol's help, "Follow Your Heart" changes from a meaningless cliché into a clear sense of direction about your path and purpose, as an individual and as a drop in the Ocean of Unity."

Keith Harrington, East Meets West Center, Vienna, Virginia

"Carol Fitzpatrick has "wowed" me over and over again with her intuition, compassion, and connection to Spirit during private sessions and workshops with her. She is a clear messenger and the most accurate clairvoyant I have ever been to in 35 years. She has touched my life and catapulted me toward my highest expression! For this I will be eternally grateful"

Robyn Hanna, Reston, Virginia

"Carol Fitzpatrick has extraordinary gifts that she shares for the benefit of humankind. She dwells with the highest energies and bridges the worlds in a unique and profound way. She raises my vibration and gives wings to my world with the wisdom she transmits from the beyond. She brings peace and great joy to my heart."

Donna Gary, Washington, DC

For my brothers and sisters of the light;
to remind them that all is well.

To Mark Torgeson;
for all that you bring to my life.

ACKNOWLEDGEMENTS

It goes without saying that this book would not have become a reality without the support and participation of my brothers and sisters of the Light. Over the years, we have played, laughed, and cried together, but most importantly, we have learned how to open our hearts and trust the unseen force of light that guides us in this ever unfolding grand adventure called life.

I have wanted to share with you, a more complete picture; of how love and joyousness is playing such a pivotal role in shifting global consciousness, for quite some time. The shear power that you are calling forth, as a collective consciousness, is impossible to fully capture in words, but here it is. Your willingness to trust the collaborative process that we have been, and continue to move through (you, me and the Guides as our master teachers), seems inadequate to describe my deep and abiding love and appreciation for who you are.

I do not consider this book a single act of one person but a collective effort. Through the wisdom that can only be gleaned from walking one's talk, your voice has been nested into the teachings and transformational tools right here along with so many others. Through the medium of this book, may your own unique contribution be heard ever so gently, but quite loudly, by the hearts and minds of light beings everywhere.

The journey to share always happens when one person hears the call to serve, then opens to receive. In my life, it was a chance meeting of Lisa Marks, the founder of Inner Peace in Richmond, VA. I had just written and self-published my first book, *Fear Not My Child*, and was seeking out speaking opportunities. As I quickly learned, it only takes one single act of kindness for one's entire world to open up. Lisa served as that link for me. She gave the book to Jane Hayden, owner of The

Alchemist, a spiritually focused bookstore also in Richmond. Jane graciously invited me to speak.

I'll never forget the ride down that first evening, and my anticipation of looking into the faces of those who were coming to hear the message. My heart was bursting with joy! I felt like I was going to meet my soul family, and I was. The excitement that evening was palpable. That first experience — and Jane's unwavering support for the work thereafter — set into motion a wave of spiritual activism that has transformed my call to serve into a deep and rich journey into the knowing of my own heart.

From that first opening, I have learned that without the mutual support of others, this kind of cutting edge message would never see the light of day. It takes great courage to champion someone whose message is outside the norm. In particular, I owe a debt of gratitude to Jane, Mary Ruth Van Landingham, of Terra Christa in Vienna, Virginia, Kya [Shawn) Supers], director of the Wise Women Foundation, and so many others who have since stepped forward.

From my eight years of working on the national level, I learned a lot about working with leaders around issues of neighborhood safety. But that schooling was no match to the power of experiencing a true grassroots movement. I have had the privilege of serving with a plethora of new paradigm leaders who, from the very beginning, understood the work, and invited me into their homes and places of business or worship without reservation. In some cases they went against religious, political or work doctrine and simply followed their heart. To Rev. Polly, Laura Fox, JoAnn Light and Karen Madison, Sandy Kalaora, Hannifah, Ann Puryear, Kevin Walters, Karen Special, Lynn Allen, Amy Storm, Terri Clokey, Laura Jackson, and so many others, thank you.

Visionaries Janna Moore, Krystal Fenn, Pat Hill, Maureen Riley, and Keith Harrington all jumped in to help set the

Community Activation events into motion. Without their invitation and involvement, the profound global healing, a few of which are shared in this book, would not have become a reality.

The events and a plethora of experiences provided the contents for this book, yet when it came to offering continued encouragement and support, I owe a very special note of thanks to friends and family who held the space for me to write the story in my own unique way. They offered a blanket of unconditional love that kept me focused on my inner voice regardless of what advice was coming from the outside. To Mark, my husband and partner in life, and to daughter and son, Danielle and James, you are my personal joy manifested. To Wendy, Christine, and Mikaela, thank you for being a part of my life and offering me the encouragement to maintain my focus. To Chris Thompson, thank you for your friendship and for keeping me physically aligned with the light, and to Dr. Sheron Marquina for bringing the body back to health. A big hug to you, Martha, for helping me to maneuver through the tangled woods of the book publishing industry and for your expert editing skills, but most importantly, for just being you. And to Malia Scanlan for doing the first official critique of the final manuscript. I owe a special note of thanks to John Hunt, publisher of O-Books, for saying *yes* to oneness consciousness, and for including me in his vision.

Dance, my heart! Dance today with joy.
The strains of love fill the days and the night with music,
and the world is
Listening to its melodies:
Mad with joy, life and death dance to the rhythm of this
music. The hills and
the sea and the earth dance.
The world of many dances in laughter and tears.
Why put on the robe of the monk, and live aloof from the
world in lonely pride?
Behold! My heart dances in the delight of a hundred arts;
and the Creators are
well pleased.

Kabir (1440?-1518)
One Hundred Poems of Kabir

NOTE

The examples of real-life scenarios used in *A Call to Remember* have come from the many specific interactions I have had through my work with individuals and groups. The people and circumstances that I use to illustrate a particular point have been drawn from memory and serve as a reference to clarify the teachings. Examples have been used from recorded group sessions, written correspondence, workshops and presentations, and submissions from those who have graciously given me permission to share their experiences. Protecting the privacy of these individuals is paramount. Therefore, when using examples to illustrate a larger point, I have altered the identifying details without losing the focus of the teaching, or have combined similar cases into one.

On another more stylistic note, when an example calls for an expression of either masculine or feminine, I have chosen to use the feminine form of she. I have also written the majority of the enclosed passages with the intention of speaking to my fellow brothers and sisters of the light. Therefore, I have chosen to use the familiar form of we or us with the exception of when I am directing my comments directly to you, the reader, for added clarity.

Higher Knowledge

There are many ways that we gain higher knowledge. Some people rely on inspiration, others inner guidance, revelation, or vision. Yet others gain wisdom that comes about from observation. The teachings and examples that I am about to share with you have been gained from my direct experience with the Divine. I am using the word Divine as something unseen but no less real than any commonly accepted physical property or reality. The wisdom that comes from such a direct experience might also be described as mystical because it is so out of the ordinary that it cannot be explained through logic. It's the kind of experience that comes from surrendering to an unseen force that guides me mostly through feeling but also through visions and words. This force is like a river of high vibration that I step into. The flow of the force feels like joyousness, boundless joy that makes me chuckle with delight. At the same time, it also brings me a deep sense of peace — a peace that can only be described as inner stillness.

Similarly, the catch-phrase from the 1960's TV series, Star Trek, "Beam me up Scottie," and the visual picture of the space travelers getting beamed back to their mother ship is a good description of how I feel when the light begins to envelop me. As I step inside that channel of light, every atom in my body vibrates at an ultra high intensity. And at once, I am filled with an amplified sense of well-being beyond measure. By doing so, I am energetically transported through an inner doorway that opens between the two worlds (physical and non-physical). It takes me from a few nanoseconds to a few minutes to adjust and integrate the higher vibration now in the body. Once I am through the inner passageway, I am aware that what keeps me in that state is my ability to hold my focus to the stillness of what guides me. By doing so, I am able to travel into other dimensions or galaxies of light with the help of my non-physical teachers, the Guides.

The physical body is pure vibration, which serves as a kind of human tuning fork. Sometimes when I connect with the higher vibratory realms, the energy shift or connection is very gentle. At other times it feels like a frenetic lightning bolt coursing through the density of my bones. As I discern what or with whom I am to allow into my sphere of influence, I have come to sense vibration down to its most subtle form. I continually feel the nature of the vibratory pattern that I am connecting with and either accept or reject the light into my body according to what I feel as my highest expression. It's my life, my body and my learning, so *anything* that I allow is purely for furthering my highest expression, which leads me to Truth.

Truth, as a vibration, is smooth as silk. The very essence of Truth is pure stillness but inside the stillness is sometimes radical, lightening speed movement. That's the beauty and magic of Truth. No need to slow down, there's nothing to hold Truth back because there is no distortion in pure Truth. Any distortion feels discordant, out of alignment with the stillness of Truth.

I have learned that the practice of discernment is the only way to know the finer nuances of Truth, and one that I continually refine down to the subtlest of oscillation. Needless to say, with no one around to act as a mentor, it has taken me years to get to know and to adjust to all kinds of vibration. Through continued exploration, I am still discovering that the spectrum of light is infinite and this way of learning is too.

The question asked most often is how can I learn this way of knowing? My answer is that it's there for everyone if you are willing to listen. Listening is the key. We have forgotten how to listen, how to go deep inside and listen to our heart, to set the mind aside and to reside fully in the knowing of what becomes us. Our outer world offers us a small ration of life compared to what can be found inside the stillness.

When we do listen, we discover a very different world. This world takes some getting used to because it's not structured like our physical world. When we simply allow, we discover an entirely different landscape, and a different way of navigating, of communicating with others. Yes, others. Just like the explorers who have gone before us those courageous explorers who discovered that the world was not flat but round, we too, are beginning to accept new ideas, new realities. With the help of our scientific community, philosophers and new paradigm leaders, and others who are willing to speak their truth, more of us are beginning to accept the idea that there just might be life on other planets, in other star systems, and in distant galaxies.

In my work, I regularly communicate with light beings from other worlds. They do not have the same kind of physical bodies that we do but they are just as real as we are and have a lot to share. They are not souls who have passed over, although, as much as I prefer to hang out in the higher realms, I do occasionally communicate with a select few on the other side (some call it heaven or after-life depending on their school of thought or belief).

There are those who wish to share their knowledge and provide us with guidance about our world from their perspective. Many have lived in this reality eons ago, or have created realities, much like earth in other galaxies of light. Some are what many of us call angels and masters: light beings who are here to help humanity make better choices. In our physical reality, we might have difficulty understanding someone who does not speak our native language. It's the same with beings from other star cultures—nonphysical beings that reside in the higher spectrums of light.

Interstellar language bases come from a variety of inter-galactic star cultures and angelic kingdoms. Non-physical beings speak to me in their native language, and if I have not already asked for a guide to do the translating for me, it takes a quick adjustment in vibration to gain the understanding in my language base and vocabulary range. If a stellar language is unfamiliar to me, I have learned to ask for a translator. If you can imagine all the languages on earth being spoken at the same time, you can begin to get a sense of what I sometimes experience. One might be multi-lingual but not be able to grasp the exact language when heard in a sea of other sounds.

There are so many differences in not only communication patterns, but also dimensional realities that it always amazes me that the translation takes place at all, but pictures really are worth a thousand words. Sometimes to aid in my ability to relay a particular message to others, the Guides will quickly provide me with a feeling or perhaps a mental picture of their world so that I can better understand how to explain where they are coming from. Since I have seen and been in so many different dimensions by now, I have learned how to more quickly adjust, through feeling, as I am being shown these mental pictures. Whether I am writing or speaking, the process is essentially the same.

Sometimes the Guides will show me a vision to convey a deeper understanding of a life situation that I am asking about. The use of a simple metaphor provides an easy way to get across very complex ideas and concepts. The Self-Inquiry section has some of the more common metaphors that the guides have relayed to me in answers to questions that have been posed on a variety of topics. They may apply to your life situation much the same way they did for others.

Those who can see the more subtle energies have told me that, while I am inside the channel, all my chakras (the body's seven major energy centers) light up as a solid core of iridescent white. In addition, some have seen small sparks of multi-colored lights, like miniature sparklers, moving in and around my throat, head and heart. I experience these small flashes as high vibrational light beings with great intelligence who are the pure essence of joyousness. Sometimes they are represented by every shape and color imaginable or show up as a visual representation of Archangels, Ascended Masters, or fairy-like beings called Devas (Devas are the overseers of the fairies who keep Mother Nature in balance). Higher beings can transform into any form that makes us feel comfortable in their effort to help us understand the multi-dimensional aspects of who we are.

Once I have made the connection that best suits me, and I'm fully immersed in the opened channel, the intelligence comes in through this flow. The streaming of light is always accompanied by a profound sense of timelessness. I have since learned that what I am doing is actually stepping into the higher dimensions while also keeping enough of myself in third-dimensional reality to maintain a physical presence. Many of us do this all the time—float in and out of third dimensional reality. Some experience it as daydreaming, others by simply leaving the body while they go off to travel, only to return refreshed and ready to tackle that long perceived problem that no longer bothers them.

No matter how I first connect, the vibration is always brimming with joy, especially when the Elohim are present. These are the beings of light that are here to help bring joy to the planet. These grand beings are actually mentioned in the Old Testament, by name, as being sent by God to serve as a reminder to humankind that we are light beings in a physical body.

Another way that I access higher knowledge is by experiencing the vibration without any communication from other beings. Over time, the Guides have shown me how to access higher knowledge by following the vibrational lines (much like the electro-magnetic ley lines of the earth) that are created by the voice. The very nature of the voice is vibration. Therefore, speech patterns are strands of knowledge all strung together. The rhythm, cadence and inflection of the voice form energy patterns that can easily be followed from beginning to end. When the vibration of the spoken word is combined with intention, you can see, hear and feel a person's entire history, present moment and projected future emerging. But the grid doesn't have to be accessed by human sound.

Whatever is connected to that sound is all there. Everything that a person has thought or experienced is wrapped up in the vibrational quality of the speaking of a single name or question. Apply this concept to group creations or entire creation cycles and you can go just about anywhere by following the energy patterns along the grid — the grid comprises magnetic grid lines which connect everything to everyone — to find potential outcomes based on any present moment reality creation. I regularly teach this skill-set to others so I know it is not unique to me. It just takes practice.

This same concept can be applied to music. I have experienced high vibrational frequencies through the intentionally created music by my husband, Mark Torgeson. He is a world-class concert pianist, but more importantly, a healer, who uses his musical gifts to tune into people just like I do. The information that comes through his music is astounding, and only magnifies my ability to see into the higher dimensions. Since we often co-facilitate workshops, I have been in the position to witness others who have had similar experiences with his music. Reactions range from spontaneous emotional releases or deep calm after an intense reaction to something disturbing, or perhaps heightened mental clarity. But most experience intense states of joy.

There are as many ways to gain access to higher knowledge, as we are open to receive. All it takes is a willingness to be open and a constant vigilance to discern what is one's highest expression; in other words, what is Truth. I maintain that in just a few years, the gift that a small percentage of the world's population currently enjoys will become a common day occurrence.

THE GRID

The grid is a magical part of our earthly existence. When we really tune in, we can realize the power and force of the individual to affect vast global change because we are all connected. We, truly, are all one.

There are actually seven grids that govern the sector of the galaxy that includes earth, but I am referring here to the grid of humanity. Within this grid are 32 very strong light centers, energetic vortexes or very focused, high vibrational centers, like energetic solar flares but of the earthbound variety. These centers serve as beacons for others and are integral to the magnetic ley lines that animals instinctually follow to get from point A to B. As more and more people begin to exponentially open, these power spots will be key to igniting, or raising the vibration of the grid. Dramatic awakenings of entire earth populations will serve to step up the vibration of the whole, and the grid is what is necessary to make that a reality. As more of us open our hearts, the entire grid shifts because it is one luminous, organic intelligent field. An inter-connected highway, that moves, transforms and heals.

Whether I am called to speak or write in a higher state of consciousness, once I go deep into the stillness, my inner world transforms into an energetic landscape that is vast in its feeling of oneness. Through feeling, sensing and seeing, I am connecting to the grid, which I experience as a multi-dimensional web. Some have called it the matrix. Whatever the chosen name, I navigate the grid by following the energetic lines that are revealed as I intend my desire to know or to see a particular aspect of the universe.

The Guides have shown me vast worlds and universes of light not fully present in the physical dimensions that we understand as earth. These other realms of light are accessed by aligning with the true nature of time. Time, contrary to our forced way of relating to life, is not a measured, linear sequence of events but a place, or a dimension that we can go to at will. I'll be talking more about the true nature of time later because it holds an essential key to transforming our future, which leads me to this next piece.

The horizontal lines within the grid, depending upon the world in which I am exploring, require me to let go of my orientation to up/down, right/left and to simply trust what I am receiving.

By letting go of the mind's way of seeing, I experience other worlds, and other galaxies of light as a kaleidoscope of sight, sound, color and sensation, which is what brings me to the very notion of prophecy. Once I learned to let go of my physical third-dimensional orientation and experience other worlds, other light beings, I reoriented my way of seeing myself in this newly expanded world. By doing so, I realized that everything is pure vibration—people, dogs, cats, air, water, trees, cars, thoughts, particles, beams, rays—everything. Vibration is in constant motion, which is what makes the grid so dynamic and changing.

With this experience came the knowing that we are as much a part of the grid as any being of light, any other form of consciousness and it did not come about by blind-faith but from living in the physical. What makes life so exciting, once we gain the understanding that everything is inter-connected, is our power to create, not by doing but through the power of intention.

Knowing that the grid is subject to our intention, the primary purpose of this book is to teach you how to transform or transcend any lower vibration that holds you away from realizing your freedom. My purpose is to help you transform and become your truest self.

The power of love activates changes and transforms the grid. As we allow more love to flow through our physical creations we further ignite the grid with light. Love transforms everything while joy is the fuel that allows love to flow. Peace is then the net result of bringing the body, mind and spirit back into balance. Our light is amplified when we adjoin with other light beings that are also living joyously and that is where real freedom is fully realized.

When it comes to knowing, I have discovered that there are no new ideas in the grid, just an infinite pool of higher knowledge that is accessible to everyone. As we set our sights on what we so desire, the answer to any given question usually reveals itself in a variety of ways.

Just as our physical world is a very big place, many of us choose to settle into a very specific area or focus for learning. We find a spot in our life that makes us feel comfortable then we decide to establish a home base for our future explorations. Our orientation to this way of learning can be likened to someone who loves the ballet but also holds an appreciation for square dancing. Chances are you're likely to focus most of your attention on the classical arts, but this does not mean that you don't also appreciate the Appalachian-styled dancing and its accompanying music. It's the same line of logic when it comes to the grid: our souls are aligned with a particular bandwidth of light. If the bulk of our focus has been in the field of science, then, as we open to learn more, we are most likely to focus our energy and inner questing within areas that support and expand our awareness of all things scientific.

And finally, a word about the sounds of the grid. When the grid of humanity is very active, you can hear it as a very thin, high-pitched sound. Sometimes, like right now as I am writing this passage, I am hearing the thousands of varied pitches, tones and pulses that change, shift, and evolve. The universe of light is full of sound. All consciousness is comprised of sound (its very sub-atomic structure is vibration) with an infinite variety of frequencies. Beings in higher realms of light, higher frequencies that we cannot hear with our five senses, communicate with one another this way, and all healing is done through sound. As you tune into the grid, you will find that your inner knowing will guide you to where you need to be. Trust the knowing.

INTRODUCTION

We are living in an age where miracles are happening all around us, and within us. Some may take the tack that we are headed down the path of destruction, but there is neither a black nor white picture that is emerging. Inside the chaos of reconfiguring everything—absolutely everything—about who we are and how we live (even the very nature of the cosmos is being reshuffled), we are evolving into a new race, and with it, a more expanded understanding of what it means to be human.

If movies were used as an indication of what is coming, we would be in for a big surprise. Hollywood's idea of the super-race, complete with super-powers is not far off from the visions that I have seen, but lacks the essential element of the heart. Most of us have been exposed to violence, the callousness of untold acts of thoughtlessness, and some experience violence against the self on a daily basis. Contrary to the mega-watt power crusher characters or the endless stream of cruelty streaming into our awareness, the version of the future human that I have foreseen is transformed because we each have taken the time to make a different kind of choice. And for those of us who know that we are spiritual beings of light having a human experience, we are the ones leading the way to realize this global shift in consciousness.

As an avid spiritual activist, I firmly believe that we, as a collective human consciousness, can take back our hearts and leave the rest behind. As we do, fear and oppression will have no place in our future. Many of us are already taking the steps to ensure that our future is transformed before we get there. By choosing differently now—starting from where we are—we are improving the quality of life in our own lives, our families of origin, communities, and workplaces.

Once we realize that we really don't have to be held captive by the status quo, we will be able to tune-out the violence. We are not traumatized like so many others. By the same token, this does not mean that we are insensitive to what is going on in the world. Most of the people I speak with are some of the most caring, compassionate people I have ever met. They have been in the trenches fighting to take back their lives, like so many others, to one degree or another. But they have also made the choice to eliminate fear from their lives by choosing a new kind of path.

Their choice for joy is the stuff of high adventure that only comes from serving humanity. That's the real satisfaction — like building a sense of new community or starting a new school, food co-op, cross-cultural movement or perhaps breaking through corporate barriers. Most find their true sense of joy by serving the greater good in some capacity and by doing random acts of kindness. They do so just because it makes them feel good, and are a part of the solution. Joy is good medicine.

Why this book, and why now?

The motivation for writing this book came to me in the wee hours of a morning meditation when the angels, along with my Guides, started to show and tell me things about our future beyond the self-inflicted pain and violence of today. They showed me the timelines and the energy patterns that are created by humanity's deep-seeded patterns of hatred and violence that are fueled by greed and how we can each do our part to change the future now. They showed me how to transform what is already set to play out, even as the darker pockets of fear fan out to infect our entire human family. I've foreseen events that are spring-loaded and ready to be triggered by that one more act of violence, for instance. But even those future events can be shifted so they will not be so catastrophic. Just like the events in our recent past, we'll be surprised when tragedy strikes, but in hindsight we'll eventually realize we could have prevented them. But only if more of us will wake-up now, can we actually transform or transcend some of the more dramatic future events that are already set into motion.

It sounds convoluted to think that we create events before they happen, but we do. I've seen the energy patterns of future events that have already been created by our thoughts and actions toward one another — tragedies even more dramatic than disasters like 9/11 or the Tsunami that hit Indonesia in 2004, the Aids epidemic or the human genocide taking place right now. And some of the more planned events by world power brokers who have orchestrated a series of events with such precision that we are voluntarily asking them to take more and more of our rights away. Some of these future events were set into motion long ago and are getting ready to culminate into an unprecedented global calamity.

The angels and Guides showed me how we can turn the tide, to change the course, if we would only wake-up and remember. By remembering who we truly are, we can once again learn to listen to our own inner voice, and do what our heart tells us is right and true, not what others want us to do.

At first, I thought what the angels were telling me was crazy. Their words made no sense in the context of my version of reality but I had long ago made a promise to listen, and to follow my inner guidance to the letter. So, there I sat in the silence and listened. I started writing as I usually did, but this writing felt different. I knew that I would be sharing it in the form of a book but I felt scared, responsible. This feeling of responsibility stayed with me, and at times paralyzed my ability to see, hear and feel what was right and truest to my heart.

I procrastinated for months. Then after a trip to India in February 2006, I cleared the fear from my heart and came home to write in the cushion of a deep and abiding love. This feeling has carried me to the conclusion of this body of work.

Now that I am on the other side of this period of learning, I fully realize that all energy is the same. Once we drop the judgment from whatever ails us, we can transform or transcend anything — anything as long as we keep our focus on unconditional love, and take responsibility for our creations.

Some of what I have to share with you will not be pleasant. It may even border on depressing or overwhelming but I encourage you to stay with me. The Guides have encouraged me to provide you with information about our history, then move through some of the most deeply ingrained patterns that humanity has already created. I will be sharing this information with you just as it was given to me. I also understand how important it is to learn from others. Therefore, I have provided examples of how some of these darker patterns are not only playing out right now within entire populations but also within us. These examples include stories of how courageous souls have transformed their lives into something much bigger, deeper, richer, perhaps, from these same oppressive energy patterns.

When the Guides were teaching me, I found that my understanding of the global patterns became key to recognizing them in my own life. Every one of us is being influenced to a greater or lesser degree by at least one of these patterns because that is why we are here: to exercise the power of the individual. We do so by tuning out the endless barrage of fear-based messages and control tactics. Instead, we focus on opening our hearts and bringing more joy into our lives. As we do, we become a part of the solution.

Take oppression for instance. Any overt display of oppression may seem like a million miles away, but take a serious look inside, and we are likely to find an element of that same dynamic playing out in our own lives. Oppression has been with us for so long that most of us don't even recognize when it's gotten a hold of us until we feel trapped with no way out. It's important to learn how to recognize any lower-vibration earlier, down to the finer nuances of the pattern that has formed in our lives so that we can break the cycle.

It seems simple, doesn't it? It really is but that's what makes it easy for so many of us to overlook the patterns. We think that life happens to us and we forget that we are the creators of everything in our world. It takes great courage and tenacity to allow old habits, outmoded ideas of who we think we are, to fall away, and open our hearts to receive the very grace that is so freely given to us. I assure you, as someone who took that first small step away from fear, it's worth your every effort to make listening to your heart the central focus of your life.

The work to transform your life is simple but will not necessarily be easy. But just by picking up this book, you are making the first move to allow more joy into your life. The examples of how others have shifted away from fear will help you to remember the life you have always wanted but might have left behind or put on hold. Perhaps you have already realized a deeper sense of love and peace in your life but want more. If any of these life-paths apply to you, I invite you to explore the teachings, and begin to understand the over-arching patterns that create interference with your ability to live from the heart.

A Call to Remember is written in the spirit of empowering you to make whatever changes are necessary to realize your greatest potential as a light being having a human experience. As you wake-up to joy, and realize that you, too, can start living in the miracle of life by choosing to listen to your heart, you are adjoining with others to shift global consciousness. In my view, the personal and the global are two sides of the same dynamic. Each one of us is like a drop in the ocean of humanity; you may not realize the affect that you are having on others in your life, but your willingness to open your heart will change the world. Once you fully understand just how powerful you are—the kind of power that moves mountains over rivers—you will have the most essential tool to realize ultimate freedom.

PART 1

WHO WE ARE

Love is who we are. Truth, compassion, acceptance, passion is what we have brought into this world. Joy is where we are going. We are here to bring deeper levels of understanding and compassion to all beings, everywhere.

1: A FORCE OF LIGHT

True power comes from Source

I have been privileged to speak with thousands of people who are awakening to their true nature as divine beings of light. They know who they are and understand that they are different. In the physical reality of life, they are artists, inventors, musicians, financial planners, engineers, administrators, nurses, doctors, bureaucrats, entrepreneurs, mechanics, architects, retired, stay-at-home moms, children, students, and teachers. Most of all they are compassionate human-beings with one thing that seems to bind them together: a commitment to bringing more joy into their lives, and by doing so, they are changing the world.

Make no mistake about it. Fear is a frequency that is on its way out, and joy is the vibration of where we are going. It sounds simple and it is, but becoming the change we so desire for the world is not an easy task in this day and age. In fact, it is nearly impossible without turning off or tuning out the constant barrage of fear-based events and developments that thread themselves into our daily awareness. By allowing our inner peace to be assaulted, we are only reinforcing learned behavior.

Shifting our focus away from the illusion of fear requires us to see through its many faces, and to make choices that reflect more of who we are. It's easier to get pushed or pulled by the chaos because it's so familiar. But that's where our version of weapons of mass destruction come in. Choice. Only we can make the choice to stop fear at our very door. Rephrasing that thought, only you can make the choice to stop fear at your door. The true power behind this collective force of light — the magnitude of force that moves those mountains over rivers — is you.

This kind of soul-level determination sets off an energetic shift that takes place as we reclaim our power. But this does not happen by merely tuning out the lower vibrational choices that we have made in the past. The shift happens because we begin to wake-up and remember who we truly are and begin the process of reclaiming our power. When this epiphany first occurs, most of the people realize that they are not crazy after all. In the inner recesses of their heart, no matter how deep they have buried their knowing, the revelation is the same. They really can play out their lives in the way they first dreamed them into being. Many have gone through their entire lives seeking peace of mind about their true identity. They have tried so hard to make sense of what they know, and to find the missing pieces to their own special life-puzzle that validates what they have known all along.

Some go crazy trying to find validation for that final piece that matches their innermost knowing of who they are. And it doesn't matter what spiritual path they are on either. I have talked with people who don't believe in God, and others who have walked their talk as priests, nuns or clergy for most of their adult lives. But somewhere inside of them, there always remained a yearning for something much richer, more profound than what life was offering up. Once they received such a soul level confirmation of what they really knew all along, this foundational knowing was enough to transform the most hardened of hearts into a gentle flowing of love.

Just a few days ago, I was in a neighboring community doing a book signing. In the mix of this blessed afternoon came a woman who stood motionless for a long time while she was either waiting for a friend or listening to the bubbling conversations all around her. As the room grew quiet, she came up to the table and pointed at the word mystic on the cover of my first book. She continued to stand in front of me like there was something she needed to say but wasn't sure where to begin. So I asked her about her life path. It seemed like a logical question given the fact that we were standing in the middle of a spiritual bookstore. She hesitated then said, "Nothing like the path you are on; we have nothing in common." It took a few more questions, but then there is was. *"Holy Spirit"* and *"nothing can take away from me the knowing of what I have experienced."*

Suddenly we were on the same page. I viscerally under-stood her resistance. She was wildly trying to figure out if I was safe given the warnings about people like me. But something inside told her that I held a piece to the puzzle for her; and the yearning to solve the puzzle was stronger than the warnings. My parting words to her were, *nothing can take your knowing away from you. And its up to you to decide just how much you are going to trust your own knowing over the outside voices that are biting at you to conform. And the loneliness doesn't have to continue. Once you decide to come out of the closet and speak your truth, some friends will fall away. But hiding your truth is what is causing your loneliness. Be courageous, and you'll find new friends.* At that moment, in popped a woman expounding about how she had just met and totally connected with a new soul sister. What synchronicity.

Just this one example is representative of the growing numbers of people waking-up to their own direct knowing of Truth. But even in their struggle to break free of their beliefs and identification with long-held expectations, they are becoming a global phenomenon. We're in the midst of a modern day revolution that is more like an evolution of consciousness than any act of defiance or evil doing.

The beginning of this inner-journey to rediscover our true nature finds us focused on getting off the merry-go-round of living life the way we were taught. We discover that we are not the stories that we have been told. Once we reconnect with the light that we are, the new knowledge cannot be explained by the limited range of navigating the world within the confines of our five senses. The more we release ourselves from the bondage of our stories we eventually, and quite surprisingly, open up. This opening is not just a psycho-emotional response to life; it's also a physical phenomenon, as you will soon learn more about.

We have come here to contribute the power and magnitude of our love for humanity as an adjoined force for the purpose of shifting global consciousness, and we are close to reaching critical mass. When this occurs, the world will experience such a profound shift in consciousness that we will transcend our greatest fear. And we are not alone in this effort. We are adjoined in vibration with those who are guiding us. As we fully align into a collective force, all of humanity will begin to step away from oppression, away from poverty, subjugation of others, greed, and cruelty. The list of what we need to shed seems endless in our present day, but with more of us waking up and remembering to choose joy there is resolve to journey from the one stream of consciousness to the other. It's a beautiful journey, and one that we have been waiting lifetimes to complete.

The evidence is all around us.
There is evidence of this shift in consciousness all around us. In our third-dimensional world, the signs of radical change are not only being felt as an energetic shift but are also being experienced as failing or inflated social systems that no longer serve the common good. It can be easy to become numb from the constant barrage of overt acts of violence and self-degradation that stream into our awareness in daily doses. It's become such a normal way of life for so many that feeling trapped in downward spiraling lives, while being emotionally

assaulted day after day, feels normal.

But for those who are waking-up and opting for something different, the challenge is to take bold steps to fix deep-rooted problems, or to walk away from broken systems entirely and start anew. The shift in consciousness is the quiet awakening of the soul's calling to be free. As we awaken, we begin to recognize that our quality of life is suffering and we start choosing a new reality, a new life, and begin to shed the outer skin of the old. From family structures in need of repair to the declining quality of the air we breathe, we are hearing that proverbial wake-up call in growing numbers. By doing so, many of us are breaking away from anything and everything that feels constrictive.

Some wake-up slowly after feeling their spirit slipping away for years, or are so dulled to the den of fear that something dramatic, like an accident or tragedy finally serves as the jolt that gets their attention. Through some 'aha' moment, they know that it's time to listen to that deeper voice within; the one that calls them to let go and begin singing their song to a more heartfelt tune. For others, it's a matter of finally saying that it's okay feeling like a misfit in a world gone mad. Just by doing so, they decide that pretending is no longer an option.

As I continue my work with people who are drawn to the teachings, I have witnessed countless courageous souls take back their lives even if it means dropping out of systems that have always provided them a sense of security all their lives, souls like:

- a 70-year-old retired postal worker who became certified in healing touch so that she could help children suffering from cancer
- the young woman who had lived in one place all her life but just knew she had made the right decision to sell

everything in order to take a two-year trek into Tibet and learn directly from her master teacher

- a leader in the banking industry who retired from her six-figure job to coach third-world women entrepreneurs while rallying support from the private-sector to finance the needed micro-loans
- the young mother who had enough of poor school systems and started advocating for higher quality education, not only for her children, but for kids everywhere, and
- the 22-year veteran of corporate healthcare who took on the challenge to advocate a kinder, more compassionate way of delivering services.

Each one of these people made the shift because when their heart called out to them, they listened.

My life has been made fuller by heroic stories of seemingly ordinary people making peace with their fears in order to pursue their heart's desire. By doing so they have taken a leap of faith into the unknown, only to find a deep well of unconditional love and often times a grand adventure waiting for them. Many more courageous souls have already broken through the bounds of fear and are actively adjoining with others who are honoring the inner voice of their heart as well. We live in an unprecedented time where the power of the individual to affect vast change in others offers us a model of what is possible.

As witnessed in other people's lives and proven time and again in my own, help is always there as we muster the courage to make the shift. Once we open our heart, we realize that we have many earthbound angels among us — those compassionate individuals who avail themselves to us in times of trouble or transition. They are the countless people who speak a kind word at just the right moment or give us that extra boost when we are discouraged. When we are in fear, it's easy to think that we are separate from one another, but the higher realms (light beings like angels, guides, and ascended masters) do not see us as separate at all. According to them, we are *all* one. They see humanity as one light, one energetic light wave frequency, one bandwidth of primordial sound, one collective consciousness. From their higher perspective, when something happens to one, it is happening to everyone. In fact the principle of ONE includes not only *everyone* but *everything* on earth, including Gaia, herself.

My experience of this knowing was confirmed when the Guides took me into the higher dimensions and showed me what humanity looks and feels like from their perspective. This knowing totally changed my view of who I am and helped me to realize that what I do impacts someone next door as much as others around the world.

A collective coming-together

The teachings found within these pages reflect the knowing that humanity comprises this collective consciousness of oneness, which serves as the basis for the work I do. My calling is to work with people who desire to improve the quality of their lives. They also understand the power they wield to shift global consciousness. I've come to call this work Activation. Whether I am speaking to a single person or facilitating a group process, there is always a mystical, magical element to the work when two or more of us come together and allow the grace of God to flow into our lives. I am not one to use the word God as a dogmatic or religious word, but it's about the only word that describes the fullness of vibration that comes through as a power and presence that transforms lives.

The Activations are deeply personal to participants while also serving to shift the energy patterns of entire regions and sectors of society. The bonding of participants, which happens within a matter of minutes of coming together inside this chamber of magnified light, is often profound and life-altering for those involved. After having both experienced and witnessed miracles happen in these settings, it is my belief that a committed group of people devoted to channeling grace to one another can create an amplified field through which healing and transformation can occur.

This amazing collaboration does not happen alone. Whether I am speaking with a single person or to a crowd, our non-physical brothers and sisters of the light, teachers and guides are always present. Those who are gathered are serving as the conduits for grace. As a facilitator of the Activation process, I act as a translator between the higher realms and the participants. These master teachers from the higher realms are always on the ready to help us transform our lives and the world in which we live.

For years now, I have been quietly doing the work with those who I have come to call new paradigm leaders. They are the healers, teachers, bridge-builders, transformers and activators of a new global consciousness. These remarkable people are shifting into higher states of joy, and by doing so are helping others to step away from long-held patterns of manipulation and control, oppression and old violent paradigms that are no longer serving the greater good. We've been getting ready to do the work of creating this amplified field, not only in our own lives but as we are called to teach or come together with others for healing and transforming the planet. The time has now come to share what we know with others.

Based on the energy patterns I have seen, the few million people who have already awakened to their innate gifts of heart will soon morph into nearly a billion people. These billion will begin moving through this same process of inviting and actively engaging grace to move through their lives. In saying this, as greater numbers wake-up, the shift will be more dramatic for them because the energy of the collective (those who have already awakened compared to those who continue to hold onto fear) is becoming exponentially polarized.

How grace flows, transforms

We are waking up by the millions now. It's an exponential shift, a mass awakening that is accelerating to such an extent that it is forming an enormous wall of light that will soon catapult humanity, as a whole, into mass chaos. The chaos is already there in seed form. All current and future reality is a result of humanity's collective past actions, which has crystallized as global patterns of thought, and thought leads to action. These global energy patterns affect every one of us, but starts with the individual. Since we are all one, what we are collectively creating is catapulting every human-being on earth into a future that continually morphs into something new.

In the midst of constant creation, we can change anything about our future if we align with what we desire. But you can imagine the task at hand. In the case of some of our most pressing issues like pollution perhaps, it may seem like I am suggesting that we get a gaggle of ducks to all cross the street at the same time. Impossible! Some might say it seems hopeless, but I have seen a different probable outcome — one that is much more optimistic. As of this writing, what have emerged are three over-riding probable futures. I'll explain each of the three in basic structure to you a bit later, but for now, it's vital to understand just how important you are to transforming the global picture.

In the bigger picture, no matter how our collective future is bound to play out, on the other end of any choice will be a new global reality. Any new version of life on the planet will be influenced more and more by those of us who have awakened to our understanding that we are all one family of humanity. As much as we love and care about humanity, we also recognize that we are a part of the larger story of souls ever evolving, growing, and expanding through shared learning. The drama of our human story is playing out against the backdrop of a vast cosmic story of light beings evolving in the infinite reality of the One.

The typical math equation is that the addition of all the parts are equal to the sum total. But when shifting the consciousness of humanity, the parts, or the contribution made by each individual, do not correlate to the sum total at all. The energetic picture is that an individual amplifies the whole, thus serving as a key element that dramatically shifts the entire human matrix. In other words, it doesn't take all 6.6 billion people to shift the entire human race. The vibration of love always trumps every other creation.

I've even seen, through a series of mental pictures, that a very small percentage of the global population will be enough. In fact, it only takes one person to fully align with oneness and channel grace to amplify all of humanity's energy field, which can then shift or ignite the human grid system. It happens incrementally all the time but we have chosen to make this next exponential shift in consciousness as a collective force. The Guides tell me that the tipping point is 15 percent of the world's population who become fully awakened and realize their innate power. Then with this power of love, as a united force, the entire human matrix will shift. I call it the joy barometer. When our collective joy has reached a particular vibrational level, the consciousness of everyone and every-thing will shift because we are all connected.

We are not only aligning in consciousness, but this shift is being aided by a physical phenomenon as the earth begins her return to a sector of the galaxy that has been 17,000 earth-timed years in the making. We are headed straight into the center of the Milky Way galaxy that will take us into an entirely different sector of the universe. As we move closer to our point of entry, we are feeling it. It may sound 'way out' there, like some kind of fantasy, but as we look at our journey as light beings, souls having a human experience, we will discover that we are on the very cusp of entering into a very different vibrational environment. This environment could push us further into chaos if we do not align with oneness.

The dilemma and humanity's cry for help

We do all kinds of things because we think we have to — a manufactured drama. Keep doing enough of those things and, as a collective consciousness, we create yet another story that ends in tragedy or loss. Humanity has been evolving this way for eons. She has created lower vibrational realities for so long that she is at a major crossroad where things must change if she is to survive. This form of surviving does not mean that life on the planet will cease to exist. It most certainly will go on, but in what form, is the question.

There are parts of our human family that are dying. Many of us are dying inside by releasing fears that we have been carrying around for years, and millions of others are dying from spiraling so far down into fear that they are eliminating their ability to survive. These fear-based beliefs turn into the realities that flash in front of us everyday — death and destruction of the body, environment, shady politics, get-rich schemes that turn out to cause harm to thousands of faithful employees. These images create the sound bites that are broadcast out into the world, which only perpetuates the myth that we are all potential victims.

Humanity is multiplying at such an alarming rate, and is so disconnected from her Source that she is inflicting pain on her brothers and sisters, the plant and animal kingdoms, as well as the planet. Her disconnect is showing up as a total disregard for the sanctity of life as she relentlessly seeks out, 'what's in it for me' greed-based life scenarios that serve only to cut off her own life force. She is quickly outliving her capacity to provide for her family, and to reproduce healthy offspring. In short, humanity is suffering the consequences of her unconscious behavior.

On a primordial level, humanity has awakened to her dire plight. What other beings in far distant galaxies are hearing, and have been hearing for some time, is her cry for help. As a response, many have decided to come and offer reinforcement in the effort to give her the support she needs to wake-up, and to help her start making conscious choices that are for the good of the entire body, not just her separate parts.

Some of the very first star cultures to respond, light beings from other galaxies, are the beings that first imagined the game on earth into form. Their help has taken the form of an energetic shot in the arm—an infusion of pure, refreshing, high-vibrational light—into her very veins. This light, having manifested as souls incarnating from other star systems, has already caused a ripple, and is about to cause a tidal wave as necessary, in the effort to move humanity in a different direction. The interjection is like any great cure all: Some go right to the source and do the job, some get lost in the struggle and weaken in their resolve, and others forget their mission entirely. That shot in the arm of light just may be you.

We are living in an era that marks a new beginning for generations to follow. As light beings from other star systems, Source is speaking loudly to us now, giving us the energetic jolt of oneness consciousness that is needed to either wake-up, or to help the others to wake-up and finish what we have come here to do. With this new current of grace running through all of us, we are beginning to strengthen our collective core vibration. We are realizing that unless humanity changes the course, the future will look hauntingly like history books filled with the many stories that are told by her few survivors.

Many of us have become so disconnected from the feeling of oneness that we have forgotten who we are. Some of us are spiritual activists that have been here all along. Others have been coming and going, and are joined by more who have only recently stepped in to serve as role models and catalysts, builders and transformers or gatekeepers. Our history as souls parallels the story of humanity but we are not that. Even though we are a part of humanity, our true identity resides with our star family. We come to know our root star origins by the way we feel when we open to receive the Truth of who we are. We are light beings, souls who incarnated into the human gene pool from other galaxies of light. These galaxies can be felt as love, and truth, unconditional acceptance of self and others, peace or joy, perhaps.

Like the stories that we have heard of generations before us — distant relatives who immigrated to a new country, new culture — we too, have our own version of this story. Like third and forth generation immigrants, many of us have been inter-twined with humanity for so long that we have forgotten our birth origins. We have grown to love our adoptive family and therefore feel we are an integral part of the whole.

As we awaken to our mission of incarnating for the express purpose of learning and thereby serving our adopted family, we realize that we cannot be effective until we shake off the illusions of who we think we are and reclaim our power. Our power is to see through the illusion that runs this world. As we begin to understand that fear is an illusion, we can begin to transform any fear within us, and then transcend this lower vibration altogether, even as others may choose to engage in mass hysteria.

Fear is a choice

If we pay attention to what is happening in the world today, there is no question that fear is running rampant. Fear, for most, may be an unconscious choosing but it is still a choice. As I have been called to speak with people, light beings, about their lives, I have witnessed many in pain, who, within an instant, have shifted from fear into sheer joy. This happens after hearing the other version of their life—the part of themselves that they have long denied. To hear their hopes, dreams and desires told back to them by a total stranger is, on the surface, a mind-blowing experience but to feel the truth of what is being said is the thing that seems to grab even the biggest skeptic. To watch the transformation play out before my eyes is often very dramatic but always touching. By now this kind of waking up happens so regularly in my practice that I have come to anticipate the change rather than be surprised by it.

One of the most profound of these kinds of awakenings occurred during a session with a beautiful but sad, and burdened woman in her early 40's. As a gifted singer, she traveled all over the world. She had a young child that she absolutely adored and was married to a husband who could not tie one shoe without asking her for help. She had been seeing a therapist for years to work through childhood trauma and abuse issues. She was deeply depressed when she came to me on referral from a friend. I could tell, as I usually can, that when I was repeating what the Guides wanted her to know, a deep blanket of peace descended upon us. The grace that came to her that day caused an energetic shift within her, but I had no idea to what affect or why.

The next time I saw her was almost a year later. I didn't recognize her at first. She was smiling, glowing, really. Her face was soft and full of optimism. She told me that her therapist of 25 years called her transformation a spiritual miracle. She was cured. I asked her what had made the difference for her. After our time together, she said she went home and changed her attitude, eventually divorced her husband, but only after repeated counseling sessions failed to reconcile the marriage. She found a new job. "It wasn't easy," she said, "but it was worth it. I connected to the joy I felt that day, and I wanted more."

The joy that comes with reclaiming our true power is the key. It's the simple but profound connection with this amplified field that transports us to another place, another time when all things are possible. Before that particular 'aha' moment, many of us go through our entire lives seeking peace of mind about who we are and what guides us. We try so hard to make sense of what we inherently know, and why this knowing never seems to match the feeling nature of what we are actually experiencing in life.

Once we rediscover the knowing and the joy that guides us, the rest of life becomes a game of mix and match. We realize that the stories we have been living are not necessarily our story but someone else's. It also changes our orientation to what other people think of us. We realize that we are not here to solve someone else's problem and we begin in earnest to love and honor ourselves.

This act of separating out from who we think we are and reconnecting with the feeling nature of who we *know* we are creates a permanent shift in consciousness. This shift sets us up to choose between the two feelings. One is discordant; the other feels like home. The challenge is not in the recognition. That's the easy part. The real challenge comes when we so recognize our Truth that only our courage is what comforts us to let go of all the rest. For most, as we let go of the façade of being only human, we begin the process of reconnecting to, and taking ownership of, our innate gifts as light beings.

Intuition plays a big role in this reconnection process as

many of us are prone to ask, "Now what? What do I do with these feelings, these visions or this knowing that I have been having all my life? Or why do I know things or see things about people and situations before they actually occur? Why do I hear what people are thinking or feeling before they do? I have a great love of humanity and feel that I have been born to help people, but I don't know what that is. Will I understand the puzzle before it's too late? Late for what?"

These kinds of questions help us to put our feet firmly on the ground and begin taking the steps to re-discover our true nature. The beginning of realigning with our truth finds us focused on challenging everything that does not resonate with what we feel inside that is right for us. Once we reconnect with the stillness that has been guiding us all along, the limited range of our five senses cannot explain the feeling of this amplified sense of self that is pregnant with optimism and wonderment. The more we release ourselves from the bondage of our stories, the more we open up to a wider field of light. And it's still much more than that.

Deoxyribonucleic acid (DNA)

Not only do we experience an emotional 'aha' moment, but it causes a physical shift within us as well. As we begin to make these inner connections, our DNA actually shifts and changes to match the vibration of who we are. The field of science supports this and is beginning to catch up to explain what many of us already know: that there are more than two basic strands of DNA. In fact they are not strands at all but light waves that form frequencies of sound that resonate together as particles. These particles group together to form a collective intelligence that provides the body (physical and causal) with knowledge. The particles can change, and are continually changing, transforming, as our core energy is influenced by our conscious intention all the time.

When we spiritually awaken it's because the body's energetic frequencies are going through a kind of quickening or reorganization. Our very own awakening is in direct correlation to particular light-wave frequencies that activate the DNA as new wave patterns form within us. The sequence connects, or rather reconnects, our consciousness to higher wave-forms thus allowing us to experience a wider bandwidth of the grid. When this occurs, we open to receive inner knowing far beyond anything our five senses could ever tell us.

When it comes to the practical aspects of awakening, sight, sound, color, and even new combinations of smells can activate DNA. When we are exposed to higher learning, there is not only a mental and emotional response to the experience but a physical one as well. This physical response fires off a vibration that triggers the DNA in our cells, which then opens our field to greater understanding and optimism for life. This directly relates to coming together with different individuals and groups, because once we experience higher vibration, anything that does not resonate with this new frequency feels uncomfortable. This uncomfortable feeling plays out as shifting interests, impatience with the old patterns, reluctance to play life out a particular way, and thereby points us into the direction of the new. Then we naturally gravitate to new friendships, new situations, new opportunities, and so on. It's all a game of vibrational match in constant motion.

The soul sends us these energetic signals that trigger the heart. The heart pulses the energetic instructions from the soul through the body, activates the DNA, and if we are listening, we react. The heart is the brain of any light being's body: not the mind, but the heart. The heart sends us signals all the time but we have forgotten to listen and we allow the mind, our human nature, to over-ride our own knowing. Knowing who we are is the key.

2: LIGHT BEINGS

Love, love, love

In any given social setting, we are often asked to describe ourselves to others. Most of us begin with what kind of work we do, then move on to our sense of play followed by the identification we are holding to family of origin, ethnicity, geographic location and so forth. The list can be however long or short we desire with as much detail as we choose to share. But in this typical scenario lies a deeper knowing of who we are that is revealed to only those select few that we entrust with this knowing. For our purpose here, I will approach the nature of who we are in terms of vibration and begin describing us in terms of thought and feeling. This process automatically turns our focus inward.

For starters, we are not the body and we are not the mind; we are spiritual beings having a human experience. Love is who we are. Love is a vibration, a light-wave frequency unlike any other vibration. Vibration forms sound and sound creates frequencies, which then form patterns. The vibrational quality of sound — constant or pulsing, loud or soft — produces complex waves or wave-forms, which create a force like a grassy meadow that is being washed by the wind. The wind is the force that forms each new wave pattern. Similar to sound, you can't see the wind but you can feel it and see the effects of the force on the meadow.

Love is much like the example above. Love forms a force that is created by the soul's sound. The soul creates a particular light-wave frequency that creates movement. We each comprise a unique love vibration. Love is the foundation of the universe, which makes our journey as souls on earth so magnificent. Humanity is a kaleidoscope of the sound of love that creates an entire symphony of vibration.

In our physical world, we sense the variety of these love vibrations through our five senses. We may believe that we are sending or receiving love but we are not. Like a tuning fork harmonizing with another, when we feel love, we are amplifying what is already within us by opening and allowing more love to flow through us. If you substitute the word light for love, many of us have a history of dimming our light to hide or to protect ourselves. Once we understand that love cannot be taken away from us, we can become aware of when we are cutting ourselves off from our own source. Love is our natural state of being, and it feels good to be in alignment with this universal love.

Our human concept of giving or getting love is not to be confused with self-expression. We think we get or give love in the physical world by taking action because we can feel the movement of love through our fives senses the same way that we can feel a cool breeze on our warm skin. But love is more like breathing. We breathe air, but we don't pull it in only to hold onto it. Love just is. Our human nature wants to believe that we have a kind of love bank that can be robbed, or lost to us, but how can we lose something that is the essence of who we are?

The feeling nature of love in our physical world is a tactile experience and is intermixed with an infinite number of other kinds of experiences such as the touch of our first born child, and the wonderment that we feel inside. As we caress our new bundle of joy, we may project our imagination into the future as we feel the hope and promise of a life of fulfillment for both the child and ourselves. Inside this same feeling, we are also swept back into our own memories of being loved, or not. The feeling nature of love is experienced as both inter-dimensional and as a physical sensation. Present or future projections of our intention and memories of our past experiences are all there within the feeling nature of that one caress. The knowing nature of love is what we realize in our most timeless state as souls living in the reality of a physical existence. In this state, love can best be felt when we are in perfect stillness. No pulling, no pushing. Just stillness. This is what unconditional love is: inner stillness even when there is great movement around us and within us.

When we can get to the place in our lives when we love ourselves and others without condition then we are experiencing our truest self. Once we get even a taste or glimpse of this knowing, it points us to where we are going-back into the stillness. Stillness is not only a feeling, but is a physical property. We cannot separate out who we are with where we are going because we are all a part of the electromagnetic field of the earth's surface, and the earth is being pulled toward a sector of the galaxy that directly matches this feeling of unconditional love.

This inward way of moving toward the stillness feels like home. This feeling of home represents a return trip because we have been there before. We are headed back toward, not only our own peace of mind, but also the realization of a collective oneness consciousness.

This sense of traveling is a feeling that magnetically draws us into a deep state of stillness. Some of us finally arrive at this place of being after making choices about what we don't want, and some naturally gravitate to this state instinctually. Like a bird knowing in what direction it needs to fly, it's a natural feeling that is already inside of us, but many have succumbed to the counter-intuitive trappings of our modern world, and over-ride them with the mind.

Even in the stillness can be found great movement. We might be making great changes in our lives, like leaving everyone we have known from the very beginning of our lives, but inside of us, we feel a deep peace about our choice. This stillness is what propels us forward as we take the steps to sell our home, leave our job, project our energy into our new surroundings by reaching out to make new friends. For others who are not making their choice inside this same state of being, they may experience these identical life transitions as painful or traumatic. As we go within and find what motivates us to move, to create, and connect to that deep inner stillness, huge quantum leaps of movement are possible without even a single care or worry about what lies ahead. We instinctually know we are safe because we can feel it deep inside, guiding us along the way. Many of us are feeling this now. The stillness of unconditional love is pulling us along the path toward total personal and global transformation.

Love is who we are and when we are out of body, as souls, we maintain our identity but are freer to merge, to align or to play off of the group. Even as we are playing and aligning we can feel a pull or propulsion of the larger flow. In the body it is much subtler in one sense to feel the flow. But go against the flow and life slams us. That's why we love to come to this denser reality because we can feel vibration in such a strong tactile sense. But that becomes a challenge for those who lose sight of the flow of love that they are.

From a physical point of view, we can tune into this flow. And just like the higher dimensional realities, where we are actually going—no one really knows, but we do understand how to stay in the flow of consciousness that is guiding us. We know it because we can feel it. We know it because we can feel the love that we are. We are to align with the feeling nature of who we are.

Love feels good to us. Peace, joy, balance, harmony are facets of the same love vibration. These are all words that describe stillness, the kind of deep stillness that comes over us when we fully and completely accept the truth of who we are, unconditionally loved by our creator, and start living our lives in alignment with this knowing.

Stillness is the awareness that is being absorbed by more and more light beings as they wake-up. And we are getting help from our brothers and sisters from other star cultures: beings who reside in an entirely different star system are sending us their love. Many of us can feel this love and support and are integrating the amplified energy into our lives now, especially when we are called to come together with others and channel this kind of grace to one another. It's a magnetic resonance. It feels like home, which helps us to remember our base frequency in its purest form. It serves as the compass setting that we have been seeking all along so that we can align with the stillness that comes with knowing that we are unconditional love. This river of stillness is what that makes our ride home so joyful.

Remembering who we are

As beings of light, we are well on our way to returning to our roots but we have come to this sector of the galaxy, to earth, so long ago that many of us have forgotten who we are. Knowing that we are a being of light in a human body and seeing ourselves as just human are realities that come with different vibrational learning qualities. One is very ethereal, the other quite tactile.

Most of us recall incarnational memories of living in far distant galaxies and our past lives on earth. These memories come in waves or fragmented visions, dreams and flashbacks. The memories can become pretty confusing if we get hung up on issues of self-limiting beliefs, but if we suspend judgment, then we are half way there. By learning to understand that reality is simply a viewpoint at any given time, we will find it easier to separate out from the fear vibrations that have held us captive in our physically oriented world.

Knowing that we are an integral part of humanity as multi-dimensional beings dramatically changes our perspective on life in general. In the reality of being human, we are experiencing life in four simultaneous realms (physical, mental, emotional and spiritual) but our multi-dimensional selves can travel in up to 27 realms of light at once (realms of light are levels or layers of consciousness). So, at any given moment in our experience on earth, we are experiencing life at two very basic levels of consciousness, one through our multi-dimensional reality filter, and the second through our third-dimensional reality filter (only by what we can see, hear, taste and touch).

Many of us already know and have experienced our inner identities as light or star beings who have come here from far distant galaxies, or have at least recognized that we are very different from those around us. Some of us have even separated out from our body from time to time and watched as the human part of the self continued to operate in the world. Some of us, especially as children, remember talking to light beings that looked out for us until we could orient ourselves to third-dimensional reality.

Throughout our incarnation cycles, we have worked very hard to live our lives out as the human stories that we have created before we got here, but now it is time to wake-up. As light beings, we have not come here to wreak havoc on humanity but to aid in our mutual choice to ascend, to break free from the constraints of the third-dimensional illusions, especially the illusions that are brought on by fear. These illusions hold the fears deep inside of us that are so immeasurably rooted in our intertwined journey of choice-making while in the physical. Our mutual story of humanity has a long history of learning through the filter of distorted versions of love that are viscerally experienced as violence, hatred, greed, malice, discontent, jealousy, or resentment just to name a few.

Recognizing that I have just taken a giant leap out of the mainstream of human evolution theory, I invite you to quiet any resistance of the mind for just a moment and tune into the stillness of your heart.

Our human expression as light beings

When I tell an audience that we are not only human but multi-dimensional beings, people either nod their heads in total affirmation of this statement or stare back at me in disbelief. There seems to be two distinct camps on this point: One absolutely knows we are light beings having a human experience, and the other knows that we all have special gifts but are firmly rooted in the reality of one dimension; human. This second camp maintains a stance of five senses with a heaven and hell, or no heaven at all, a finite existence of one world, one reality.

We are multi-dimensional beings of light inhabiting a human body. The human part of our consciousness (the Guides call it the body consciousness) does not fully under-stand the difference between the two levels of awareness but willingly accepts the higher-vibrational being as a part of the whole that makes up the self. As we make peace with the body consciousness, we will find our way to express freedom as a light being more clearly, which then allows the feeling nature of who we are to permeate the mind. By doing so we will transcend or rise above the body consciousness, and separate out from the fear that rules the mind.

Some describe this lower part of the self in physical terms, for instance our reptilian brain; that part of brain that is still a part of our DNA structural make-up. But for our purpose here, you will find me referring to the totality of our physical and energetic make-up in terms of levels of consciousness.

Since I have made the assumption that you, the reader, are attracted to this work because it holds the vibrational resonance of who you are, I refer to the light being part of the self as *we* or *us*, *light being* or *soul*. The human aspect of self is referred to as the *body consciousness* or *human nature*. And finally, I refer to the self as the inclusion of both. In the physical creations of both, you will find me referring to our higher nature as *heart*, and the lower nature as *mind*. Some call the mind "ego", but I find that the ego is more complex than the human part of the mind. The ego comprises, in part, the personality matrix, aspects of which you take with you when you transition out of the body at the end of your life on earth.

So here we are: the body consciousness that moves and drives the human experience and the soul, the light being that we are, steering our earthbound mission of learning. However we may choose to identify with this timeless aspect of the self in this present moment, we will gain access to this part of the self through direct knowing. This knowing stems from our ability to feel, to sense, to see the truth of who we are.

Many of us have recognized ourselves as beings of light for as long as we can remember. From our earliest beginnings we remember feeling very different, alien, in a way. Most remember making a choice in early childhood about getting along to survive, thrive, seek approval, acceptance and so forth. Most of these choices signal a shift away from the soul's identity in a physical body, toward the peacemaking as playing human in a human family. For others, we made a choice to deny or to compartmentalize this knowing at an early age. The one aspect of this knowing is that we made the choice to pretend to be human by the age of five or six but no later than seven. A second choice followed the first usually by the age of nine to 14. The actual ages and set of circumstances differ with everyone, but the zones of learning are more consistent across the board.

Some struggle with this identity shift their whole life, but most go back and forth in fits and starts until they just can't handle being human any longer. That clear, strong, consistent Inner Light just never goes away. I liken it to a child being born into a black family but raised by a loving Hispanic family. No matter how much this child is loved, even without seeing another black face all the days of her life, she will always know she is different. It's the same way with star children. They just know they are different. No matter what the human family context is or is not. The difference was not planted as an idea. The difference is in their light matrix, their DNA.

This perception emanated from our core identification as light beings. The path to reverse or to uncover the game that we have come to play can get very convoluted until one day we get stopped in our tracks. Most of us come to realize that we just can't keep playing the mental game of fitting in like everyone else no matter what the stakes. It's the "no matter what" piece of this revelation that brings most beings of light to me, and to others who are actively working to awaken our brothers and sisters of the light.

Even the term to awaken is a misnomer because no one really helps anyone to awaken. We each have our own timeframe, like a blossom knowing when to burst forth from the radiance of the sun. Somewhere deep within us, we know who we are and when it is time to open to a deeper truth. We inherently know our own unique timeframe for doing so. Once we finally determine that we can't stand sitting in our chosen mental box any longer, we recognize that we will never look at our human family the same way ever again.

As we stand in this knowing, divine love flows through us; this grace amplifies our field, and we awaken. As we awaken to the truth of who we are, we initially spend a lot of time moving through all the memories of who we are not — the learned behaviors, the misperceptions at first seem endless.

After we have come to fully recognize and begin to take ownership that we are different, we begin to seek out others who feel the same way. This point of our waking-up process is thrilling as we begin to understand that we are not alone. Finding others who actually feel the same way that we do is magical and soul enriching to say the least.

What seems to be a grand awakening, in essence, is a remembering that is as laid out as any textbook on geography. We know the contour of the land because we have been here before. We've tasted the air, walked the earth, and dug deep into our subconscious to recall what we already know. When one wakes up, it opens the field for us all to do the same because everyone you have ever known, especially those you have ever loved, get a blessing because we are all one. We are all one even when we don't believe that we are.

On the surface, these self-discoveries seem a long way from creating in a new way but they are not. We've been here before. Before we were born, with the aide of our teachers, our earth-bound guides, we laid out a learning path for our life in the physical with special remembrances for when it would become the time to take this road, or make that choice.

We are to fully remember not just a part or a fragment of ourselves but everything. As we discover the clues that lead us to know the bigger pieces of the worldly puzzle, we realize that we have already created this picture in our heart. Now, in the physical, we are creating from what we know, and what we know creates within us as we honor our imagination. For all of us here today, we have already imagined the end result of our choices long before we arrived at this place right now. We chose the body, the family, and the surroundings where we reside. We planted the clues in the little things, the smallest of details and larger-than-life remembering. We said, "Yes, when I am there, when I get there, when I meet that person, see that sight, I will remember to go this way, to open, to see, to be a part of my life in the way that sets my heart free."

I often find it quite amazing when I speak to people about their own set of clues and memories of how often they are surprised at first. Then with time, they tell me, "Yes, I do remember and what you told me is not a surprise to me at all. I knew it all along, I just chose to believe that it was not true until I was ready to accept what I already know. I thought I was crazy for thinking this way. Now, I accept what I have realized about myself all along." The comments of mock-surprise are always so touching as I watch the soul expand out with excitement from this form of inner recognition, especially as the self-discoverer celebrates as soul-level memories come flooding back into consciousness.

We have come to a place in our lives where we have begun to realize that there is no escaping the directives of the soul because the soul communicates her desire directly to the heart. As the soul sends light impulses to the body consciousness, we can feel it as a flush of inspiration or through mental pictures. The heart is the embodiment of the Divine and there is no escaping its innate wisdom. But unlike the survival-focused quality of the mind, our hearts carry only the feeling of expansiveness. The mind is the part of our human nature that carries with us the memories of trauma and fear. We are to make peace with the mind by seeking out the stillness. As we do, we will find that there are vast arrays of change and transformation that take place within us. No longer is the mind searching for a way out of our imaginings, but acquiescing to our expansive nature as divine beings of light. Now, this is not to say that the mind simply falls into a deep slumber never to awaken. This is not the case at all. The mind has a very important role as the follower of the heart. The mind is to carry out the reality that the soul so clearly communicates to the heart. By carefully listening to these impulses, the mind sure-footedly sets the desires of the soul into motion.

Doing is a vital and instrumental part of our world. We are here to liberate ourselves from the confusion between mind and heart, and by doing so we are to ignite the passion of freedom within us. Rather than holding ourselves back from recognizing and actualizing our heart's desire, we are challenged to liberate ourselves from limiting thoughts and beliefs. Just look around your world and see what you see. As you do, you will recognize the inner pathways to your own brand of freedom.

Freedom is felt in many aspects of life but is personal to each one of us. We have come through our learning patterns in a way that is unique and specific to us. Therefore, only you can decide what is right for you. Your joy, love and peace looks and feels differently, and expresses uniquely only to you. This self-directed state of being is meant to open up vast arrays of heartfelt remembrances within you, even as you might actively work to root out the many emotionally charged stories in the continual effort to let go of who you are not.

Many of us are moving through this period of life where others in our world tell us that what we feel within us has no place in the world, but that is not true. There is always a place for righteousness even on the most basic level of our worldly existence. As you begin to awaken to your own version of joy, you may begin to actualize the truth of who you are from deep within your imagination, which begins to open when you let go of the fear of being judged.

It takes great courage to reveal your heart to others. As beings of light, we are not to let anyone tell us that we do not have the right to express our truth. This world is merely a stopping point along the road of a much bigger awakening process and in large measure is a part of why we are here: to shift the global consciousness by flowing with grace, the kind of grace that comes with speaking truth.

In short, light beings may look like mere mortals in a human body, but we are so much more. We are very clear about what we have come here to do: to channel more Light, more grace, into the planet. It's a very simple task once we become clear, but then again the task of getting clear is an enormous effort for some, and is the mark of a continual evolution of the soul. It takes patience and perseverance to drop the masks, the defense mechanisms that we have developed over time, and face the world with resolve to shift our own version of humanity's story from fear to joy, but we are ready to liberate ourselves and to transform the planet.

3: THE EARTH AND THE ROLE OF MOTHER NATURE

Our earth home and the consciousness that governs our stay here

Even without the expanded backdrop of who we are, precious few ever venture out beyond the confines of what is face-valued knowledge to better understand our earth home let alone our galaxy. We have a growing library of pictures that astronauts have brought back from their journeys and astronomers through telescopes have so freely shared with us. Through their eyes, we have seen distant galaxies and star systems not otherwise visible with the naked eye. The sun, the moon and the stars suddenly make sense in this larger context but I can't even begin to tell the story of our involvement with humanity without taking a moment to talk a little about the earth herself.

She is the very reason why we are here. She provides the physical home, the reality creation of being human within an environment of beauty and variety. Mother Nature, you will learn through experience, is directly tied to the earth and provides us with a way to stay grounded, centered and balanced.

Earth is the Mother to humanity and light beings alike. She provides us with a place, a home to learn in a tactile, visceral kind of way. Many souls incarnate over and over again just to gain positive experience in the dense realities of earth's field of gravity yet we sometimes get so caught up in our journey here that we sometimes forget: All experience is for learning. Our life here on the planet has been seeded with many different learning patterns within the vibrations that govern our spectacular earth home.

As the Guides say, energy is energy, and it is the energy of love that guides and directs all of creation but many of us have become confused about this knowing over time. While earth provides us a home, Mother Nature helps to bring us closer to the feeling of oneness and thereby keeps us balanced and harmonized if we are willing to listen.

The earth is a living, conscious entity. She is the most dynamic of all creations because she has the capacity to adapt, to adjust to any struggle or transgression taken against her. In fact, all of life here on the planet stems from her ability to evolve. In the larger inter-galactic picture of the earth traveling through space, I have often found myself telling others that we, as a collective consciousness, are not to worry about the Mother, she will adapt. It is humanity that needs to regain its balance. Humanity's constant barrage on the environment is the potential precursor to its demise. The earth will continue to adapt and adjust to humanity's abuse, but we may not be sustained. Humanity is inextricably linked to her Mother.

We are not here to be a part of the grand play of life in a way that steps on or ignores our role as playing human but we are to understand that all is truly well. Mother Nature is here to help maintain balance and harmony. I do speak about Mother Nature as a separate consciousness from that of the earth because she is. We can think of the Earth as the body and Mother Nature as her heart.

I invite you to take a look around your immediate surroundings to find evidence of how Mother Nature is there to support you. As you do, you are bound to discover the many facets of her magic. The endless waves of creations come and go like a tide washing away the last remnants of a storm gone awry. We awaken to a new fresh day and take action in the midst of nature's ebb and flow. This way of creating is meant to awaken within us a unique form of love and grace in action that is available to everyone. Just as we might remember the rocking motion of a baby in its mother's arms, the earth cradles us in her embrace as well.

The consciousness of Mother Nature comprises the very fabric of the plant and animal kingdom. Humanity is not separate from Mother Nature; we just think we are. Without the consistent creative life force of the planet we would cease to exist. Mother Nature is the earthbound version of unconditional love flowing through us.

Allow the multitudes of her voice to speak directly to you, "There is a delicate balance between Mother Nature, as we have come to be called, and the human species. We are not the determiners of the game of life but we are here to perpetuate the balancing of the more harsh with the meek. We can be found in the chaos. Amidst the harshest reality creations are also peacefully co-existing. Within each creative flowing of the natural law of creation can be found the central sun. Many souls, now awakening to the central sun's influence within their inner being, are finding this core feeling even in the most chaotic creations of human consciousness."

The vast call to return to the honoring of nature reconnects us to a strong sense of oneness. Immersed in our human experience, we are beginning to awaken to an Inner Light and are aware of our earthbound mission. We are no longer called to create as victims and perpetrators, instigators or manipulators and aggressors against others. Mother Nature calls us to come to a place of peace within the inner ways of creating. Each action born from the inner realm of being depicts a life, in human form, that is balanced and harmonized with the worldly way of creating.

Calling on Mother Nature to keep grounded

Many souls are slowly awakening to the need, or desire, to return to nature from time to time for learning, rejuvenation and rebalancing. I count myself in the mix of those who are starting to more fully awaken to the need to create more balance and harmony in my life. It has taken me years to get fully back into my body. I'm prone to jumping out and away at the first sign of aggression or fear that feels the least bit life threatening. I really didn't understand what I was doing. It took me time to recognize the signs. But once I started taking trips into the mountains of rural Virginia with my expert guide, my husband, my nerves began to relax, and my spirit started to feel okay about being here fulltime.

Since that time, I have met many people who cannot seem to stay in their bodies. If you find yourself feeling out of sorts and out of touch, here are some signs that you may want to consider:

- light-headedness,
- inability to focus or to form coherent, consistent thoughts,
- lack of drive or motivation,
- feeling lukewarm about life in general or even lethargic or
- (on the other end of the scale) emotional about every-thing,
- feeling the other's emotional body more than yours,
- leaving a part of yourself behind when you are not feeling safe. (Those who have experienced abuse, especially in childhood, have learned at an early age to separate out from the body consciousness. Their bodies cannot escape so they simply go somewhere else to get away.)

If any of these symptoms apply to you, the very best thing to do is to, first recognize where you are in relation to your body. Second, go take a walk, spend some time, real quality time, in Mother Nature. The Guides have always said that running water is the very best way to clear out the cobwebs of confusion. If you are clearing out emotional confusion, find a moving body of water, like a river or stream and walk upstream. The energy coming off the movement of water will calm the emotions, and bring clarity to the mind. A sense of peace is bound to settle in. If you are out-of-body, go find a big rock and sit on it for a while or find a sunny place to lie flat on the ground. Then tune in; allow your whole body to relax into it. In all cases, let go of the mind and meld into the natural rhythm that only Mother Nature has to offer. Your mind will want you to get up and get going, but just be. You'll be so glad you did. The more time you can find to appreciate the ways of the natural kingdom, the better.

During the times when you just cannot get out and commune, try meditation and sink deep into the body while you imagine yourself to be safe in the Mother's arms. Practice deep belly breathing, in a relaxed manner, as you find your center, the center of you in your body, as another way to get accustomed to being in the body. Many people talk about getting grounded but I see it a bit different than that. I feel the earth, now, like a big warm blanket that keeps me balanced and harmonized with where she is going, where we are both choosing to go together. I know that I can leave at anytime because I am very practiced at consciously coming and going from my body, but my choice is to be here now. Once you make your conscious choice to be here, ask Mother Nature for help in staying here.

In the coming years ahead, she will play a more dramatic role than she does now. Many more will begin to connect the dots, that humanity and Mother Nature is inextricably tied together in a kind of yin-yang creation cycle. Universal law was set up from the very beginning this way. As we come to better understand the Law, we will begin to see the patterns play out in a way that will help us to bring our human family back into balance and harmony with the natural laws of nature. Mother Nature is a gift to humanity. As we learn to adjust to the energetic waves that pull and push as we are pulled home, she will bring balance to the chaos, harmony to the disenfranchised except as we resist her loving embrace.

As someone who has grown to love Mother Nature, Maureen Wright of Amelia, Virginia has been sharing her sentiments with me, and now she shares them directly with you. She writes, "The most beautiful music can be heard in the sounds of nature: in the songs of birds and crickets and wolves; in the flowing of tiny streams and waterfalls and ocean waves; in the wind, both wild and gentle; in the quiet messages that the trees share with us; and in the majestic silence of the mountains.

"If you are open to Nature and are very, very quiet, you can hear the stars conversing with each other at night, and the early morning sunshine laughing its way through the trees, and the snowflakes bumping into each other during a snowfall, and the fairies dancing in the moonlight. But you must be very still to hear them. Such is the magic and majesty of nature."

PART 2:

OPENING THE DOORWAY
TO TRANSFORM

The river of light moves from mountain to valley before flowing into the sea. By the time we are all together, we will ignite the passions of love and joyousness within all beings everywhere. We come together for love, for light, for increasing our awareness of joy.

4: THE SEEDING OF LEARNING PATTERNS

The life of a soul is always about learning

We cannot really appreciate this shift in consciousness until we have recaptured a sense of our early learning and how we came into being from other planets, other galaxies of light. Every religion and culture has its own unique teachings on where we come from and where we are going once we leave this plane of existence. My energetic teachers have shown me many other galaxies of light, and I go there on a regular basis to help people here better understand where they are from, where their loved ones have gone, or what and where we are all moving toward. I love traveling into the higher realms of light and talking with the light beings that are doing their part to share their knowing with us.

The more I learn, the more I love being in the body right now at this time. It's such a pivotal time in our evolution. The story of our evolution and the way we have been created as souls to learn has already been an incredible adventure that only gets better. Everyone on the planet is influenced by this collective adventure whether we consciously know it or not. Many of us have fragmented memories of times gone by, or flashes of anger and hatred toward others that make no sense in the context of our lives today. Some us don't want anything to do with particular places, groups, or occupations, or we feel pain or constriction in our bodies for what seems like no reason at all. But the reasons can be traced to past life experiences and yet it is even more than that. Part of why we are here is to transform or transcend the fragmented parts of humanity's collective consciousness but there is more, much more, to this part of the story than simple learning.

Versions of our human history can be found in a variety of

sources. The official ones always tell the story from a skewed perspective. Unfortunately, the very best history books are merely the restating of perceptions and beliefs as seen through the eyes of those doing the writing. In my view, all stories are just that. They are created to tell a story to convince, or to deny an aspect of humanity that does not agree with a particular point of view.

Many times, we have seen entire retellings of stories, well after the fact, that are very different from what actually occurred. We see this happening in our world today as warring factions wipe out entire legacies with a single stroke of a pen. But it is the verbal retelling of stories that never truly dies. They are there to share the learning, the lessons of old with the creators of the new. If we listen to the messages that are handed down from generation to generation, and create anew from the perspective of learning then the history of humanity can take on a different form. It becomes useful in the now moment.

You will not find this version of our history as souls having a human experience in any history book because I received it from following the energy patterns of our current day happenings back to their source. That is the magic of the grid. With the help of the Guides I went into the higher realms to see how the game of life here on planet earth was created. This telling is to help us better understand how to accept grace into our lives and to channel grace to others. By understanding our journey as souls and how we learn and how we create, you'll better understand how to heal or transform anything about your life now.

Early earth learning cycles

The earthen leg of our evolutionary journey began in the midst of a long lineage of souls playing out realities in far distant lands, within other galaxies, other worlds. Many of us, here today, are a part of those who dared to venture into the new, away from the familiar hierarchies of light. Souls have always evolved through a constant but organic system of chaos into a new order of evolution, and when evolution is realized, expansion, growth, and new creation emerges.

We can remember who we are and learn as souls when we are in our sleep-state and go home to play with those who are guiding us. But as for the way that we create, two creators, two collective forms or dynamics of light that formed a dualistic way of learning established the precursor of the world we know today. The two represented vast arrays of high vibration that culminated in the creation of souls from other worlds, other dominions. The central source of all brought these two creators together to form a new hierarchy for the purpose of developing a way for souls to experience dynamic movement. Souls recruited for this innovative way of learning would eventually inhabit the new planet (earth) that was forming in a galaxy where vibration was first felt then transformed through the marriage of pure consciousness and a physical body.

This was an innovative way of accelerating soul evolution. The creator felt that the consciousness of very young souls could be developed through the emotional component of the human species thereby accelerating the growth of the light being and the human consciousness. The evolution of the dark planet, as the earth came to be known, eventually evolved to such an extent that the creator decided to merge the two creations of reality together for the purpose of evolving the race of what came to be called humanity. Scientists today have named this timeframe of our insertion into humanity as Homo erectus.

The first group of young souls entered the body consciousness during this era of human evolution for the specific purpose of experiencing life through a series of physical sensations and nothing more. What they discovered was a wonderfully organic, delicious world of outer-creationism. This body consciousness ran with the animals and created as one. There was no difference between the creatures of the sea, land, and air, and that of being human.

As the group of young souls continued to inhabit the body in a watchful state, the creator decided to engage the soul with the subtle dialogues or inner prompting that took place over four more cycles of evolution. Within each of these cycles, the creator decided to ensure a greater degree of involvement with human consciousness and by the time of the fourth cycle, humanity was given enough support from other dimensions, other galaxies of light to shift into an evolutionary pattern of exercising free-will.

At this juncture in the game of life on earth, all souls incarnate in the body were given a choice to remain imbedded within the body consciousness, or to leave. Many decided to leave. In their place, souls incarnated with a very different level of consciousness, a different approach to learning. No longer was there to be a watching way of learning but a total immersion in the evolution of the human species. This was the planting of seeds, new souls, in the game of life we know today.

What followed this tactical shift, was an enormous interest in what became known as humanity (light beings merged or imbedded with the human species) by souls from other galaxies of light as she began to awaken to a higher purpose. The merging between souls inhabiting physical bodies and those who continued to remain outside the realm of light became known as the after-world or heaven. These light beings took on an ever-increasing and active role of guiding those who became more deeply immersed in the human game of life.

Our central sun, the consciousness that governs this sector

of the galaxy of light, once played the role of creator for all the star factions. These factions were great hierarchies or systems of governance (to use our current day equivalent), and created realms of light that extended far beyond the galaxies of light known to humanity. It was not until the creator adjoined the two hierarchies that formed the dualistic nature of our earth-bound learning that so many other star systems began to take notice. This is the heart verses mind learning that we now experience as felt through the human emotional body while also maintaining the flow of light through the heart.

They came to realize the possibilities of foresting the lands and creating animals and other life forms that would support the vibrational frequencies that would sustain their galaxies of light separate and apart from the central sun. Therefore, they began to inculcate their galaxies' light beings into the body consciousness for the sake of manipulating and controlling outcomes. The intended outcomes of these star cultures were self-serving in nature, and before long, the beings of light who inhabited the body consciousness this way, were whisked away by a great wave of devastation that, in its wake, surrendered all human life to a new expression of creation.

Some modern day theorists depict a life cycle as continuous, which it was. But in the context of the human species, there were many breaks in evolution where one being or one particular light culture would come into the domination of the species, then another. As time in the life cycle of earth progressed, there were so many competing factions that the inter-councils of light decided that all sectors of the galaxy were to take responsibility for sustaining human life on the planet.

These inter-councils of light comprised formations of vibration. Like the United Nations on earth represents a collective vibration of member nations, these councils brought together entire clusters of star cultures that were developing in their own way. This early coming together was not born out of a sense of righteousness or doing what was right for the planet, but came from the desire to create a practical solution.

We have been taught the story of the ascended masters. Through the ages, the many different star cultures that have sent souls to inhabit the planet have done so as a way to harvest light wave patterns necessary to move vast arrays of star technologies forward. On earth there are particular frequencies not available in the higher dimensional realms of light such as fear. These frequencies would then be taken back to their seed colonies and cultivated for use in developing entirely new formations of light.

The remnants of this behavior, which first started with the souls that represent these star systems, can be likened to the miners who mine for gold — those who take natural resources out of the earth never to return it again. We are not divorced from this ancient influence either. In modern-day terms, we are witnessing the profits of the relative few who pump oil out of the ground for the expendable use of many. The earth is quickly being depleted while the greed of a few is being satisfied and the multitudes continue to buy into a form of economic enslavement. What the ancient star nations realized is that this method of taking does not sustain a civilization, and at some point, the entire system begins to break down. They finally understood that the key to sustainability was to systematically produce light as a self-regenerating life cycle.

It's interesting to note that humanity is at the same juncture in our earth life-cycle that separated the ancient light cultures out from the "take and not give back" mode of creating. It comes as no surprise to those who are watching this game of life from afar because the remnants of the behavior from the early actions taken by these same, now evolved, cultures were allowed to remain imbedded in the human mind. By remaining in thought and influence as a frequency of light, they were not permitted to leave the planet until this vibrational quality was evolved on all dimensions, not just the higher. Therefore the penchant for self-destruction, as an element of the human race, still remains.

We are seeing the results of power and manipulation being played out in many facets of our modern day society. The cultural ties to these early light cultures can be found in our inner drive to succeed at all costs, our propensity to subjugate other human-beings while sacrificing personal integrity, the division of the sexes, and governing structures built on the construct of authoritarian rule. We can even see democratic societies that continue to portend ruling dictatorships or monarchies by establishing rules for the masses while exempting the rule makers and their cronies.

We find energetic strains of these ancient star cultures in our bedrooms and in our corporate elitism boardrooms. There is no escaping the cultural strain of both consciousness and behavior. These roles are played out for our collective learning, and no one is better or worse than another. Each of us, here on the planet today, is making choices based on a complex code born from early soul-level programming.

Along with severing the energetic ties that allowed the various star-cultures to interfere with the human game of life, the central sun repositioned the way the light beings could play the game of life with one another. The expansion of their light technologies for self-gain was eliminated from their evolutionary cycle.

The star systems feeding off of one another were propelled to go inward and create cultures of light that were self-perpetuating, and built on a system of non-judgment, non-violence, and self-acceptance. These new formations of light formed our current system of soul groupings. Soul groupings are pods or pools of souls who are grouped together for a collective purpose. Some souls are birthed into being to learn more about compassion or to experience greater degrees of unconditional Love. Others are birthed into being to teach, to heal or to lead in times of great change.

You might say that as we look back and arrange our hearts to accept a deeper history than one that contains apes and man, we are looking back and witnessing the true power of creationist theory. But we have forgotten that we are, in part, the very creators who set this way of creating into motion. This is where the process of fully awakening sometimes becomes difficult — to separate the energetic strains of consciousness out from who we are, and the energetic strains that were imbedded into the part of the human consciousness so long ago. Our hearts know that we are light beings, but our minds have become convinced that we are human, an integral part of the earth animal kingdom.

The influence of star cultures on the soul's learning

Our human mind is ruled by fear but we forget that we are not our human nature. It all begins at the first breath we take as human and does not stop. This form of learning has been going on in a repeated cycle of birth and rebirth for as long as we have been coming to the planet.

From the very instant that we are born into the world, most us hold tight to our soul identity before the door shuts and we are thrust into our new third-dimensional reality. Some of us hold our awareness open anywhere from the moment we are born to up to five to seven years of age. However, most of us surrender our identity as a light being along with the feeling nature of where we have come from beyond that early age.

Whenever we decide to shut our memory of our more expanded identity down, we choose an ally in our earth world, someone who will protect us or keep us safe until we find our equilibrium. It's pretty tough to break through the illusions of our earth world when everyone else is playing the game of life by a very different set of rules than what we inherently know. In the spirit world, all is joy, love and laughter. But once we are here, even as newborn babies, we can feel the density, the fear, the tug and pull of worry of our caregivers.

Most of us learn to protect ourselves by taking on the identity of these vibrations to conform. The Guides call this act of protection a hall of mirrors. Many of the people I speak with are still working on dispelling their version of untruth — the versions of life they adopted growing up — as they reach deep inside to remember the feeling nature of their soul. This work is constant and some have a very hard time remembering at all. But some find the desire to open too much and shut down in favor of surviving.

Because of the dramatic difference between the two realities — our light home and earth home — our need to adjust with no way to get back home, is a necessity for most. This need to forget in order to survive the distortions of the denser reality does not happen in just one lifetime either. We have slowly given in to this grand illusion, one traumatic life experience at a time. Many of us participated in the human games by becoming the oppressed, the downtrodden or perhaps the martyr for the sake of transmuting frequencies of a particular soul group. Some would call this mad, others noble. Before re-entering the lower density world from our higher perspective we were so sure of our mission to clear the planet of darkness and distortion that we said, "Never again. Never again will we allow ourselves to transmute the light this way." But each time of regrouping or relearning between lives cleared the earthbound distortion from our fields to such an extent that we were encouraged to return yet again, and again with optimism and hope.

The central sun does not dictate the terms of human

engagement. A soul may choose to return as many times as one wishes. Most of us began our journey into the lower frequencies of third-dimensional reality learning only after we had mastered the inner qualities of holding the light solely within the higher self. Only then did the teachers and advisors on the council level encourage souls to incarnate into the earth's physical plane.

Most of the people I speak with first came into the body as a soul having a human experience between 5,000 to 3,000 BC. They incarnated to become a part of the shift in consciousness that was set into motion by ascended masters (souls who broke through the third-dimensional illusion during their incarnations on earth). These light beings that mastered the density of this world led the way for the rest of us. By doing so, they dispersed their light into five sectors of the world. The souls that followed opened to receive wisdom through the masters' earlier earthbound experiences who, by that time, had opened up vast reaches of higher light for others to integrate into a higher awareness.

As a part of this soul group, many of us were dispatched to what was once known as Eurothia back in the days of knights and wizards, but now called Europe, and lived out life after life as earthbound champions of social justice and equality. Among the people of the African countries in what came to be known as the land masses between the Indian and Atlantic oceans, the masters created the energetic frequencies of compassion and wisdom.

Three more zones of learning were established. One was placed among the people who spanned what is now called the Aegean Sea; the other two were placed among the people to the western part of what we now know as Russia and China. The transmigration of humanity within these five zones became the focus of modern day scholars but the real learning was created within the inner landmasses of the ocean floor between what are now the Americas.

Each zone of learning was earmarked for the soul groups to descend into the darker regions of the planet to begin transforming the energetic frequencies by allowing the life force of the higher vibrations to integrate into the body consciousness. This process of integrating higher wave-forms of light into the lower vibrations of the human body has been going on for eons. Some of us got so good at doing this that we wanted to come back into the body again and again.

Against that backdrop, at some point, we began to intertwine our energetic structural make-up with the DNA of the body consciousness. From our ground-level view, we felt it would offer us a form of protection against the marauding councils but in the end we discovered that it was a way, designed by the star-councils, to keep us earthbound through thousands of incarnations of intensified learning.

The essence of this collective choice provided the body consciousness some relief. During times in our human experience when life became unbearable, we provided strength to the body consciousness to help the human species understand what was happening from a higher perspective. We, in turn, became more aware of the deeper levels and the role of emotion while immersed or intertwined in playing life out through the filter of what it means to be human. In fact, many of us became so enamored with this way of tactile learning that over lifetimes, we grew to forget the higher wave-forms from which we came. It's like the ultimate human version of co-dependence. We feel the body consciousness so much so that we forget the very essence of who we are, and therefore begin resonating with what is happening to us instead of maintaining the integrity of our core identity.

Fast-track back to the present, and we are currently entering into a time where we realize that it is no longer necessary to play the game of life this way, ever again. We are to under-stand the nature of our earliest beginnings, and begin to make our way back into a feeling of oneness consciousness — not by holding ourselves down for the sake of evolving the human species but by waking-up and breaking away from the denser reality creations.

There are many star cultures who will try to persuade us to remain steady, to stay hidden from our true identity, but we are to rouse out of sleep anyway. The fear cultures of our current world governments, many of whom are still aligned with the old paradigm of the early star cultures, are sending out messages of impending attack and reprisals. It's like a broken record that plays over and over again. Even though it's an old creation cycle, it's easy for so many of us to forget that this way of learning is finished. It's over and we can be free now.

From our earthbound perspective, these same star cultures have taken on positions of power, but in all of their blustering, we are not to be dissuaded from our mission of reuniting with love and unconditional acceptance of self and others.

There will be many opportunities to say no to fear in the coming months and years ahead, but for now it is time to change the way that we learn. Your courage is the very life-blood that will liberate you from your karmic learning (learning while in the body), and your higher awareness of who you are is needed now to liberate our fellow brothers and sisters of the light. For this purpose, humanity is being primed to let go of the lower vibrations that keep 3D life in high-drama mode as well. But as history is our witness, this may not be an easy task. Letting go of the very fabric of pain that by now is familiar will not be comfortable. Humanity has already gotten a taste in recent years of what it means to let go, but more is coming. She is about to undergo great waves of sadness as swells of devastation will envelop many who are not prepared to accept the ways of Mother Nature.

Mother Nature's job is not only to help humanity maintain balance but to help maintain harmony among the many inter-galactic star races still submerged in the souls incarnate on the planet today. There are over 17 star species remaining out of the original 32 that have been here all along. Many of us have had a plethora of different lives as human but originate from one of these 17 light galaxies.

Like names that have been created to identify earthbound landmass, star galaxies have names like Siria, Pleiadia, Orion, and Aranu, Arayu. Cultures are the same. We might identify our national or cultural heritage with such names as French, Italian or Canadian, but these star races have names like Octurian, Centurions or Hawthorn. The same is with cultural and national identity. Many of us, whose forefathers come from far distant lands like Russia or Israel, also choose to identify with our new nation. Light beings from star cultures are no different. We each have multiple energetic strains of the originating consciousness imbedded within us and can easily be identified in a variety of ways.

The way that I have come to understand these star cultures are through light, sound and color. There is also a root learning quality associated with each star culture as well. Siria repre-sents truth; Pleiadians, peace; Orion, high intelligence; Aranu, compassion; Arayu, joy. This is a very simplistic way to identify our ancient roots but it's a start. As an aside, when I first learned that I was to form a new partnership with my husband Mark for the work we were calling forth, I learned that the name was to be Arayu. I've since learned much more about this sector of the galaxy, the star tribes who first inhabited this part of the universe and what part they have played in the evolution of humanity. The Star of David plays heavily in its configuration.

If you would like to understand your soul's primary purpose for being here now, all you have to do is to ask. Our birth origins may seem like those far distant galaxies mentioned but the feeling nature of where we come from is easily identified when we get quiet and go inside.

Here is a simple way to find out: Inwardly ask "What color am I?" Then be still and listen. When you do you'll find a feeling waiting there for you. You can amplify the feeling by putting your hand over your heart as you ask. You'll be surprised at how quickly the answer will flush into your awareness. If you find that you are pushing with your mind, step back and get quiet. Ask again to be sure that you are not thinking your way into your answer but receiving it. Just color, alone, is loaded with all kinds of other information but for the sake of finding your soul's origin, this is a good place to start.

The next question to ask might be "What qualities does this color of (green, blue, aqua for instance) carry for me?" Then let go of the mind and see what comes to you. You'll know the answer because your heart will open, and likely tears of recognition will flow. That's when you'll begin to understand the core of who you are. That's how we, as light beings, communicate but once we are in the body we get confused. We are taught to react to the world and by doing so, we begin to think that the world defines who we are. We are in the world but we are not of the world. We are to go inside to remember who we are, and from that orientation, we can always find our way back home.

At anytime you feel out of balance or off-kilter with life, all you have to do is tune back into the feeling nature of who you are then follow that very thin energetic cord from your heart to where ever it goes. Just trust, and you'll see. You can go on to ask your higher self what your role is here on the planet and a plethora of other questions. It's all there if you are willing to trust what you receive. I have taken people who attend my workshops and tele-sessions through this same process many times. The revelations are always delightful and at times quite surprising. Here is just one example of what someone who did this exercise discovered about herself: "The color cord that flowed from my heart was beautiful, a beautiful shade of translucent soft pink, nearly iridescent, but it was really how my body reacted to this. The opening was amazingly incredible. I feel so ready to be a channel for this energy. I am so happy."

As curious as most are to find out their birth origin as a light being, just as many have asked me, "What relevance does it have on my life today (in my life on earth in a human body) to know what star culture I come from?" The answer the Guides gave to me during a recent group session was telling. Like any genetic make-up, we behave in a certain way and have a leaning toward a life path because we are acting from what is already inside of us. Just like a caterpillar doesn't have to think about its life as a butterfly, we too, don't have to doubt what propels us to love and honor one another. Some of us have come here to bridge the gap between who we are and what we are experiencing in life, and others are here to teach what they already know. Understanding your true origin only adds a depth of peace and resolve to keep your focus on listening to your heart.

So not only are we souls who have originated from other galaxies of light that have exotic names which can be seen as we stare into the Milky Way galaxy on a clear night, but we never really lose our connection to our source. We are multi-dimensional beings whose souls remain fully present in both our galaxies of origin and communicate to us through our heart.

Our intuition is the navigational guide for the soul having a human experience. Most of us have come to understand that this feeling emanates from our heart-center — not our physical heart. The heart I am speaking of is an energetic one; a small opening or channel behind the physical organ that acts as the central pump to keep us alive. We instinctually know how to find it but we often get lost in the sea of confusing signals that are coming at us from all directions. Even though it cannot be located like a muscle or major artery it is magnetic and can be felt. It's a master conductor of the body's life force, prana, that flows from source through the body to earth and back to source again. This central receptor of the soul's directives is also the true intelligence that keeps us informed up to the nanosecond of any change of direction.

As you seek to live from your heart, be patient with yourself. Make sure that you are not pushing with your mind. If anything, this will serve as the start of discerning the difference between the mind and heart. It sounds so simple but life gets busy and we have schedules to keep. Before you know it, we are lost in a sea of mental confusion. Finding our center (the truest part of the self) requires us to know who we are, and knowing where we have come from helps us to seamlessly navigate through life. Knowing who we truly are cuts out all the confusion of trying to fit in. We just get right to it, and this knowing is what will guide us through the chaos ahead.

I've met many different people. Some have similar colors. Some have followed similar soul paths, but no two light beings are alike, even when they discover that they are twin souls. That's what makes life so magical. No matter how much you learn there is always a new adventure right around the corner just by looking into the eyes of another.

5: CHANGING THE WAY SOULS LEARN

Separating out from the lower emotional body

No matter how many incarnations we have had on earth, or where we originally came from, we are all now being inwardly propelled back toward the stillness. Moving back over the physical layout of the most recent part of our journey on earth, in my visions, I have seen our central sun as the seventh star in a system or group of stars known as the Pleiadians. The earth's sun is one of the stars that comprise the outer perimeter of the Pleiadian star system. As the earth moves around the sun, it is being drawn into a newly formed stargate that will propel us toward new sector of the galaxy. A stargate is formed by an energetic shift in the ionic polarity between the magnetic forces that define physical matter. Once formed, stargates serve as portals of light that remain open for a time and are set to a specific light-wave frequency.

The Pleiadian star system does not only occupy time and space, but comprises an entire star race of beings who have a very special relationship to humanity. They have been offering the human race help and assistance since souls from their star system began coming to earth for learning eons ago.

The stargate and the incremental gateways (also known as energetic openings or doorways)
Not all star species can see or feel the stargate or its incremental portals of light, but all can move through them once they have adjusted their frequency. The Pleiadians are attuned to a very highly refined frequency of peace. Most of us who can feel these frequencies relate to them as the highest states of God-realization by the ascended masters. Some of these masters are worshipped as Gods or way-showers in some of humanity's major religions, yet there are many more than

those identified few. In my knowing, the Essenes, an ancient Jewish mystical sect, were a people who most successfully held the vibration of the Pleiadian star culture, and learned to live in the body for as long as 900 earth-timed years. Some of the souls who incarnated from 30,000 BC to as late as 7,0000 BC were greatly helped by the Pleiadians in developing what we have come to realize as ancient healing techniques.

The earth is fully engaged in her accelerated path and is heading back toward her galaxy's galactic center, and it is the Pleiadians who are helping humanity to assimilate each step up in vibration, as we near the zero-point of the quantum shift that will occur in late 2012.

Beyond 2012 to early 2013, it will take the earth 12 to 14 years to move through the first leg of the stargate. During that time, the human body will move through a period of biological repatterning (DNA reconfiguration). The repatterning will be a product of the vibration that will shift everything on earth, including earth, as she moves into a new sector of the galaxy. This new sector is vibrationally very different than where we are now. To help us to adjust incrementally, the stargateway has been set up as a series of incremental openings that will provide a way for humanity to come into balance with the new resonance by 2012 and beyond. These openings allow us to ease our way into the shift as the earth moves through this new vibrational terrain. For those of us who are already feeling the physical affects of the shift in vibration, and are living our lives in joy, our lives will continue to expand.

There is tremendous light coming into the planet at this time. And with any high vibration, it can feed you or crush you. If you are choosing to open up and allow the love that you are to flow through you, you are likely feeling just wonderful. You may have parts of your life where you are not in alignment with who you are, but, for the most part, you are channeling vast reaches of light out into the world by just showing up and becoming more present to life. For some of us, this is quite enough. But for the lion's share of those I meet, they feel compelled to channel the grace they are receiving by becoming a part of the global solution. They have long held visions of new communities, or teaching, writing or perhaps counseling others. They are ready to do so and know that it's time. As we listen to our heart and are called to serve, there is only one rule of engagement: Do no harm. This practice calls us to take total responsibility for our own life choices and not blame anyone or ask someone else to do our bidding.

As the earth moves through this 12 to 14 year period, humanity, as a collective consciousness, will come into contact with her new home for the next two thousand years, a sector of the galaxy called Arayu. Arayu is governed by a highly evolved light culture and comprises one of the 17 star councils that heard humanity's cry for help and came to her aid. In the context of our human experience, we can feel or sense Arayu as a very high frequency of joy. The finer qualities of joy are immeasurably still like a first fallen snow, when even sound seems absent from life outside. The star cultures that reside within the Arayu sector of the galaxy are highly evolved beings whose frequencies comprise one of the purest forms of oneness consciousness ever realized by a collective consciousness. Most of us who are here now have been to this sector long before we incarnated as human or have experienced the shift while still earthbound.

Not all souls will be allowed to move through the portals of light that have been set up to ease our inner passageway back to oneness. Only those who match, energetically, to the codes that are embedded in the human DNA structures will gain entry into this sector of the galaxy. And it's more than that. Only those beings that have been activated will gain entry. The activation occurs by moving through a series of energetically aligned gateways. As light beings having a human experience, it's like a game of vibrational match that we are all engaged in. As we open to receive light and channel it to others, our DNA activates inside an amplified field that is created when we open our heart. The body's energy field ignites or implodes with amplified vibration: Grace. Our energy body shifts and we move up the vibrational spiral and through the gateway.

There's a second element as well. By the year 2012, the earth will be the closest to her sister planet in the Andromeda galaxy since the inception of both galaxies. The two planets will begin energetically merging. This coming together will match everything together all the way down to the finest particles of physical matter. What does not match or resonate with the higher vibration will be transformed or transmuted into another galaxy of light. This happening translates into life, which I'll be explaining in a moment, but for now, if you can just imagine your life as vibration then you'll understand the game of learning as it was originally designed. Love is a higher vibration than hate, compassion lighter than jealousy.

We have all picked to be here now, as a part of this grand adventure to create an opening to take that quantum leap and by doing so shift the entire matrix of humanity. It's a magical process of adjoining as a collective consciousness to exponentially propel the entire human race up the vibrational spiral.

Separating the energetic experience from the physical

We are certainly here to play our part in this most exciting time in human history, but no matter what happens next, life will continue to evolve. Creation is infinite and will continue to expand and grow no matter how our particular effort plays out. I had to come to this conclusion when I saw the big picture and how we are each called to play our part to change the course of our human family. For a very long time, I was so concerned about the scenes of death and destruction that kept flashing up on my mental screen. It took me a very long time and a concerted effort to parse out the pictures that I had already seen come to pass from ages ago, and the mental pictures that are a part of our current collective consciousness.

There are a gazillion different realities to tune into if you so desire. But my goal has always been to reveal humanity's highest expression, whether that involves an individual, a group or our entire global family. In order to see the highest probable future, I have had to learn to get out of my own way. I believe this process is true for all of us. We each have our own way of stepping back away from internal judgments. That is why it's important to separate out what is going on energetically from what is happening physically. Our journey as souls from other dimensions, other realms, is interdependent with the history of humanity and the earth. What one does affects the other, but the evolvement of the physical does not dictate the outcome of the ethereal. To illustrate my point, how a rock reacts to gravity is not the same as what a helium balloon is inclined to do.

The Guides tell me that the light beings involved in this next phase of life on the planet will go on no matter what. Some will leave the body and help from the higher dimensions; some will ascend while still in the body and merge in consciousness to form a new race of human. Others will remain for a time before returning to their root star system. Even though we are bound to experience chaos through physical death, earth pattern changes, societal upheaval or disease, energy is energy and everything will transform or transcend. The question is how?

As the years have gone by, what can be seen is a fuller picture of our probable future. This one reveals glimpses of a humanity that looks more like a merging — a merging of new ideas, new formulas and new inventions — that will be realized as we get closer to making contact with our original DNA blueprint.

What has changed? Not only have so many of us opened up to allow more joy to flow through our lives, but the help on the other side of the veil (higher vibrational realms beyond our five senses) is so present that it is hard not to know that we are being buoyed up by our star brothers and sisters. As the energy of the planet is stepped up in vibration, many are responding to the unconditional love that is pouring into our lives at this time. We are actively learning how to transform or transcend our lower fear-based reality creations to such an extent that we are collectively transforming the energy patterns that have already solidified into physical manifestations. I am so very humbled to play an active part in this as I work with groups of enlightened souls who so willingly open their heart in selfless service to others.

Here is just one example of what can happen when a small, focused, committed group of people get together to cause a shift in consciousness: On an early September morning, a remarkable group of woman adjoined hearts with one another in what turned out to be felt by all. Of particular interest to me were five healings that we were guided to do around the issue of two star tribes, groups of souls from two different star systems. These souls had purposely incarnated long before the stories of gods and goddesses ruling the planet came about. The Guides called this work the telling of five secrets.

These two star tribes were charged with bringing more light into the planet. Instead, once they incarnated in waves of new souls who arrived to seed the planet with light, the density of the earth, at that time, overpowered them. Of course, this is our story. Many of us here now were a part of this early seeding of light. If we weren't actually on the planet then, we have greatly benefited from those who did.

This process started as early as 8,000 BC as souls were being born in to what is now known as the Middle East. One soul group came from a star culture known as Siria, a huge race of light beings that came to teach truth to humanity. The other, the Pleiadians, who came to share peace. On a side note, Christ came through the Pleiadian star system to the earthen plane, from which emanates a cosmic ocean of peace. His mother Mary came from a sister galaxy called Occasio, which fosters souls to embrace some of the deepest forms of unconditional love known to humankind.

Rather than accept these beings who came from these higher vibrational worlds, the people on earth lacked the understanding of who they were, and instead, saw them as gods and glorified them. The stress of being treated like this pushed many to separate out from their bodies or to hide the light they came to offer humanity fearing their human counter-parts would abuse the power. They were right. For those who did not hide, their power was used against them or taken and used to control others through hatred and killing. Some became confused by the density on the planet and abused their power; some fled. Most from Siria splintered away from their captors, and went through Egypt; the Pleiadians disappeared into the nomatic life as in what came to be known as the Essenes. Their heirs eventually incarnated through the royal bloodlines of Europe.

As we sat in the silence of this knowing, the Guides spoke to those who represented these two star races, "Now is the time for you to come back together as one to heal the breech. It's no longer necessary to hide the truth of who you are from humanity."

It may be a different time but the dynamic of hiding our light is still the same. The Guides spoke to us about the need to realign with truth and compassion, to bring them back together as one light, and to honor Mother Nature for the healing of hatred among all people. "The division must be healed."

For those who incarnated through these two lineages, we had long ago created secret codes to keep our separate alignments safe, hidden away from humanity, and with good reason. We were persecuted because of our light. Over time, to maintain the purity of the light, we hid the knowing of unconditional love deeper within us, while still passing our innermost secret along to others through these mysterious codes.

We continued to anchor the light but out of sight, underground. The anchoring processes turned into rituals, which were also eventually forced underground. It became a real danger to amplify the light. It was seen as threatening to the way of life at the time. But even this wasn't the answer to what we had come here to do. Like any story that is passed down from one generation to another, both star tribes had forgotten the other half of the equation. We were to have united the two qualities of the Divine, so no one lineage had it right. We were never meant to separate out but to unite.

I found this teaching and subsequent healing fascinating because many of us remember lifetimes or have snatches of memories of underground caves, inner chambers, or standing in underground tunnels with a single light shining on us. These are all residual memories from lifetimes that have been carried forward from one lifetime to another, each time remembering just a little less than before.

You might be asking yourself now, "How does this apply to me?"

I find that many of us have trouble speaking our truth or fully trusting others. This reluctance to speak up or to openly share is actually carried forth from other lifetimes. These are the result of promises made so long ago, and played out incarnation after incarnation. The traits of hiding, not being good enough, unworthiness, and other core traits become a part of our identity. Therefore, we invariably react to new situations almost as if our life is in danger, and with good reason; keeping our version of the truth safe was a matter of life or death.

For those who stood witness to this healing, we channeled grace to one another to bring the two races, two dynamics of light, back together again as one. "Know that you are not going to be persecuted any more. You are free."

We learned through this experience that the encodings that contain the vibrational frequencies of these two soul patterns can be activated as one heart aligns with another. All it takes is an open awareness as one amplifies the light and the other allows her heart to remain open rather than cloaked or masked.

In the group processes I am led to do, this kind of soul-level activation is often transferred through the eyes. But in this particular case, I was guided to show those who participated in the initial activation, particular hand positions before they were invited to activate the others in the room. No one was left out. And it continued. Less than a month later, we found ourselves in Washington, DC. There we kept the activation going as we were guided to spread the light to others. It was quite amazing to consider the exponential shift that was about to occur as each person in turn carried this new vibration out into the world.

What was reinforced within me that day was that we each serve as a vital link to fix the broken chain from events that played out so long. Because of the participants' willingness to channel grace to one another, the rest of us became the benefactor to some of the purest vibration I have experienced to date. This kind of modern-day alchemy takes us back through the portals of time and places us back in the open doorways of our ancestors. What is most heartening is that healing and transformation is going on all over the world, but we are not out of the woods yet. There is so much more joy to be realized.

Like any quickening of consciousness, everyone has a choice to make. Unconditional love may feel good to some, but if you are not used to receiving, it may be just too much to handle. Many who have not yet come into total alignment with our original DNA blueprint will be drawn into a different configuration and will be pulled into a different orbit, a different global reality. These are the visions where I have seen catastrophic deaths occurring around specific timed events, or mass exoduses by those who are not in full alignment with the freedom that comes by residing in the stillness of joy. Freedom, for some, may prove to be too much to bear and that is okay. This freedom we are flowing in is a cosmic river of a particular light-wave configuration.

The encodings that are embedded within us hold the key to fully aligning with joy. As we draw closer and closer to the time of the masses shifting into the higher octave frequencies, the activation of our DNA provides an opportunity to attune to each new energetic wave that enters into our world's atmosphere with ease and grace. Many of these same star cultures, the very star cultures who first seeded this world with souls, are positioned just outside the Arayu gateway. They are here to help guide us home.

We have experienced exponential jumps, or shifts, in the human evolutionary cycle before, but this time will be different. We are being called to separate out from the part of our DNA that is shared by both light being and body consciousness: The emotional body. This is quite easy for some and a mired challenge for others. When the current rotational cycle of the earth enters into the outer dimensions of its parent star, many beings of light will be called to leave humanity completely. Beings of light who are still embroiled in the human fear games, those who are representing warring factions born from these 17 star light cultures, will be called away from their incarnations on earth. Their departure will serve, in part, to lift humanity into a new state of awareness.

Once these old, interfering star cultures have been extricated from the world, humanity will evolve into a kind of super human, which will then merge or meld the best of both races — human nature with our higher nature. With this merging, humanity will begin to channel her source through her heart, and the beings of light who have shifted into oneness consciousness prior to the time of the total merging of the races will be adjoined as one race. This will take time and, at times, will feel like the human race has gone mad, but we are not to worry. We are to reside in the stillness at all times.

Many of us who have come here to aid in the extrication of other warring light beings, have also come here to hold the magnified light until we get to this place in our mutual journey. After the merging of higher consciousness is complete, we will remain in the physical for a time of rebuilding and reconfiguring the human heart. Once the earth comes into the outer reach of Arayu, many, regardless of our individual instructional sets, will feel the pull toward the central sun. Whether we are called to remain incarnate or to leave the body entirely, this meager yet powerful energetic gateway offers a way for all light beings to come home.

It's interesting to note that each of the original star races that comprise the governing council for the planet has a different targeted outcome for the time of the quickening. As I have already mentioned, the quickening is to occur in late-2012, earth timed years, just as the two galaxies of light begin to energetically merge. I have seen it as a huge wall of light being pulsed into the planet. Anything that does not resonate with oneness consciousness by that time will be forced out, even as each star race will try to sway the outcome to evolve the earth into their star system's desired outcome.

You might be asking at this point in the retelling of our history, what significance does all this have on my life right now, today, or even for my future? Just getting up in the morning and going to work and raising my family is enough to worry about. I am assuming that you are reading this book because you are already aware that there is much more to your life than meets the eye. If you find that you are experiencing resistance around this information, then I invite you to get quiet and allow your heart to speak to you in the stillness.

You might wish to pause for just a moment.

One moment.

Our human nature and need for discernment

We are more than the body and the stories we have been told but there is a part of us—a bigger part—that identifies with our human nature. It's hard to tell this story on just one level since there are so many facets to it. But for the sake of explaining the nature of us, as beings of light, we cannot ignore that we are also human in the way that we currently identify with living in our three-dimensional world. This different viewpoint of living life out in a linear world wreaks havoc on our ability to comprehend the multi-dimensional aspects of what we inherently know.

The question begs to be asked, what does it matter if we are multi-dimensional beings? What does it have to do with our lives here on earth? What can we do about what is unfolding anyway? It is important to reorient ourselves to the feeling of the self because that is the part of us that will begin to take precedent in the coming years ahead. The physical property of our earth, air, water is changing and so are we. Our human nature represents the lower octave of vibration that is calibrated closer to the earth's inner rhythm.

On an emotional level, our human nature has resonated more with fear, anxiety, safety and security, which is reflected in our continual focus on societal expectations as we worry about our place in the pack. On the mental level of our human consciousness, our human nature is more likely controlled by what someone tells us to do. We can relate to our world from a logical perspective but the roots for our reliance on fear to warn us of impending danger runs deep.

Remembering that we are multi-dimensional beings of light, the human nature part of the self is also a reflection of our history with the star races but comes from a separate group of star beings than our light brothers and sisters. Therein lies the issue of discernment. Who are we are to listen to — when and why — are questions that abound when we are focused on the emotional qualities of our lives.

At this time in humanity's evolutionary cycle, a plethora of other star races are still here pursuing their self-interests and will stop at nothing even though intergalactic treaties have been signed to stop any and all interference with humanity. Soul harvesting (pushing fear into humanity's creation cycles to generate a particular bandwidth of light) has been going on for eons. It is still going on under the radar so to speak, especially in our two-dimensional world (the landmasses beneath our feet) where souls are forced to create dense, fear-based thought forms that influence the mass consciousness in our three-dimensional world. The struggle is not over yet.

Other star races from other galaxies are here to harvest the light from their own souls getting ready to return to their source. The earth plane is filled, chock-full of star races from many distant galaxies that are here to learn. That's why it is so important to stand clear of any fear-based programs still running through your human story. Release the stories and the fear falls away.

We can effectively use those same fight or take flight

survival skills that we have learned coming through the human gene pool by looking deeper at what we are experiencing. By practicing discernment, we'll more easily realize when something more is going on beneath the surface that is pushing us to create in a way that may not be honoring of the self.

Within the context of this larger more complex picture being jockeyed about by the star cultures, and the influences of physical changes taking place, we are being challenged to change the way we play out the game of life here on earth. We will find that with each new magnetic wave, or push/pull from the star races trying to influence the outcome of this earthbound revolution, that we are bound to feel the affects of these changes within our emotional, mental and physical bodies.

The impact of these ancient star cultures on the world today is like that of a falling star: The ball of fire eventually lands somewhere and wherever it lands, one and all feel the magnitude of its impact even without conscious knowledge of the event.

Four energetic shifts in consciousness set the tone for today's world.

If we look at the influences of these star cultures on light beings in terms of energy, (the energetic shifts or waves of consciousness that influence our lives on the planet), on the many earthbound soul groupings, we will continue to discover a very different view of history. Many light beings living out incarnational experiences on the planet today continue to be affected to some degree by the changes introduced to humanity in just the past half dozen centuries. We have been deeply affected by three major energetic shifts since that time. These shifts were not designed to bring about pain and anguish but to introduce more light into the planet, but any time a higher vibrational frequency is introduced to humanity; the lower frequency must surface in order to be released from humanity's collective consciousness.

Today, we are still being influenced by three energetic shifts that were introduced to the earthen plane starting in the early 15th century. Remember that when any higher vibration is introduced, anything that does not resonate with the higher is either released or played out in the physical. The first of these three waves were comprised of unconditional love. The Greeks were the first to feel the affects of this higher wave-form but reacted by playing life out as oppression as late as 1478. For those of us in the body at that time, as acts of oppression spread out across the land, we infused our light bodies with deep waves of compassion as the insurgents, known as the marauders, invaded the great landmasses known as the Americas.

The result of these raids was the discoveries of ancient native people like the Incas, first conquered in the most southern tip of the Americas. The discovery of riches set off a race to end the rule of the monarchies. The ruling kings and queens of Europe ordered the invasions. The European dynasties were direct reflections of remnants of star cultures that valued the acquisition of land and subjugation of others. Their raid and subjugation of other cultures continued well into the 19th century.

Many of us, during the incarnations that took place under their reigns, learned to integrate unconditional love from both sides of the coin—as conquerors and the conquered—which is why many in the west are now so hungry to experience and to remember the ways of the ancient cultures. Many of us were a part of the native culture at that time, and yearn to regain conscious memory of the star-culture knowledge that was passed down to us at that time. Through time, we submerged this higher sense of self into subconscious mind for safekeeping for another time, another opportunity to bring peace to humanity.

The introduction of the second wave of unconditional love into humanity caused a shift in mass consciousness beginning in 1897. This occurred when we passed through an energetic doorway (doorways have been described as openings which result in the culmination of a particular soul-level learning cycle) which set off what we now remember as the industrial revolution. The world has never been the same since. We are still working through the dramatic shifts in consciousness that came about from such an infusion of high frequency light. You can trace the influxes of light back through the grid by taking note of inventions, the arts, music, and philosophical break-throughs by souls who specifically incarnate to introduce these vibrations into the physical.

Most of us who lived out lives during this time, channeled deep pockets of oppression through the physical expressions of their lives in a desire to help bring more light into the planet, and accelerate their own soul's learning. But those were still dense, hard times. A lot of the people that I have worked with are still transmuting some of the darker, more convoluted patterns of oppression and are working to infuse their light bodies with more unconditional love. If they didn't clear oppression from the body during that time, they brought the learning patterns back in to clear in this lifetime. I see a lot of people who were learning through the filter of emotional starvation or poverty from programming they picked up from around the turn of the century.

The third wave, that began coming into the planet in 1952, gave humanity the final infusion of unconditional love, which prompted her to begin releasing long-held patterns of oppression. By doing so, these frequencies began to break away from her conscious awareness. This big push played out on the global scale in cold war scenarios as humanity worked through issues of good and evil. She focused so hard on duality that the threat of blowing up the world became a potential reality. The belief in duality was held firmly in place by mass consciousness until the early 1980s. By 1984, oppression (as played out by the many doom and gloom scenarios) finally began to give way to peace and love as an alternative reality.

As you can see, this one singular shift in global consciousness did not happen over night. It took a series of strong influxes of light by our star brothers and sisters and generations of incarnate light beings to transmute the energy to create the shift. But in doing so, humanity's collective perspective is continually changing, evolving.

The introduction of these three recent energetic waves into the planet stirred up some of humanity's deepest wells of oppression that are still playing out today. The continued effort by light beings incarnating to help humanity transmute some of her lowest vibrations prompted many to come back into the physical as early as the beginning of the twentieth century. Even with those three major influxes of light, oppression is still very much a part of our lives. It is interwoven into almost all facets of our modern-day society.

Some of us who have played the incarnational game during some of humanity's darkest hours as oppressor and oppressed are here all together again, but this time we are here to clear the planet of this dense energy once and for all. These are the souls who played out their lives as victims or perpetrators during the major conflicts and wars from 1924 through 1945. Some of us remained entrenched or trapped in the body until as late as 1952 but liberated ourselves enough to re-incarnate as early as 1964. Those who did carried with them vast spectrums of fear only to discover their light in a way that freed them to begin creating joyfully with gusto.

There are other souls, light beings, who carry these same patterns of oppression with them, but decide to come back into the body with little or no past life memory. They still carry with them the very same traits and disturbances from prior incarnations but choose to use their soul-light to hold the frequency of unconditional love for others. In some cases, they are not here to clear the energetic pattern for themselves as much as to channel in soul level awareness for shifting the collective consciousness of the planet. I find that when I have been called to work with these individuals, they have no conscious awareness of what their soul is here to learn, only that they totally love humanity. Most are enmeshed in helping others. They are compassionate, loving human-beings that are holding the light for so many others who are lost and cannot see their way through the fog of oppression.

By the same token, many of these same beings who held the light during these first three waves of high frequency infusions, have developed the capacity to hold and channel very pure forms of oneness consciousness. In doing so, while still on the other side of the veil, they intoned virtues of integrity, honesty, kindness, compassion, for instance, into their DNA encoding. This kind of hardwiring aids them in bringing these vibrations in to the denser reality in service to humanity. Like a radio station beckoning to others, we amplify these higher frequencies out into entire soul groups who are also working to align with oneness. I call these light beings activators.

I have met many activators in my time, as I'll explain more in detail later, but for now, I'll share this one person's story with you to give you an idea of how the soul brings light into the planet. One of my favorite examples is that of a young woman from Europe. She is married and the mother of three young children. She has the voice of an angel. In fact, it's obvious that she is an angel. She loves to open her heart and channel grace to everyone she meets. At a recent event, the ascended soul of a divine master (some know her as Mother Mary) started to merge with her physical body. Months earlier, she had connected to a vision of herself holding her arms open wide and intoning peace to a room full of people seeking solace from fear. There she was in the middle of a community activation doing exactly that but this time it was unconditional love she was emanating. I couldn't help but to be humbled by the knowing that her master teacher and guide is the Mother Mary. Through this remarkable young woman, this master teacher is here to bring unconditional love to the world.

I've seen this kind of merging in others but never as an over-soul to someone. After that experience, I realized that no matter what was going on in this young person's life, her soul was quite aware of and in charge of the role she has come to play.

I invite you to connect with what you, as a light being, are here to teach. When you do then your history as a soul will reveal itself to you. You will learn how you best operate in your world. Just your conscious awareness of who you are will transform your life. Shifting your focus away from life happening to you and putting it toward what you are experiencing from a higher learning perspective will simplify all the choices you are called to make about your life. As you begin to understand that you are so much more than the body consciousness, that your mind is not in control of your life — your soul is — then you will begin to open up to a whole new world.

6: THE QUICKENING OF LIGHT DRAWS NEAR

Moving up the evolutionary spiral

As you have just learned, we have experienced dramatic jumps in the human evolutionary cycle many times, but this next jump will be quite different. Given our early journeying into the emotional qualities of being human, we are entering into another cycle of exponentially shifting in vibration once again. By doing so, we are embarking upon a new wave of mass ascension, which is actually a series of incremental shifts that will occur in the coming years until we have reached critical mass. Many of us have already been called home; many are aware of the change; others remain numb or asleep. Wherever you are in this cycle, we are all in the process of being magnetically pulled toward the central sun. By virtue of our awareness, as we have now discovered, we are bound to shift the consciousness of our human family as we adjoin together in our highest expression of love and joyousness.

One might ask the question, "Why are we called to awaken now in preparation of a mass awakening?" The answer is multifaceted and much more complex that can be answered within this medium but the simplified version is because we are ready. We are ready to release ourselves from the grip of the body consciousness because humanity, as a whole, has declared herself ready to embrace the truth of who she is.

This exponential shift can be likened to the teacher and the student. Eventually with hard work and discipline the student then becomes a teacher in her own right; and so goes the learning.

Many star cultures are awaiting this change to humanity's evolutionary cycle with joyful anticipation. Some are not. There are many that wish to keep the game of life on the planet the same so that more of their souls can continue to reap great reward from experiencing human emotion, but again, that part of the game is over; the war has been won. Now it's just a matter of ensuring that all parties involved learn about the truce. Mother Nature holds the key. In my visions, I have seen a cap of light placed around the earthen stratosphere. It's an energetic light, like a bubble. What is already inside the bubble stays inside and plays out with everything else. Like cooking a pot of stew, once the lid is in place, all the ingredients cook together.

So here we all are. As, light beings, we are poised and ready to do our part for fully awakening to joy. The star councils, as of this writing, have finally ratified the contractual agreements they made with one another at the beginning of the fifteenth century to allow humanity to work through these cycles without any outside interference.

Mother Nature serves as the force that binds all parties to this agreement. She is the governing body that disallows any universal law to be violated by outside influences. From our earthbound perspective, we have witnessed her mighty hand as she responds to humanity when it has violated natural law.

The four energetic gateways
There will be many times to look back and remember these exhilarating times but for now, it does not necessarily feel good or comfortable on the body. We are remembering who we are at a very fast rate. The many beings of light, who are here to represent their perspective star cultures, are coming alive with new ideas, new inventions every day.

The incremental stargates will only accelerate the activation process. The path through each passageway serves to speed up or elevate our ability to access higher knowledge and channel more light into the world. These gateways were established long ago. They were put into place by our forefathers and can only be activated as we remember who we are, and what we are here to do as an individual and collective force. As we move through the gateways, we will begin to gain full and direct knowledge of the skill-sets that we have accumulated over lifetimes of learning.

When I first encounter my brothers and sisters of the light, many are still occupied with confusion or focused on past misgivings. But once they begin to wake-up, rather than spend their time grieving over the past, most dive head-first into calling forth their inner strength, and wisely so. This time of coming together for the purpose of awakening an entire planet of light beings is not an easy task for one, but knowing that we are all together brings them comfort as they realize that they are not alone.

The outcome of this era will determine how the game of life will be played out on other planets by other light species within other galaxies of light far away from our beloved blue planet for star generations to come. It's our human thought patterns that bring us pause, but when we settle back into our hearts, we know who we are and that grace is guiding us.

The Guides say that there are many physical properties that are transforming humanity. Thought patterns are what is shifting the consciousness of the planet. They have often referred to our world, less as a galaxy of light and more as a process of awakening.

"In all of your worldly creations you are moving toward a collective consciousness of oneness. There are many who will tell you that as you are creating, and as you are aligning there will be many who will create within the reality of oneness. For you see, it is oneness that is guiding all of earth-plane consciousness. You will not find this feeling to be anything less than a total union with the Divine light that guides you. There are no grand awakenings needed to create within the oneness, just a willingness to allow your very heart to open to the inner spaces, the inner realities of all there is.

"As you awaken to the feeling of oneness, and create within the knowing of well-being, you will find a grand sense of adventure awaiting each self-discovery. There are many who will tell you that it is not alright to be speaking to the many beings of light who come to this sector of the galaxy. But you will find that as you do, and as you create within the reality of all there is, you will find us there with you.

"You are ready to be free, as a race of nations, but you are also wanting to band together within the feeling of oneness. It is not necessary to belabor one truth over another. You will find that as you allow for all truths to flow forth, and to see beyond the veil of your own understanding that you will begin to shift in consciousness to a point of view that is allowing of all thought, all feeling, to rise to the surface of all your human interactions. You will find that as you do, and as you allow these sensibilities to guide you, to direct your own inner knowing, that there are many who will see their way to a very different plane of existence."

I have often received this way of speaking from the Guides. Their message is always very clearly aligned with peace as they speak to the need to align with the oneness. We each offer the key to the puzzle of the game of life as we are playing out within our own stories. But in saying this, I often find that we do forget that we are more than just our stories.

As you work to bring more light into your life, it's important to keep your focus on the moment-to-moment, day-to-day choices, while also holding your intention for oneness. By doing so with purpose, the feeling of oneness will guide you through each choice with ease and grace. So here we are, and we are ready to liberate ourselves from the roadblocks of the mind first, then allow joy to carry us along to awaken our brothers and sisters.

New energy gateways propel us further up the evolutionary spiral

On the soul level of our awareness, we have already chosen the reality we wanted to play out long before we came into the physical. Now, as we are prompted to consciously wake-up, we are called to make yet another choice. This choice is one that will separate us out from the illusion of the game of life itself. It's an individual choice to awaken, but when we do, we are provided with the opportunity to adjoin with others who are also making their way through a series of energetic doorways that will help us regain our sense of equilibrium even as we remain in the physical. These energetic doorways are not unlike the gateways that have been opened to us in the past, but the goal is different. This time, we're not just here for soul level learning then to leave and come back to try again. We are certainly back again to clear the lower vibrational qualities of oppression from our energy fields but the rules of engagement have changed. This time, the goal is to clear the lower vibrations, not by acting like a human sponge, but by transcending the lowest of vibrations entirely. The only way that we can do so is to fully align with the stillness. Once we are aligned with oneness consciousness, we will be called to ultimately merge into the amplified vortex of light that will then propel us all the way through the stargate to take us home.

There are four incremental gateways that will be opening over the next four to 18 years to those who are ready, and the ticket through this inner passageway can only be realized through intention and alignment with the stillness. The prize is expansion of our awareness into ultimate realization of oneness as a collective consciousness. Just feeling around the edges of this grand awakening brings me a total sense of joy.

Oneness is a knowing that is felt through the heart. It is a very different feeling than humanity's current dualistic state of hatred and malice born from fear. Oneness is also different but more closely aligned with the highest levels achieved by the masters who have come before us as teachers and guides. The difference between these two vibrational qualities (oneness or fear that is brought on by a belief in separation) is polarized on several fronts. For starters, oneness is felt through the heart while fear is experienced through the solar plexus. The two vibrations are almost complete opposites in feeling, but not quite. Tuning into each vibration is one way to discern but we also have third-dimensional evidence of both. In our physical world, oneness can be seen in patterns of undisturbed areas within the context of Mother Nature, while those who are into the control and manipulation of others for personal gain project fear as the root cause of oppression. We see evidence of this in malnourished children, poverty and starvation in contrast to elitism, material excess and obesity.

But there is help on the horizon. The star councils have created not just four gateways, but also a series of energetic zones or vortexes that are designed to propel us up the spiral. Each of these vortexes serve as a kind of pool of cleansing water that allows the soul to rest, the body consciousness to awaken, and the co-creation between the two vibrational frequencies to merge.

These are pockets of energy that are made available when entire soul groupings come together to create a magnification of oneness consciousness. These groups are light beings in the non-physical coming to the aid of their counter parts in the physical. These non-physical light beings hold light for their third-dimensional counterparts. When the consciousness of the earthbound group has come into alignment with a particular frequency or the Guides decide that humanity as a whole is ready to shift, they push great waves or oceans of high frequencies of light into the planet.

The planet is a passive participant in humanity's unfolding. But as the earth continues on her path and is pulled back toward the central sun, we are feeling the affects as she travels toward this new sector of the galaxy. Add all these factors to the interjection of the star-councils and their specific agendas and you can see that there are complex energies aligning and pulling us apart all at the same time. It is no wonder that we find ourselves so confused by life at times.

With this being said, I have outlined an over-riding framework to provide you with an energetic roadmap of where we are going and what the world around us will look like, and feel like, as we move through these cycles. The most important thing is to keep your focus on your heart. Follow the stream of oneness and know that all is well. The world will take many twists and turns but you are not to worry about your life at all. When you do get worried, stop; get quiet and find your way back into the stillness. So here we go.

The first gateway

The first doorway opened in early 2006, and with it began to pull souls into a formation of oneness by as early as the fall of the year. We are obviously past the time of its opening, but this gateway will remain open to all who wish to step forward for help with their inner awakening and to gain a deeper understanding of who they are. What does it take to step forward? A willingness to set aside earthbound worries and fears, even if for only a moment, to begin creating within the space of peace. As we step through this first doorway and awaken to the inner light of unconditional love, we feel a sensation or begin to see evidence of higher frequencies of light threaded all through our physical reality. The feeling is unmistakable, even as we are called to release the lower fear-based learning. We will find that as we do, and as we are called to create in this more open, receptive manner, that all co-creation with others will take form as a feeling of one-heartedness.

We are multi-dimensional beings of light and we are here to guide humanity to a very different aspect of herself but cannot do so without bringing clarity and purpose to our own lives. As we step through the first doorway, and begin to shift in consciousness, we will find that many individuals are there with us. Together, as a collective consciousness, we will begin to feel the affects of our higher vibrational creations in their fullest forms. We are singular in our choice but come together with others who are doing the same, and life takes on a lighter, brighter feeling altogether.

The second gateway

The second gateway began to open in mid-2007. This was when that inner-dimensional treaty from 1478 was finally ratified. The agreement made among the star cultures to practice noninterference solidified humanity's path toward oneness consciousness. And because of this, we started feeling the affects of the shift in consciousness peak during mid-summer. By late summer our star brothers and sisters had created a cap of light that gave us the boost needed to seal our fate.

We will not realize the transformational affects of this boost until we pass through a great wave of sadness that was triggered by the last kick of oppression that began playing out in the latter part of 2007. It manifested as economic turbulence as the world financial markets went into flux and schemes of trying to unite the Americas against an invading enemy continued to play out. It took us through a year of turbulence — hardship and losses for many — but just remember that what is protected stays hidden and what is out of balance needs to fall away.

On the governmental front, the very hawk-like nature of the West will continue to serve as the catalyst for what will begin as an inner turbulence before the world financial markets ignite the passions of the East. The West's fall from grace on high will prompt the East to rise up and retaliate against the interference that has long been imposed by the West on their way of living. Therefore, the West's dictatorship of the East, through the veil of global policy, is coming to a close. Once the West has been extricated from the East, the East will come to a place of peace by signing truces and reconfiguring their governments to realign with time honored traditions of one heart, many minds.

As world governmental and economic powers realign around more harmonious energetic structures, our focus will be turned outward for a time. Our individual expressions, for those who have already passed through these first two doorways, will take form as love and joyousness in the face of adversity. The world events, as they play out, will serve as the catalyst to call forth vast global changes, but they are born from our hearts calling forth freedom. Therefore, for those of us who have already claimed victory over fear and oppression and have brought our lives back into balance with our hearts, our interpersonal worlds will not be affected by the global chaos that is playing out around issues of power and economic control. If we are listening to our inner voice, we will know where we are to be in the flow of life.

If you find yourself out of balance in any area of your life, even in this present moment, think again. Go to that sense of feeling stuck and ask your heart to show you the way out of the woods. Ask and you will receive. Just be ready to accept your answer and go with it. Like many, you may be willing to move but get confused about what to do. Here is an example of one person's inner questing to listen to his heart, and the solution that follows. "I look at my current creations and I am feeling uneasy in my partnership and ambivalent about my work. I feel uneasy and know my heart is telling me what to do but I feel fear about this change. I fear the unknown. I am unsure what to do first since these situations are interrelated. My inner guidance tells me to love myself. Is that my true inner work at this point? This process seems so simple. Why then does it feel so confusing?"

Sound familiar? Your heart will always guide you if you will listen, but your mind wants to focus on what to do. The conflict between the heart and mind is classic. But the heart must lead the way. The solution is very simple, but sometimes the heart as it prompts you to change can push you into mortal fear. The solution for this person is the same for you and for me. Get quiet. Listen; then to do exactly what you heart calls you to do. Love the self. By first loving yourself, the rest of the steps that are called for in any life situation will fall into place, joyously.

During the first stage of passing through this second gateway, there are many who will tell us that we are to be quiet, to be silent about our knowing. But instead, we are to be quite vocal about our belief in oneness as we share, in feeling, the many ways to create within the collective, and by doing so we will help the others to recognize the knowing for themselves as well.

In other words, speak your truth when you are prompted without judgment of the self and without reservation. Here is an example of someone who just recently connected with this knowing about speaking her truth: "I once received a very clear, audible message to share what's in my heart with the world. I realize that this may not literally mean *with words*, but that heart-achy feeling to be of service in that highest expression comes for some good reason. The feeling is similar to the fluttery fear, but that immensely exciting feeling you described [on the call tonight] with an urgency to it. It was so strongly felt during my experience before the call that it brought tears of what felt like longing."

This person obviously has connected with her desire to speak her truth and is ready to do so. But many of us are still holding on to traumatic memories of getting our heads lopped off or maimed and tortured for speaking out for love and honor. Now is the time to release the fear and begin speaking your truth but many don't know how to get over that fear. The primary force that will get you over the roadblock is to know that all is well and that this time is truly different. As I say to most who cross my path these days, the time for heavy emoting and processing out lifetimes one by one is finished. Allow all those heavy, fear-based emotions to flush through your system as pure energy and move on.

There is a process you can use for this. It goes like this: When something unpleasant comes up, you can express it as simply as a sound ('Oh!', for instance) or another expression without going into the details or searching for the root cause. Just honor the feeling with a simple sound of recognition. Then release it from your mind by breathing it out with a deep sigh, 'Ah'. Don't give it anymore importance than that. Breathe in the fear, then let it out. There are many different variations on the same theme. Pick the one that works the best for you and use it as often as something comes up to thwart your resolve to speak your truth.

This may sound harsh and unappreciative of what you might have been through to create such heaviness in your heart, but this is not the time to wallow in fear. Do what you must to move it out of the body. I have found that healing does not have to be painful. In fact, it can be downright joyful and relatively quick. Moving energy does not mean that we are not honoring the learning. Simply work on blessing the learning then release it. Stop the judgment. Blessing and releasing all judgment puts the intention for fully realizing joy into motion. (Using affirmations like *I let it go* are effective.)

If you made this shift in consciousness, and physically aligned with your soul path by mid-September 2007, then your way has been made so much easier. If you waited to make your move because you were resisting, you will find your shift in consciousness a more dramatic ride through the gateways because the energy is continually stepping up in vibration. That is why I say there is no time like the present to begin trusting your heart. Go for it!

All beings of light must enter through the first doorway in order to recognize the second. Once the recognition is made the rest is a flow toward the co-creation with others as a part of a collective consciousness.

The third gateway

The third gateway opens in the later part of 2008. This is an energetic doorway designed to push vast quantities of higher vibration into the earth plane, which will cause great waves of love to caress those who are fully aligned with Source. Others are pushed further into chaos or find themselves unable to catch up or withstand the polarization between the two frequencies (oneness verses oppression) so overwhelming that many may decide to ascend by transitioning out of the physical body altogether.

The third gateway serves as an exit point for the masses to shift into a very different state of being entirely. With this dramatic shift arrives both a renaissance of heartfelt remembrances of who we are by those who are releasing distortion from the light body, and the experience of terror striking those who find themselves in continued cycles of creating within the reality of pain and anguish.

The Guides have described this time as the Rapture. This is how they describe it: "When the soul and the personality part of the self meet, the lower aspect of self becomes consciously aware that he or she is the soul having a human experience. The music [they provided] helps us to merge with the light of the truth of who we are. As you awaken to your life's purpose you will be seeing within yourself what many are now experiencing as inner chaos. As you are seeing and feeling chaos, learn to allow your heart to be your guide. You will be waking up to a very different reality when approximately 15 percent of the world population have moved through the same process. This aligning will cause a dramatic shift in the consciousness of humanity. We [in the Angelic Realms] are adjoining with you to help humanity to quicken this process so that the others can experience this shift in consciousness as well."

Like a massive body of water being pulled toward the cliff of the waterfall, we, as beings of light, began feeling the pull of the third gateway before it's eventual opening as early as late-2007 as we entered into a new phase of growing into the collective consciousness of oneness. By the summer of 2008, because this feeling of being *pulled toward the cliff* of the third gateway feels intense, the numbers continue to grow who publicly toss about the idea of environmental catastrophes, impending doom and gloom. But those of us who felt the pull toward the gateway early on were not worried at all. We understand that the stronger the initial pull, the less the resistance we will all feel once the full force that accompanies this third gateway once it is fully open. And it will continue to get even easier. The big push of any new opening is always the most dramatic. But because so many of us began the aligning process early, the big push of the third gateway, is made much easier even as so many others continue to be tossed about by the force of light that comes with this kind of mass awakening.

As we continue to feel our way through these gateways, mass consciousness will play these scenarios out in the reality of their lives. But those who are aligning with the stillness of this force will simply witness the more dramatic affects play out in the world. Like great waves of light that have come before us, we are schooled to see, hear and feel these portals of light open — we feel them as waves, energetic shifts in vibration — prior to the actual crash into our physical bodies. It is all a grand playing out of the collective consciousness and one that was pre-ordained but not meant to be controlled or calculated by any one force or star race prior to our arrival in the physical.

The opening of the third energetic gateway in the fall of 2008 leads to vast changes in our society as the final energetic push of oneness consciousness suddenly becomes a kind of push, or pulling, from the polar opposite end of the spectrum of light. Of course this depends on what kind of vibrational mix you are holding in your light body at this time. Once the third gateway fully opens, humanity will begin to play out the many scenarios of hatred and malice hurled against the collective self as she works to bring herself back into balance with the oneness.

For those who enter into the first gateway before the time of the third opening, their coming together forms a collective light force. This united field of love and joyousness serves to lead the others into a heightened state of oneness, which then opens the door for the others to follow the energetic trail. As the numbers of light beings coming into alignment with the higher consciousness begin to grow exponentially, by the year of 2012, we will begin to realize a unified field for shifting the entire grid.

This field is already energetically aligned with the 32 vortexes of light, or light holders, currently positioned around the world. They are fully stabilized and ready to be fortified by others who will be adjoining as a collective force of intensified joy. The light centers are entire populations of people who are drawn to particular areas of the world. Many of these vortexes have long been established with new light centers being added as needed to shift the entire grid.

As a part of this global movement to fortify and to bridge the gaps in the human grid, you may find that — in your own life — you may be inwardly prompted to move at least three to four times before the fall of the great wall of oppression. This cycle of breaking down the physical creations that were born of humanity's incarnate patterning eons ago is very challenging to release from our collective awareness, but by entering through these energetic gateways, your path will not only accelerate but will serve to amplify unconditional love throughout the grid.

Evidence of this kind of mass movement happened from early- 2005 to late-2006 as light workers by the truckloads were suddenly called to the West Coast of the United States and Canada. Areas such as California, Washington State, New Mexico, and Northern Idaho suddenly were all on the map. The Guides spoke about the Ring of Fire, a series of volcanoes around the world, becoming active as the tectonic plates began to shift. But with these people heeding to their inner direction, their move to these areas served as a stabilizer. You wouldn't think that one person driving up the backbone of California to eastern Washington State in the middle of a blizzard would have such a strong impact on an entire region but it does. We are all connected to other light beings who are working with us and through us to affect profound change.

Another call is bound to go out in early part of 2010. Person after person who has been led through a guided meditation in the workshops I lead has described this time in the Spring of the year as their call to leave, to go to higher ground. Years later, in their visions, up to 2032, they find themselves living in very simple housing. Most are looking out over vast vistas of water and connect to a deep sense of appreciation for Mother Nature. They report that they are alone or sense very few people are around them, people that they do not know but for whom feel a deep connection. A sense of oneness is what pervades the feeling of humanity at this time.

If these visions are correct, in order to help mass consciousness break the pattern, we may very well experience a dismantling of the lives we have become accustomed to. As we listen and allow the inner stillness to be our guide, we will know how we are to shift our vibration and by doing so follow a different road or go down an unbeaten path. This shifting is likely to show up as a physical move, job or career change, or perhaps a reconfiguration of primary and secondary relationships.

We are not to worry about our physical well-being at all because we have nothing to worry about. The Guides are constantly reminding us that we are to know that all our needs are met before we even have to ask. It's easy for them to see, but because we are the ones doing the living and making the choices, it takes an enormous measure of trust during radical times of transition so trusting our intuition is the key.

With the help of Mother Nature, by the early part of 2017, humanity will begin to fully align with balance and harmony. Remembering that Mother Nature's job is to bring everything back into alignment that is out of balance, you may find that in your own life, a change in weather patterns may prompt you to go to another town or region, or perhaps another continent. It's not surprising that the weather will begin to factor in to the choices we make.

Mother Nature is bound to play a pivotal role in ensuring that the light beings are fully positioned on the grid by that time. We will discover that these 32 energy centers will be fully formed and activated with the help of those who are guiding us. Even as we are called to remain steady, we will feel totally connected to the grid. There will be many, between now and then, who will begin to explain these basic concepts to the world at large, but we are to know that there is a particular band-width or frequency that we are to align with now. Not everyone is to be tuned to the same frequency. We all have different jobs, different alliances, but we are all aligned to the same frequency together for a time before being asked to go our separate ways. This requires us to listen, to be still. As we do, we will know where we are to be and how we are to align.

A quickening of light

As the ramifications are felt in our physical world by the opening of the third gateway, and the galvanizing of the light that is realized from greater numbers coming into a collective consciousness by 2012, we will experience an exponential shift in consciousness. Prophecy tells us that there will be a great quickening of the light around this time through early 2013. By that time, the intensity of the field that activates humanity is so brilliant in its refinement, as a frequency, that the earth begins her shift to attune to oneness as a whole. As a direct influence to this shift, as the planet is taking in more light, she begins to slow down for a period of years as she transitions into a new rotational cycle.

For many, we will feel the affects of this incremental shift by the weight of our bodies; we will feel pushed and pulled about by the change. We will feel it in not only the stepped up magnetic force but also in the undulations on the earth's gravitational force (see entrainment later in chapter 8). The air will begin to thin, and many of us will feel as though we are breathing in the equivalent of high-mountain air. Our metabolisms will change as the composition of our bodies transform to take on more light. This will reduce our tolerance for lower vibrational foods, and toxicity in our earthbound environments. Needless to say, many will not adapt and therefore transition out of the body.

Over a period of time the shifting of the magnetic poles will begin to migrate by approximately three to five degrees. This magnetic realigning of the earth's energy grid does not occur in the direct pattern or sequence that has been theorized by social scientists. She will take a turn for the worst-case scenario, from humanity's perspective, as she begins to purge hate and violence from her crust starting as early 2013. Many people have interpreted the time from 2013 - 2024 as a great time of austerity, for which it will be, but it will mostly be remembered as a time the earth adjusted to the higher vibration as she passed through the Orion photon belt. Even as she moves through the stargate (which will appear as a tunnel of light), we'll experience longer days and nights, up to 22 to 24 days at particular intervals as we make our way to our new galactic home.

In my visions, I have seen mass consciousness experiencing a grand awakening. The awakening becomes so intensified that it takes on cathartic-like qualities in many sectors of society. It's a collective 'aha' moment where even the most ardent disbeliever in the Divine shifts her viewpoint because there is no mistaking the transgressions that humanity has taken against herself—transgressions that she has been allowing all along—come up for one big purge.

During the time of the big shift, for those who have not allowed their hearts to experience pain and suffering from their own unconscious actions, there is no escaping. The vibration on the planet, by this time, will be so high, so refined that distortion will have no place to hide. Many that have been living strictly through their five senses experience grand revelations of the Divine. The contrast in vibration before this quickening of light and after is unmistakable, and not just those who are looking for it. Everyone will experience some level of conscious awakening to joy.

How the events unfold, and humanity's reaction to such an infusion of light, is unknown to many at this time, but I have seen great lights coming from the sky. Many are bound to interpret these lights as angels, angelic hosts, coming to sooth the masses as humanity experiences great waves of sadness. These waves are reactions to physical events that play out for the purpose of prompting humanity to let go of some of her deepest levels of fear and trepidation.

I am always aware at any point in the sharing of prophecy that our human nature is mortally afraid of change and therefore has a tendency to interpret any unknown as potentially tragic. This happens all the time in my work. But in my experience I have found that speaking about what we have already created in our future—through the actions we are taking today—serves to ward us off the course of diving into the abyss, and to steer us toward a kinder, gentler journey. I have also found that through this kind of speaking, the Guides are actually helping humanity to release the many fear vibrations that we hold in the body. When I am called to speak with individuals about their creation cycles, they are just one person responsible for one life. Multiply many of these group creation cycles by the number of people on the planet, and you can see the challenge in getting the group dynamic to fully align with the stillness. It may seem impossible on the surface, but with the help of the grid, key individuals of very high vibration can shift an entire family, community, region or nation. I have met many, many people whose role is to serve that very purpose. They are awake and very aware of what they have come here to do. Their excitement is infectious, especially as they discover the deeper levels of what their roles are all about. In my view, humanity is in good hands.

For creation cycles that affect everyone, multiply this factor out by the world's population and you can understand the likelihood of changing the billions of collective creations that have already been set into motion. With that being said, this great infusion of light during the time of the quickening cannot be underestimated. It will open up humanity's collective sight and encourage everyone to begin stepping into the knowing that we are all one.

Adjusting to the opening of the third gateway

Once the third gateway opens, it will at first feel very dramatic, chaotic or like a rush of heat moving through us. For others, it will feel traumatic as their lives reorganize around the higher frequency. Just as some people thrive in hot weather, others become cranky and uncomfortable. Take this basic feeling and amplify by about a factor of ten for every year after 2008. The magnitude of the shift in 2010 is 1000 times greater than what it was in 2001. Many of us who can remember where we were and how our lives dramatically shifted from as early as 1998 to 2002 can relate to this thousand percent factor. For those who are already adjusting to the stepped up frequencies, each incremental shift will feel exuberant if we are aligned with oneness, and willing to release anything that does not feel joyous or peaceful. No one situation or relationship, for instance, can be left out of this equation. Everything is up for clearing.

In contrast, during this same period of time there will be many physical deaths because of humanity's resolve to hold to beliefs in duality. We see this in our steadfast resolve for some to hold to the belief of a punishing God. By the same token, these stepped up vibrations will cause many to repent and by doing so, find their day of reckoning. There will also be many that will be drawn to these higher frequencies so powerfully that they will walk away from their homes, their families, and begin to create anew. This pull back toward oneness will become so strong that during this transition time, we will witness miracles-acts of kindness not yet imagined.

Even though the entire spectrum of our human expression will be all around us, this is not to be viewed as doom and gloom. Anytime we make a change for the better, we are called to let go of what no longer serves the greater good. In our highest collective expression, as humanity begins to adjust to the higher vibrations of love, and begins to let go of her fear-based creations, societies will start rebuilding around time-honored wisdom. The wisdom keepers, as they were once called, will become known as truth-seers but will cease preaching to others. Great peace councils will begin to form from early 2022 forward as a way to further shift mass consciousness.

In humanity's highest probable future, beginning in late 2012, approximately 15 percent of the world's population will become awakened enough to begin working toward realigning with the higher currents of love. But it will take another generation to realize a full cessation of hatred and violence, as we now know it. By 2037, for those who are left, humanity will be at the dawn of an age of global peace and harmony. It will harmonize with the vibrational match of Arayu.

Again, it's an organic process and one that will, at times, take on Draconian-type qualities as mass consciousness begins to shift into the higher dimensions. Of course, I have mentioned all along the very feeling nature of our experiences will amplify the vibration of oneness throughout the grid of light, and we will only become stronger in our resolve to hold this vibration for all beings, all worlds, all reality creations.

While we are still moving through the third energetic gateway, we, as a race of light beings, will become so enamored with the oneness that is invoked by joy that we will begin to shift into different states of being enough to leave the body. But we will begin to feel the affects of our intentional creations on the whole of humanity.

By 2026, once we have passed through the third gateway, the fourth and final one will not open for another 14 years. There will be many faceted changes to our way of living by then. Mass consciousness will have worked her way through a sequential timeframe of mass chaos, and by the time of the opening of the fourth gateway, she will have come into a form of new order complete with new truths having filled in the gaps of old superstitions.

Within our highest probable future, there will be many aspects of society that will fall away beyond the time of the quickening. Everything beyond the time sequencing of events which are played out will be like a new invention of thought being checked out ready to create a different paradigm to shift mass consciousness. It will become common place, by the time we have spiraled up into the higher realms of light, that many awakenings tell us what is coming, and how to begin to shift lower seeded reality creations into yet higher vibratory patterns of thought. But for now, anywhere from 14 to 27 years beyond the time of the quickening, we will be focused on just getting through the chaos even as many of us are already receiving visions of what is on the horizon. Many more are already prepared to begin creating new communities, new light technologies. They are ready to become a part of building new social structures that will rise up to replace the old. As the old falls down around us, we are to look just beneath the surface of the chaos, where we will find the footing of the new already taking place. But for now, let's walk our way through the transition from the old to the new and look at the choices we are called to make.

PART 3:

THE BIG SHIFT

Shifting any dynamic, whether it is the flow of conversation or the course of human history requires us to make a different choice than the one before, and the one before that. It requires us to take total responsibility for the reality we wish to create. Like any great nation, it takes leadership from the individual to steer the ship, so that we can chart a different course.

7: HUMANITY'S PROBABLE FUTURE

What will you choose?

When it comes to the collective consciousness, what has emerged is the creation of three over-arching aspects to our global picture. Another way to say it is, humanity's destiny lines have one distinctly highest probable future, but she has not clearly made her choice on all fronts. To say that choice is finite is also a mistake. Like someone who has traveled down the road with the intention to get to a particular destination, she is now at a crossroads. Humanity has been cruising down a particular byway for quite a long time. She has her sight set on getting there, but there is still a part of her that has not decided whether or not it will be the bumpy road, the super highway, or the dirt byway. Her focus on the grittier aspects of her beginnings reminds her of her journey as a foot traveler but that doesn't predetermine her choice. All three are perfect choices and no matter what she chooses, it will result in learning. Who's to say which is best? Is there a best? She may wish to stop and change her travel plan entirely.

In the above scenario, those three choices represent our collective choice in the kind of future we wish to create. Most of us are sure that we will arrive home but how we get there is the question. This simple metaphor helps us wrap our minds around something that, on the surface, seems very complex. The dirt road represents our unconscious learning, the bumpy road, duality, and the super-highway, oneness consciousness. Each has merit and there is no judgment in whichever way one picks.

Humanity, the Guides tell us, as a collective consciousness is sitting squarely at the crossroads having traveled from the dirt to the bumpy road. The road that is paved in duality. Everything about duality splits us apart or pits us against one another in some form. Yet humanity can always make a different choice.

On her current path, she is still steeped in the death and destructive mode; other parts of the self are confused and a very small part of her collective consciousness is fully awakened to what lies ahead if she does not steer a different course. When it comes to reaching her final destination, she is destined to stay the course using the easy way or the hard way. We have all experienced the hard way before, so you know what I mean. When we are stubborn, and refuse to listen to our inner guidance, we reap what we sow, which is usually harshness brought on by confusion. If we listen, and go with the flow, life is a breeze and our transitions are easy. But that's a subject to dive deeper into later in our time together.

Humanity, as a collective consciousness, has already created her future on many fronts. I'd like to share some of those with you then dive into the over-arching themes separately. I've shared the flow as we move through the energetic doorways that propel humanity further up the evolutionary spiral, but how will our lives be affected by what the collective, particularly mass consciousness, is creating? The answer to that question lies in terms of where we are in the midst of that continuum right now.

First, let's hear directly from the Guides. "There are many collective choices at hand. Currently, the human race is creating within the confines of hatred and malice, but as this frequency is cleared from your collective reality, you will find that there are three over-arching creations playing out in your world. One is to destroy your planet of origin by harboring pockets of hatred built upon the frequencies of world domination (schemes of supply and demand; have or have not; get or be gotten) currently being played out in your day-to-day reality. This reality is splintered or fractionalized and your clarity of thought thus breaks down between two sides, two opposing forces and two opposites.

"The second overriding preponderance of reality creation speaks to survival at all costs. This creation is played out in your world dominance over Mother Nature with schemes to create a reality of ruling the natural kingdom without any regard for the planet herself. Like holding dominion over a power structure, humankind decides indiscriminately to search and destroy any element of the natural environment for the purpose of human consumption. The consequences of this choosing is already self-evident as your weather patterns change, the forests cease to grow, the ocean animals stop their cycles of procreation.

"The human waste cycle pollutes your water, shifts the landmasses as you dominate over your domain to the brink of self-destruction of your people. Again, the planet will adjust long after the human race has eliminated itself from this choosing.

"The third choosing speaks to oneness through the varying aspects of balance and harmony. We each [here in the higher realms of light] see this vibrational frequency through a different prism but for the same end goal — that of realizing oneness, a harmony in every thing and every one. Long after the void of understanding has come and gone, we will all realize that the only way home is through the gateway of oneness.

"All patterns of violence will have short-circuited. The critical mass will have been realized by lesser means but to the same end goal. All peoples everywhere will have realized that the warring factions, the world dominance themes must go if you are to survive as one race of people.

"This third probability does not come with a panacea-like way of creating. There will be hard choices to make. No one will be spared one's choice. As you relate this choosing to your life now, you will find you can no longer go with the flow of mass consciousness. You have entered into the frequency of oneness, and within this frequency demands of you a choosing—a choice—with each and every moment of your earthly expression.

"You will not find your choice the same as another. Do not expect it to be so. You are to keep your own counsel. As you come into a greater coalescence with others who are choosing of like mind, you will be swayed into choosing right along with the collective, but do not be dismayed to find vast differences in seemingly similar surroundings.

"The mindful practice of discernment is a most pressing adornment to your path as a spiritual being of light. Even as you are experiencing great joy through your stepping, you are to be quiet and to remember your early beginning with all your heart.

"As the earth begins to enter into this sector of the galaxy [where we are], you will feel the pulling sensation of home calling forth deep memories of belonging. You will want to come home to us but you are to remain silent by feeling the stillness deep within the physical depths of the body. You will find that once you dive deep into the body, you will feel the oneness settle into your day to day reality creations. You are not to worry as you will be witnessing the other two realities begin to fall away."

There are many nuances to the probable futures that the Guides speak of. But for the sake of relating to you the overarching aspects of our collective future that has already been created, I have addressed these patterns in terms of governance, economic, social, and environmental, and combinations of the four. Sectors that address specific facets of society yet benefit of the whole, for instance, the contribution of star children and their caregivers and healers, have been included as well.

Since we have come here to steer humanity toward the third probability, I'll begin with the super-highway and work my way back to where we actually are in present moment. Needless the say, the third probable future has yet to be realized, as you quickly learn, but signs are cropping us to show us the way.

Global Patterns

The first probable future (the dirt road)
We have almost completely shifted away from the more dramatic earth changes. This probable future shifted in early 1981 as the collective consciousness woke up to the reality that we really were on the brink of blowing ourselves up and something had to stop, and we did. We stopped and looked at the insanity of our leaders' actions, and said enough. With that collective 'aha' moment we began to turn our attention away from the reality creation of total annihilation of entire populations through nuclear holocaust. Instead, we have channeled remnants of this self-destructive cycle into other less fatal but just as insidious behaviors.

Humanity as a whole has taken responsibility for derailing this more dramatic future, and has implemented safeguards to ensure that she does not fall back into this darker reality creation. However, she is still working through various scenarios of death and destruction which would leave the earth and all her inhabitants to create a new future that does not include 90 percent of the human population by the year 3037. This probable future is, in my view, well on its way to becoming a future reality because the seeds are so firmly planted (literally planted) by the dramatic decrease of our food and water sources. Through depleted nutrients from the continued use of commercial fertilizers and pesticides, the continued dumping of toxic waste and pollution of air and water, we are obliterating our ability to feed our growing population. When this kind of prophetic information comes through, it is always dramatic but the Guides tell me that this kind of probable future may be in full swing but it doesn't have to play out so dramatically. We can still change it.

The second probability and duality (the bumpy road)
As of this writing, humanity is currently seated squarely in the energy of the second probability with signs of struggle to grasp at the possibility of the third. Like a flower trying to open, humanity is fighting the very signals of Mother Nature to open and to allow her creation to come into a greater degree of balance and harmony.

The second probability is being driven by a prevailing belief in duality. An example might be someone who thinks that in order to get to heaven she must die, that earth is a separate place from the higher realms. Belief in duality says that where there is good there must also be bad. Where there is black so too must there be white. Belief in duality holds humanity to a polarized reality creation.

Here is what the Guides say about duality: "We come to you as emissaries of peace. We are the Divine Masters who walk as quiet as the heart dares to hear. Your human heart beats with the history of humanity. Your inner knowing is as rich and vast as your cultural ties to your precious earth. We are not here to encourage you to separate yourselves from the many leanings to be free from strife-ridden ways of creating. We are here to help you in times of great change.

"You, as a race of nations, are cultivating the death and destruction of millions of your peoples by the way you dance the dance of duality. This form of duality takes form as poverty or wealth, sickness or wellness, intelligence or ignorance, domination or submissiveness. We are here to help you to create a society that is unified in heartfelt ways of creating. We are here because you have called us to you. We are of the light-wave frequencies that you currently study from the perspective of history. We are all gathered here, within your inner being-ness, as a collective consciousness ready to be made whole by your choosing to be free. This freedom that we speak of cannot be realized by traversing the halls of doubt and indecision. The self-realized act of betrayal can only be actualized as you surrender your fears to God.

"Your higher-self commands your destiny. Your God self, the true aspect of your physical expression, creates a light-wave frequency within the physical confines of your imagination. It is your gift born from your own choosing that is bound to set you free.

"As you recognize your place within the realm of freedom, you will begin to recognize our help and inner guidance. We do not seek to dictate the terms of this form of freedom yet we gently provide the inner opening of your heart. As you begin to open, we are there to greet you. As you align with your soul's inner calling, we are there to co-create with you.

"We are there when you cry out for change in your life, and we are there to open doorways of understanding so that you may see ever so clearly. We are here now. We are here now. Are you ready to lift the veil from your very own eyes and to claim victory over your human nature?

"As you realize your choice to release yourself from this inner bondage called duality, and begin to recognize that the very survival of your human species calls you to unite under a singular feeling of oneness of being-ness, you shall begin, as a race of nations, to claim victory over death and destruction. Your warring nature shall be replaced by peace councils. Your farmers, growers and harvesters of the sea shall be replaced by nature's bounty.

"As you seek out solutions within this framework of oneness, solutions shall be discovered among the ashes of strife as old paradigms of competition fall away.

"Your scientists now seeking answers to nature's way of creating heat shall be converted to alternate waves of light spectrums. No longer dependent upon artificial means to heat, cool and to generate light source for your modern conveniences, your populations shall begin to spread good news of freedom in all forms of living.

"Look to Mother Nature for the answers, my dear ones, and know that, as you create as a unity consciousness, we shall be there with you."

Economic / Social

In this second probable future, the plan for global domination ends in failure but in failure it takes the world longer to come out of the devastation that follows as failed social systems scramble to reassemble and fall into new order. Structurally, from 2008 to 2052, social systems, governments and economies struggle through issues of division. The East and the West polarize against one another, not unlike what we are currently experiencing but to a greater degree so that by early 2010, the world populations experience deeper pockets of economic strife, which then leads to total economic breakdown.

In the US, we experience this breakdown as crushing national debt for playing out failed war games to such an extent that by the time our notes are called in, we cannot pay the debt and the East applies economic sanctions against us. The world populations do not sympathize with our plight at all, especially after the years of arrogantly commanding our way into other economies for our own selfish needs. What affects one most certainly affects all, so we all lose.

With this dramatic erosion of the world's economy, the

earth's populations begin the process of reorganizing in myriad ways to continue trading and bartering to do business but from a flattened organizational structure. In our current day scenario, as we sit inside the energetic parameters of the second probable future, the domination by the East of the West does find its way into equilibrium. But in this more turbulent climate, balance takes 25 to 27 years and plays out in deep cycles of hatred and violence, economic depression, and fractionalized social structures well beyond the time of the quickening of 2012. In our highest probable future we transform issues of chaos into a new-world order within a relatively few 14 to 17 years, and it doesn't have to be so harsh.

Families and Children

As we play out our second probable future, families across the board are currently polarized, and will only become more fragmented as the world's social structures become unstable and crumble under the stress of trying to serve more and more people who will find themselves in need. Wide swaths of humanity within particular geographic, social and economic areas of society will experience deep pockets of chaos more than others, and pull on the world-relief systems as a whole. Children and those who cannot care for themselves are always the most deeply affected by any change, especially in families that reside in economically or politically turbulent climates. In the coming years ahead, this outer turbulence will become even more pronounced. What then?

As the second probability plays out, segments of the world's population will continue to put the needs of our most vulnerable last. Children and the weak will be the first to be affected. But we are already seeing the affects of this form of polarization now in the form of dumbed-down educational systems, mindless mass media designed to push fear into the mass consciousness, and economic exploitation of the masses to breed a new level of consumer ignorance to name just a few.

In our highest probable future, especially as we near the shift point, the core value is to put the welfare of humanity's children first; to create as a global society stable, well-balanced family environments with strong educational systems that support and nurture the child. However, in the second probability, not unlike what we are currently experiencing but more dramatically so, families struggle to survive as we stretch to make ends meet and keep one step ahead of over-riding social manipulation and control mechanisms. These social structures instill fear in the hearts to weaken the collective's constitution and break down the wall of resistance so that there will be greater numbers to be controlled.

These kinds of controls feel subtle at first but are then stepped up to chokehold status so that it feels as though there is no escaping. An example is that of a typical western family that buys into all the bells and whistles of cardboard diets. Couple the lifestyle and mind pollution with high stress debt and workaholic hours. Before long someone gets sick and can't work or the pressure only increases by the added debt load. Who suffers the most, the parents or the children? In my view, everyone.

In the second probability, the affect of economic stress becomes so crushing that children feel the affect of stress on their parents and are forced to fend for them selves to the extent that they take control. Children raise children. Older children raise their younger siblings right under the noses of their fractionalized parents. This is playing out now in families all across the globe, and will only become more polarized before we collectively take a moment, look at the writing on the wall and take concrete steps to make changes that begin to honor the child. Unfortunately, through the energy patterns I have followed, this level of stopping the madness does not happen until entire cities and towns are under siege from economic and environmental influences that play out as control and manipulation of the masses.

Environment

Environmentally, we are well on our way to experiencing dramatic land mass changes but not so dramatically as one might expect. The mental pictures I have seen look dramatic on the surface — and they are — but I am constantly reminded that we experience these changes over time. Seeing them in mental pictures with years attached provide a progression of thought that can still be changed. We are not to stop the movement of the earth's land masses but change our behavior. This has not been possible at this juncture because we are not, collectively, in enough pain to realize the inevitable.

It is no secret. Just look around our world and remember the decrease in the animal kingdom. It is a rarity to find large herds or flocks of wild animals in natural areas. You have to go looking for them. They don't exist in great numbers the way they used to just a few years ago. This trend will continue as the world's population continues to exponentially increase, but what we are counting on is the world's food source being enough to sustain the growth. As we stand in our present moment, food and water will become our biggest concern.

In the second probability, the greed factor takes over and the use of pesticides and genetically altered seed serve as the foundational frequency for famine and starvation. I have also seen vast reaches of society dropping away, not because of premature death that comes with natural catastrophe — that is most certainly a factor that plays out in population reduction along with war — but starvation from reduced nutritional value from our food sources becomes the bigger issue. We literally starve from within or going without entirely.

Greed continues to be such a driving factor that entire populations are poisoned and through compromised health standards, new disease sets in. Disease in the human body runs rampant from contaminated sources gaining entry into the world's food chain. Health and pharmaceutical industries jump in to play their part because there is too much profit in keeping us sick.

But direr than poor nutrition is the state of our most precious natural resource, water. In the second probability, water will take center stage after the year 2012 as we begin to realize that with the magnetic poles shift, the underground rivers will begin to change direction. What was there will no longer be, and with increased population growth and continued contamination of water by human pollution, our focus will turn to water. We will move to create stabilized centers for drawing water in to manage our cities, but with the increased demand that will be placed on man-made filtration systems, the lack of purified water will wreak havoc on entire populations.

In the second probability, you will not only witness people killing one another over oil not unlike what we are already witnessing as one nation pits its might against another to control the oil fields. But oil and gas struggles will become distant memories compared to what will take place around water rights.

On the very basic level of survival, we will all be moving through a time, beginning in early 2013, where water will be the topic of the day. Our focus on water, specifically, our ability to secure and make available a daily dose of purified water for human consumption will consume our day to day world for the next 38 years, especially for those who are still living in cities by the year 2024. By that time, we're going to forget about oil, and forget about gas. Water will become our most precious commodity.

In the context of global warming, we are already beginning to rally around water as a factor in our survival as a human race. If you are on the planet today and are under the age of 60, it is likely that in your lifetime, you will experience the eastern most ice caps melt and the oceans rise. This rising of the ocean waters will first affect the eastern landmasses of Europe, Indonesia, Asia and the Netherlands. Remember that gravity is not evenly distributed — some parts of the world experience more of a gravitational pull than others — so we will see some land-masses that are higher in elevation flood before some that are lower. In all logic, Hawaii should be one landmass that floods, but I see her totally untouched in the year 2037. In fact, it's the same with some shorelines along the coast of South America. But in North America, I have seen a very large mass of water flowing through parts of Canada and the United States creating a new continental divide down the center of both continents. The last time this occurred, the Guides tell me, was over 30,000 years ago.

The environmental doves, as the Guides call them, are playing a pivotal role in the shift of this more dramatic unfolding as they work diligently to spread awareness for the sake of waking people up to impending catastrophe. They are doing their part to wake people up and to begin making different choices. There is a power dynamic at work here — to wake-up humanity — and the Mother is doing her part.

In my visions, I have seen a lot of tectonic plate movement in our future. I realize that they are moving all the time but by early 2024, the plates shift to such an extent that the world map is once again reconfigured. The world scientific community has tapped into the many shifts that occur. But in the second probability, the movement of the underground plates causes humanity harm simply because the masses do not take action before it is too late to transition into a new life flow and the lands underfoot begin to shift. With land mass movement come volcanic eruptions through the Ring of Fire, but unlike we have already seen, and massive earthquakes to relieve the pressure of the earth's surfaces as she adjusts to her new rotational cycle.

The earth is a living, breathing entity and she reacts to the organic re-mixing of her underground world. Once she is in sight of the photon belt, as she nears the electromagnetic pull of her sister galaxy, the Andromeda, the earth will begin to change her rotational speed, some might say imperceptibly so. In this slight slowing down, the underground rivers begin to shift and change in their direction to match the magnetic pole shifting. With this comes weather-pattern change, again to slight variation at first, then more dramatically as she moves closer to her final destination inside the galactic center, a magnetic ionic negative state. For a time, everything that has a positive charge will begin to shift to neutral then negative, and what is negative becomes positive. During this 14 to 17 year period, while the earth is moving through the galactic center, life on the planet will undergo a time of reorganization. What feels right will be left. What is top will feel like the bottom.

During this time of reorganization, especially during the years beginning 2024 through 2052, the world's population will begin moving. What was hot will be cold, what was cold will be hot, so entire populations will be on the move to shift, to relocate to temperature zones that are best suited for their liking.

The third probability and the pull toward oneness (the super highway)

In the third probability, the quickening of light that occurs in late 2012 is very strong, sure footed, which takes us into a much shorter period of chaos. The example of this is like a child who has a Band-Aid that she does not want peeled off, but if she allows it to be pulled off quickly, the shock to her system is shorter-lived.

The catalyst to this big shift into oneness consciousness

takes place as a singular event in our now future. In my visions, I have seen great flashes from the sky that shake people into the awareness that there is more to life than a future of war and poverty. Everyone experiences this global happening at the same time. It takes our focus off death and destruction and the warring nature of people hating one another. It serves as a focal point to create another collective 'aha' moment in our collective awareness.

No matter how we react to this event, we come firmly into a clear distinction within us that we are beings of light having a human experience. A greater degree of understanding is realized. We begin to have conversations all over the world. Some of us are already having these kinds of soul-level dialogues with one another but it will begin to happen on a global scale. Questions like, "What does life actually mean to me? How does this awakening change who I am?"

Because a greater percentage of the world's population will have made it through the first two gateways by then, the energetic pulse of light that comes into the planet becomes such a push, that it serves to shift humanity out of the fear-paradigm. By doing so, everyone stops in his or her tracks. No matter where we are in life, the question for many who have been enmeshed in fear up to this point will be, "What does this feeling inside of me now mean for my life, and my family? Why do I want to conquer?" So many will walk away that there will not be enough to fight.

In my visions, I have seen on a particular day in our collective experience that humanity finally takes a deep breath and decides that she just can't keep the killing going. There must be peace. Once humanity experiences this profound energetic push to stop the violence, the world does not resume with business as usual. The heart of our human family begins to transform. What follows is a time of reorganization. Chaos felt on all levels of our global society will then transition into a deep reshuffling of humanity's priorities.

Even without this primal shift in consciousness, unlike the long, protracted period of chaos in the second probability, chaos can take on a different form. In our highest expressions, chaos serves to bring humanity together to reposition her heart. External turmoil is unavoidable. But no matter how dramatic the future unfolding of world events will be, they will be relatively short-lived. Some will see the light and change; others will find themselves caught up in the continued warring only to put down their arms. There will be more pressing issues at hand. Those engaged in violence will eventually find no one to fight and will walk away.

The nature of chaos in the context of the third probability is best explained in terms of a metaphor: When a wave slams into the shore, the land is not harmed. The sand absorbs the water and the water retreats. So the economic changes that are coming will not harm but change, cause a shift in the way that we are purchasing, saving, transacting.

Chaos, of course, is not just felt on any one particular front. We are the benefactors of this form of chaos as many of the ideas coming from the East are crashing into the West. Ideas about who we are and how we are to best create. Ideas are clashing and concepts are clashing on all levels of our conscious awareness. When they clash, the hard edges get taken away and we begin to understand on deeper levels who we are. We begin to open up and accept change in a positive way by going with the flow. The third probability is all about our coming together. The clashes become very intense and as they quickly become very aligned, there's a strong equilibrium that is realized as a result.

I've seen this play out in the people making big choices about their lives. Some wait and piddle along and life gets muddled, difficult to pull away. Others see the writing on the wall, feel the internal connection with their heart and take their leap of faith. These are the success stories. Like a star rising in the night sky, they shine brightly with joy after having made their life-transitions in one fell swoop.

Going back through the same global dynamics, the highest probable future, as the group creation plays out in the flow of grace because the realization of oneness becomes the prevailing energy of what awakens the masses to realize this profound knowing.

Governance

Old paradigm leaders, those who are still in power by the year 2011, will experience along with everyone else, a tremendous amount of societal upheaval. The East will still rise up and economically crush the West but this kind of wave crashing is generally positive as the world economies reorganize themselves around flattened economic trade structures. In our higher probable future, this flattened system will become self-evident by early to mid-2014 and in full-blown reality creation by 2024.

In the new paradigm societies, the great thinkers of old will not be leading the masses. New paradigm leadership will be realized by many coalescing into the power as one. Until this new form of leadership is more widely accepted, there are many lands and many peoples who will try to subjugate this de-centralized power brokering by forcing key restraints on the individual. They will also persuade others to anchor in the old, outmoded pyramid structure of pushing energy to control and manipulate outcomes.

As our newly formed global communities take root, struc-turally, and socially, our current day judicial system will transition into peace councils by as early as 2022. By 2037, huge jail populations will be a thing of the past. When a problem needs to be solved, the people will come to a peace council to seek resolution. They may look, on the surface, like our current day trial system but they are vastly different in their approach. These councils will comprise 10 to 15, up to not more than 30 drawn from every corner of the community. They listen to the person(s) involved. They do not exact punitive action. They invite them into the circle to envision the outcome together. We begin to understand more and more about vibration. We begin to understand that we have the ability to transform matter, consciousness.

Social / Religion

The new paradigm of thought will also move into the realms of spirituality. Religions, by 2008, have already taken a turn for the worst, in their view. But in reality, the shift, in both philosophies and structures, is a positive one. No longer is there to be an insistence on cooperation and corroboration over the inner voice of the individual.

The legacies of the light species that came into humanity eons upon eons ago speak to the subjugation of the human species. The seeds of their awakened states have already been planted into the collective consciousness. Many beings have already begun to align, energetically, to determine outcomes for entire populations of people. The affects will be felt in the way one relates to God as a higher power, and to one another, in the belief of oneness of all united in heart.

The barriers of thought through conformity-beliefs and perceptions of one God being better or funneled through another to realize truth, redemption and liberation has already been broken. The seed thought in consciousness began in 1952, and was brought into the light through the unified field in early 2001. What began to show up in the physical was a mass outpouring of wrong-doing by trusted leaders (priests, rabbis, ministers, lay readers) who hid behind the cloak of structure after violating those they led.

The manifestation of corruption, and the fall from self-made grace on high, speaks to the paradigm of self-righteousness. All physical manifestations, as they are first created in thought and fueled by feeling, must find their way into physical form some way.

Religion has taught us this linear process (and is still teaching us) but now with one exception: We are beginning to understand that it is the power of one—the power of the individual coalescing with others through the feeling of oneness—that transforms even the most hardened of hearts.

Once this basic precept is rooted in mass consciousness, the grid of light that ignites the passions of love and joyousness among all people, everywhere, will activate fully and completely. Therefore, in the third probability, humanity realizes that all spiritual paths are a united front for the individual path (individualized learning) for purpose of opening the heart and achieving a higher state of awareness. We will enter into the age of self-empowerment in its truest form.

Social / Environmental

Well before 2024, with weather pattern changes and dramatic events having been fully realized that forces people out of the cities, we will be living in small communities. By that time, through attrition, malnutrition, natural catastrophe and war, over half of the world's population will be gone and by 2037, humanity will be one-third her current size. These clustered communities will comprise of smaller enclaves nestled in the natural world and will feel more like family to us. Mother Nature by that time, will be a very present part of our lives. We will appreciate her so much more than we did before the quickening. Her significance in maintaining overall balance and harmony will have, by this time, sounded a very big alarm.

We will find one another through discerning the vibration of the group much like we do now, but with a deeper awareness of the collective consciousness. Also by 2024, our monetary system will become even more integrated into a myriad of barter systems. It may sound like, in this third probability, that we are returning to the many post-catastrophic visions many seers have envisioned but a way opens us up to realize a new system. It's a strong push into a new evolutionary building cycle, and a very positive one. In this higher probability, there is a deeply felt appreciation by all that live this way.

Economic / Governmental

After a series of turbulent changes in 2008, by early 2009, entire governments scramble to fend off the crush of economic collapse of world markets financed by corporate global alliances. By late 2014, the world populations begin to rally around decentralized commerce and grassroots enterprises as globalization by the little guy spring up as old structures collapse.

New ways of representing the group call forth vast changes in status quo bureaucracies. Cash-strapped systems vie for military control but begin to step back and away when bombs drop on unsuspecting regions to deflate growing innuendoes. There are many who will say, "I saw it coming all along," but most will be surprised by the great flash in this sky. All will see the rememberance of the light when the forces of Nature deliver a final warning of global implications to all of humanity. It will not be the bombardment of one people onto the other that will cause humanity to stop the hate, but Mother Nature.

There will be no intervention by outside forces, no takeover strategies. Humanity will be called to save herself. As the realization of wholeness, of oneness, begins to set in to even the most hardhearted human-being, we will see vast changes in our society begin to take hold by as early as 2013.

Even as the mass quickening in consciousness begins to appear in evidential form by early 2009, the years following this shift in consciousness will be quite austere at times. Pockets of hatred and malice will be felt by the collective consciousness from 2024 through 2027. Then, once again great waves of sadness are experienced by humanity as the rising waters flood the lands of the lower regions near the ocean shoreline dispelling doubt about our ability to come together and consciously make different choices.

The Tectonic plates well beneath the ocean floor will have shifted by then leaving great wastelands of land-masses with strewn buildings within the communities laid barren and empty. A return to simplicity in communities will give way to great wave patterns of love and compassion for one another. The divisional nature among the races will give way to cooperative problem-solving for the sake of the collective.

As the earth begins to experience the shifting of the magnetic poles, it will cause a massive trans-migration of people coming from different countries. Starting from early 2010 the temperatures will begin to dramatize our plight and we will see that the world's supply of water will become so scarce that wars will be fought over water rights.

Our dependence on oil, by early 2037 will seem like an archaic idea by the time we are there, because water will consume our minds by as early as 2017. Water rights will be challenged by those who are used to having, and suddenly will have not. Those who have are used to getting what they want and by exerting their power they will cause skirmishes to occur in places that would not normally think to cause strife.

Mother Nature will react in ways that will cause humanity to stop fighting because there will be no time for hatred in the new paradigm. With our focus off of natural oil and gas, free energy will become a mainstay. New technologies will replace warring factions as solutions are found to tap into underground sources and find uncontaminated waters.

With the ozone layer being depleted, we will expect to see more harshness in our weather but that will not happen. In areas of the world where there is snow, there will be water. In areas where there is sun, there will be cold. The pole shifting will reverse many weather patterns to such the extent that we will see many animals leave the planet and never come back.

Future catastrophic events are not unlike what we have already experienced through feeling, but in the third probability, they will play out in a different way. We will be able to anticipate the events prior to the time of the unfolding, because we will feel a deep quickening inside ourselves that will feel a kind of pulling or magnetic sense on our bodies. Mother Nature is tied into everything we think or do, and with this knowing we will begin to form councils, loose knit weather watchers who will send out alarms to others. We will tune into the vibrational quality of what is coming and send calming rays of love and oneness into the masses to help them to deal with what is coming. Our job is not to shift what has already been set into motion but to witness outcomes as different.

Social / Environmental

Humanity's way of killing one another will change from warfare to survival just like the current precedent in the animal kingdom. Mother Nature already provides us with a valuable way of surviving in harmony without having to inflict pain on one another.

By 2010, we will see the world's shorelines begin to flood inland waterways to such an extent that entire cities will have to be evacuated. First to feel the affects of this will be

Indonesia. At first, the West will not take pity but then when our own eastern shorelines are eaten up by the rising waters, we will sound the alarm and ask the world for help. It's all a game of yin and yang. Eventually, we will begin to recognize that thoughts really do have the power to create, and we will begin to adjoin with Mother Nature to listen, to gain insight and knowledge to what she wishes to tell us.

It's all a game of balance and harmony. Humanity is grossly out of balance, and it is the role of Mother Nature as the earth's surrogate to bring her creation back into harmony.

The revelation that we are not alone

Common to all three probable futures, it will become more commonly accepted, by 2012, that we are not alone. This concept is creeping into humanity's consciousness now, but vast reaches of populations will accept this fact because everyone every where will experience it for themselves as a single event. The *we are not alone* part of the equation is a comforting one to me personally since much of my life is spent in the higher realms. But the Guides tell me that by early 2027, the veil will be lifted from the collective consciousness to such an extent that many will come to witness other worlds, other beings of light, as a normal part of their day-to-day lives. These higher dimensional beings will play an invaluable part in the rebuilding, restructuring of many of our social systems. They will also help us to develop, as they are already, new light technologies that will be applied to solving issues of health and wellness.

A very small percentage of the world's population has already worked through most of the more obvious pitfalls that come from holding onto hatred and malice born of oppression. As growing numbers realize that oneness consciousness is what will not only allow humanity to survive but thrive, we will begin to see more evidence of humanity's awakening.

The pull toward the joy of oneness is getting stronger, even now, as we continue to vacillate between buying into the validity of our physical reality creations or listening to our heart that tells us to be on the ready. No matter where you are in your journey toward this mode of deep listening to the inner wisdom that guides you, you are bound to feel the oneness propel you to jump into the deeper river of stillness in the coming months and years ahead.

The very nature of the third probability is helping us to understand that the chaos at the shift point does not have to be so painful even as it may very well play in the above described dramatic ways. How the creations are already playing out is mostly out of our individual control at this point, but how we react to the change required of us is our choice.

8: TRANSFORMING OR TRANSCENDING DUALITY

The courage of the individual to affect vast global change

As you can see, the three over-riding probable global futures have common themes but are destined to play out a bit differently depending on what our human family chooses right here in our present moment. The force that drives these futures is the individual who holds the power of love as a force of light for change. We may not allow love into our lives, but we are still propelled by it even as we might be haunted by fear. Just remember that as you begin moving through these group creation cycles. It's easy to get caught up in something that feels so much bigger than you. But we are powerful beings of light and love always transcends fear.

Within the over-arching themes are the energetics that push or pull us into particular life-choices. It's important to understand what the group creation cycles are about and how they are likely to play out given current-day reality. Therefore, this section will take you through a progression of specific cycles to provide you with a clear picture of the mind verses heart choice associated with world events that have direct impact on our daily lives.

Again, remember that everything is energy, and energy is only matter that first is created in thought, which is then expressed as emotion and played out in the physical. As group creations form, these emotional qualities become calcified as entire populations begin repeating the same emotional patterns. Patterns become perception then quickly turn into beliefs and are eventually adopted as fact by entire populations. Once these creations become a part of the cultural norm, it is nearly impossible to change any dynamic without a catalyst to cause a shift. As the Guides have repeatedly said, there must be chaos before new order is realized, and that is what the energetic shifts are designed to do. Shifts allow us to channel more light. But most of us are more afraid of chaos than the pain we endure to conform.

Many souls are born into families and societies that have endured particular creation cycles, like oppressions, for thousands of years, then within a generation, the soul group experiences a revolt or uprising to shift away from it. Why? Because the souls coming into the physical are programmed to accept the challenge of creating movement, and second, the energetic climate transforms to provide the support needed for the group to implement the change. That's where you come in. As you read through this next section, it is designed to help you to see where you are in your own life. Use this next bit of information as a guide for transforming your life as you learn how to shift in vibration.

Any creation cycle can be dramatically shifted, transformed or transcended but the likelihood of that happening in a way that will completely change the collective direction is highly unlikely simply because the malaise of the core vibration already resides in the deeper levels of humanity's collective unconscious. But just by understanding what is going on and holding others in appreciation, know that you are doing your part to help others to shift. However, there isn't anything that you are called to deal with that isn't also inside of you, which leads me to my next point. Before you can transform any learning dynamic, it first must be brought into your conscious awareness. Some of these creation cycles have been a part of our physical world for thousands of years. In some cases, they have served as the underpinnings of societal norms for entire populations. But even so, energy is energy.

Transforming or transcending established global patterns

Oppression and freedom

We cannot talk about issues of transformation or transcendence without diving into a deeper look at the very nature of oppression since this vibrational quality has long been a part of our human experience. Many of us now understand the nature of the impact oppression has already had on humanity. I cannot understate the influence that oppression has on the warring factions that govern this earth plane. These factions would rather destroy than rebuild the unity of humanity because division—dividing and conquering—where they are concerned, is what matters most. Many of us fall prey to the vibrations that come with this dynamic simply because it is so familiar to us. Even though the feeling of oppression is repulsive to us by now, we have had deep experiences with hate, malice, discontent, control, manipulation, and subjugation—I could go on—but the familiarity with oppression can lure us in. Our disgusted reaction to it, when it shows up in our lives renders us fearful. This kind of drawing something to us out of familiarity then pushing it away or getting ensnared is a kind of Catch-22 in action.

In the coming years ahead, I encourage you to root out this quality in your life and to take note of others who are attracted to co-create with you. Over the next five to seven years, most of us will be striving to transcend oppression that will first take form as economic oppression. This does not mean that suddenly you will be poor or thrown out of your job or way of living, but it does mean that you will be challenged to follow your heart and not make choices simply to protect your pocket book.

The Guides say it this way, "It is not an easy task to break free from the more oppressive creations in your lives but as you begin to identify your soul path and purpose, the many grand awakenings will begin to guide you along the way. You cannot see beyond the moment to moment feelings in your present state of beingness, as the actions of a few will play out to affect the entirety of your society. It's quite all right that you are not aware of the next enfoldment within these reality creations. You are simply to trust in the moment of your earthly expressions and remember the truth of who you are at all times."

The Guides go on to remind us that the mind might question the inner realities of our world but our heart will create the solutions of the day. As our soul calls us to be free, we are to reflect this knowing in our own choices despite what is going on all around us. In short, our personal struggles with oppression exist because we have allowed our minds to run amok in fear that is rooted in the dynamic of being intimidated by others.

Oppression as a form of social reform and control

The oppression that plays out in all three probable futures will continue to manifest as hatred and malice, complacency and terror. It becomes such a strong force that by as early as 2010 we witness stepped up degrees of the backlash from these group creations. Again, as humanity acts out the more dramatic creations, Mother Nature will do her part to bring humanity back into balance and harmony.

By early to mid 2026, what the Guides call *the vile nature of subjugation and control* will be virtually gone from the planet. But in its place will be tracking devices that will electronically control outcomes and constrict movement by one controlling group over another. What will start out as convenient or logical solutions to logistical, modern-day living, will spiral into the surrender of personal freedom to the extent that societies will form a new cast as slave and slave owner.

The beginnings of this new caste system has its roots in our current polarized economies where a small percentage of the world's population is living in relatively high standards of living while entire regions of people go hungry. In the West, we are not living out that same degree of exaggerated duality, but with the influx of the use of credit we are headed in that direction as we begin witnessing the credit markets crash into our system of living on borrowed money. There will always be a way to circumvent a system but many of us in our modern ways of using plastic money will begin to realize that the basis for this system is to promote addiction and control over our lives. Taken to the extreme, this form of automation is one that will create an entire industry of dependencies of loan sharks and loan hunters for the sake of exculpating oneself from the subjugation that comes when the former change of life no longer matters.

Human kind will always devise ways to create. Our world of matter propels us to invent realities built on the desire to serve others. As we collectively awaken to grand possibilities, we will begin to orchestrate change at will, but that is where we are headed. We're not there yet. Issues of control and demise will first play itself out in grand style and contribute to the chaos before new order is realized.

Any central intelligence group or organized thought cannot control this kind of group orchestration of change. We can only devise ways to circumvent devices that create hardship within the reality of what we are physically experiencing. The realities of mind control and the imbedding of electronic tracking devices within the context of entire populations — to track and to control their physical movement — is an integral part of humanity's present moment, and plays out in the future as restriction of human rights. These same devices may speak to the harshness of thought but will never control our soul.

Human tracking devices are already in play, which

inevitably lead to deeper levels of control. The animal population has been tracked for years by rice sized computer chips imbedded under the skin. The next step is to imbed the device in all newborn children (already being done on a voluntary basis). If you own a US passport after 2011, you already have one. Next to be introduced into the unconsciousness is the national identification card followed by the rice-like computer chip.

In a broader sense, the old controlling ways of manipulating people's emotions (like sending out daily doses of fear then periodically staging acts of terror to get the masses to give their rights away) will be replaced with more modern-day technologically sophisticated behaviors. These tactics and devices will try to influence our thoughts, our beliefs and therefore plant the seeds of destruction of individualized thought patterns. Mass consciousness is well on its way to believing in what a small, controlled corporately-sponsored showcase of violence is doing for the purpose of shifting us into a defensive, divisional nature.

Only time will tell if the backlash to this form of subjugation and control will tantalize even the most ardent supporter of these methods of control. These same supporters may begin to encourage the masses to break out of this same divisive pattern once they realize that they have not only given others' rights away but their own.

Regardless of which over-riding probable future humanity moves into, the pattern where oppression is concerned was created so long ago. We know that there will be no new vibrations to offer up interference, but these tendencies are already in full swing and will play out until it is complete. The task at hand is to transform or transcend these cycles that are counter to oneness-consciousness. As you clear them inside of you,

you will not become ensnared in these lower probable futures. Allow joy to be your guide.

The Yin/Yang of oppression and how creation cycles play out

Like a pendulum that swings back and forth, every creation cycle swings back and forth. But in the balance of life, the swing is usually consistent, which maintains an overall sense of equilibrium. In life, we like it when we are in an up cycle or find ourselves on top of the heap, but we can also find ourselves in a time of deep sadness even as we have made our choice for joy. Some people may define this back and forth cycle through the filter of universal law — through the law of cause and effect — but it's more complex than that.

For instance, we may gain our physical freedom from incarceration but if we continue to carry the burden of this feeling of being caged long after we are liberated, then it's almost the same as still being incarcerated. These more ingrained creation cycles, like oppression, are like that as well. Even though humanity, for all intents and purposes, has already gained her freedom, she is still playing it out as though the war has not been won.

She'll play this game of liberation out one more time before she finally gets it. In the year of 2027 there will be an energetic shift where all souls adjoining as one frequency of light will realize a very specific form of freedom. Oppression, at that time, will have fully played out as freedom from economic oppression. There are other soul groups working to realize other forms of freedom but this example will help you to understand how the pendulum always swings back until we finally get it; the lesson that is. Use this next example to discern how you are to best move through your own creation cycles.

Those of us who incarnated during the years of 1917 to 1967 are evolving toward our ability to recognize oppression that takes form as manipulation and control of the mind. We have already experienced oppression through our involvement with those wishing to exert control through social structures. Many of us were either there or hold vivid mental pictures of emaciated people being liberated from the Nazi concentration camps. That was the most recent yang part of the cycle.

We have a strong residual memory of this experience of oppression because it prepared us to begin moving through the yin part of the cycle. The yang part is very physical, action oriented while the yin is quiet, receptive almost. When the pendulum is in the yang part of its swing, we are outwardly reactive, participatory. When it begins to swing back we are seemingly caught in mock surprise, as it seems that we are receiving the vibration. Our modern day version of this yin/yang dynamic is playing out now.

From 1924 to 1947 oppression played out as overt violence and subjugation of the collective self. This time, the yin of oppression has taken form as apathy, hopelessness and despair. In many parts of the world, people who wear this face of oppression, hopelessness, for instance, is pervasive. To become ensnared in this vibration requires no particular social standing. Even as so many of us remember the overt violence, this yin part of the wave or curve is actively playing out in all social structures, nationalities, world cultures, and ages. The yin of oppression is especially swinging back as harshness in the face of social conformity.

And just like the WWII troops who liberated those who were still being held captive, the continued reduction of our rights is setting the stage for liberation as entire populations wake-up and break the pattern. Realizing freedom from oppression in this yang phase of the pendulum swing is a core life path, especially if you are working to clear any of these more pervasive forms of oppression from your own life.

Right about now, you might be asking, "What causes these

feelings (apathy, hopelessness and despair) to pervade my peace of mind? Most are rooted in long forgotten or stored trauma but they don't have to hold us hostage. The point is to get these vibrations out of your body so that you can move on and create the life of your heart's desire and contribute to the shift in others.

Waking up to who you are is the first step to realizing liberation. It just seems like some cycles are more intense than others to break because they have been with us for so long. For some, we have wrapped ourselves in guilt or self-hatred, for instance, throughout our history on the planet. Where the soul is concerned time is not a factor. Learning is the ultimate goal.

Where these more recent memories of oppression are concerned, most of us have suppressed the trauma from other lifetimes. We bring these vibrations in to heal and transform but before we do, many of us make choices that border on insanity or worse, self-destruction. The next example is not pleasant but I think it's important to understand the human dynamic that plays out to help us to wake-up. This is a story of how past trauma influences the present and how remembering transforms.

Greg is a very bright, creative thirty-something professional who works in a busy office. When I first met him he was consumed by the kind of insecurity that comes from extreme shyness yet wanted to act out sexually. At the same time he had an irrational fear of being attacked. Coupled with his shyness, it caused him to avoid people as much as possible.

As we discovered, buried deep inside his subconscious mind was locked away the horrors of being raped and defiled by German soldiers. In 1937 during his former life, he was a young beautiful Jewish woman who was very shy. Once forcefully separated out from her family of origin, she was taken to an internment camp. She was spotted by these soldiers and bandied about because of her purity but more because of her shyness. The humiliation was so unbearable that she took her own life.

Having so quickly come back into the body so that she could rejoin her soul group, she decided to return as male to protect herself. But she retained her female identity along with the feeling nature of the trauma to afford her the opportunity to heal the emotional wounds.

Once Greg recognized the source of his fear, he also began to understand that his life-path was to let go of the fear that held him captive. By doing so, he began to make sense of his irrational fear and his sexuality. His life began to calm down and a sense of peace came to him. The last time I spoke with him, he said he'd always wanted to design sets for the theater, so he had joined a local theater group, and had just completed his first play. He loved it.

This same process of awakening to remember who we truly are is still being played out over and over again. If you are experiencing unexplainable fears, fragmented dreams that don't make sense or deep wells of sadness, depression, anxiety, then consider that it may be hidden soul memories of trauma. The tools for transforming these fears are just ahead.

Another more recent wave of mass awakening served to break through the more protracted physical manifestations. Beginning in 1964, this light infusion caused a great wave of celebration that took form as the Cultural Revolution. People all over the world began breaking away from long-held social norms of conformity that had, up until that time, been all about protecting the group. This new wave broke through that barrier and began to recognize the value of individual self-expression.

This new influx of light led to freedom of expression. We now celebrate greats like Martin Luther King and Gandhi but back then they (and many others like them) were considered a threat to the status quo. At first, this push for self-expression was met with resistance and experienced as violence by those who didn't accept the change. But mass consciousness eventually embraced their message of love and non-violence and with this acceptance-followed chaos. The chaos gave way to reform and birthed a new social order into being. The East and the West are still working through the issues of separation and segregation on many different levels as they move toward a more equitable way.

When this new wave of light first came into form, women and children were profoundly impacted as their warrior husbands; fathers and brothers took to the streets to protest the violation of the many sacred trusts that had been broken. Trust played a big part in this cycle. The hide and seek policy-makers of the day epitomized the defense of broken trust between those who wielded power and those who reacted to power. But this cycle also gave way to enlightened knowing 30 years later. Even today, there are many who reacted to power during this time of radical change who still hold onto the habitual ways of defending and protecting social structures and positions of power that no longer serve the greater good. But that's what learning and moving up the spiral is all about. You've got to know when to hold fast to a particular learning pattern, and when to let go.

By the late 1990s, humanity was poised to move through a second shift in her collective consciousness. This time, many more beings of light were called to wake-up and move through the chaos. The status quo way of hiding out was no longer workable. The vibration coming into the planet had radically shifted. Even some of the most ardent light beings who were rooted in the five senses were called to awaken. Those who had already awakened in earlier cycles were poised and ready to help. Just like now, the teachers, the activators, bridge-builders are helping others.

By early 2000, grace poured into the planet — great waves of grace. This time it caused an exponential shift in consciousness that is in play in our present moment. Grace poured in, and rage and anger flushed up to the surface of our human expression.

An act of terrorism is born from the energetic dynamic of subjugating the self. When one aspect of humanity dishonors herself, rage sets in and one part of our human family pits itself against the other. In this case, the energetic of terror was birthed from the hatred of those who engaged in domination of others.

By the fall of 2001 the influx of this light caused the world to shift into chaos. Some souls saw it coming and chose to leave. For those who did choose to leave, the door was opened and many transitioned. Many allowed their collective light to be used as a beacon to help entire populations begin to see their way to freedom. The events that unfolded from 2001 - 2004, were a part of the greater story of humanity's cry for help, and the higher realm response. There were millions of souls who transitioned over that three-year period for the purpose of warding off a more dramatic learning in the coming times ahead.

The series of catastrophes (record storms, earthquakes, and tsunamis) that were unleashed by Mother Nature within that same timeframe was just the precursor to what is on the horizon. Those who participated in physical ascensions during that time created a cap of light that encircled the globe. As they did, they co-created with their brethren on the other side to circumvent a more dramatic future of more terror and land mass shifting. Along with Mother Nature, humanity's collective future was thereby radically shifted into a gentler, sequencing of earth-timed events.

My personal reaction to the events from that time forward was, in part, what led me to open up publicly, and begin sharing what I know about how we can avert a more dramatic future like the events that played out during that three year period. What I witnessed was a massive light that provided humanity the energetic shift needed to create our highest probability. Like a rocket booster propelling humanity beyond the confines of hatred and violence, we can learn how to use this grace to realize global harmony.

It's been almost seven years now, and I have rarely spoken about this deep knowing, and my reaction to the events, especially during that three-year period. The souls who were so suddenly called home, helped to divert a much more catastrophic ending. They helped to create an unprecedented opportunity for humanity to finally remember her collective call to awaken. The events served to avert a global holocaust, and set into motion our collective journey toward oneness.

Over the course of the next few years, I took note of how the events that followed played out. They served to swing the vibrations of hatred and violence back toward love and forgiveness. Even today with wars still raging, millions more are choosing love and forgiveness. The angels and Guides have been emphatic all along that there is never a right or wrong in any given choice—there is no such thing as good or bad—just choice. They told me that they are here now because we, the light beings in human form, have called them to us. We are ready to listen and to begin to make the shift in consciousness the easy way. We have already experienced enough pain and hardship to know what that feels like, and now enough of us are ready to begin creating our individual and collective reality with love and joyousness.

There is proof of that happening everywhere. Most of us, who have already crossed over from mind to heart, can already feel the difference in our own lives and are seeing the signs of change everywhere.

The events that have unfolded since that last energetic

opening have been nothing short of miraculous. People, the world over, are waking up to compassion like never before. Entire countries of people are coming to the aide of the other in record numbers. And it's not just the governmental leaders but people of all nationalities who are stepping forward. The level of humanitarian activism, the world over, is unprecedented. We are a race of nations in the middle of rebuilding our global society.

And yet, there is so much more to do. The pain of self-inflicted violence as evidenced in war is miniscule compared to the millions killed in other parts of the world right now. The child poverty and starvation rates are staggering. Economic woes compare only to disease striking entire populations. We grieve our losses close to home. Many of our hearts are breaking. Amplify this feeling out to everyone and we have a global family still deeply grieving while at the same time striving to save ourselves.

That last shift has set the stage for a grand awakening of a different sort. As geopolitical landscapes begin to shift and take on partisan politics throughout inter-governmental structures, people everywhere will begin to declare their governments broken, defunct, oppressive and out of touch. With this choice will come great waves of sadness that will once again prompt many to leave the body in a variety of ways: some by falling victim to poverty and malnutrition, others by landslides, earthquakes and water poisoning. Others will play out their demise in political uprising and revolts and thus die under the banner of martyr, or other familiar patterns of cause-related learning. But that is the yin part of the creation; the yang may very well play out as peace. That would be our higher probable future as the pendulum of oppression makes its final swing back into balance.

The end result of the oppression cycle leads to an opening

for humanity to create differently. We all learn by example and learning through the act of terror is no different. The net result, after the trauma settles and the wounds have healed, will be deeper levels of connection. Like any organic process, even as whole systems are showing visible signs of decay, already springing up from a variety of sources is a global-kind of inter-connecting of ideas, philosophies, artist happenings and commerce. Grassroots community building is already on the rise and challenging patriarchal stances, in some cases, for the first time in hundred of years. As governments falter, private sector interests will take over, and the individual will begin to drop out, and break away from status quo once again.

On the individual day-to-day level, by the time you recognize the learning that you have gained by being a part of any aspect of oppression, you will always transform whatever it is into freedom by unconditionally loving the self and everyone else involved in the creation. Freedom is fueled by the desire to honor all parties involved. As you set your intention to love every aspect of the self, especially whenever oppression shows up, you can be guaranteed that freedom is just a pendulum swing away.

Global stewardship transforms world dominance

Oppression has been playing out on the global scale for as long as people have been alive. It seems to be human nature to want to control or dominate one's environment. Today is no different. With big business and big government dictating the terms of our environment, it's pretty easy to buy in to the belief that we have no power. But that is only what is on the surface of life. In our world today, global dominance by one super power over another played out in dramatic style in the early 1950s until the mid-1980s. The power games continue but now they are so out of kilter that people everywhere are waking up and asking the big question. Why does it have to be the way that it is?

Some ask the question because they are hurting, and others because they have so long been dominated that they have had enough. Others see all the mayhem that happens when the power dynamics turn to total disregard for human life and they jump in to help make it right.

On the whole, humanity is in the midst of transforming world dominance but over the next five to seven years it will not look that way on the surface of our lives at all. We are feeling, and seeing evidence of this transformation as people take to the streets and defy control politics by stepping in to help those in need, or rallying around rainforest issues by planting trees where giant forests once stood. Others have seen the writing on the wall and are seeking out safe havens to build new models of community. Whatever the motivation, we are in the midst of rebuilding community even as the old is crumbling around the edges. Economic chaos is looming large these days but right behind any big crash is the multitudes already rebuilding around new ideals. We are all part of such a grand creation. It's an organic process that emulates the ways of Mother Nature. Anytime a grand old tree falls to the ground, there is new growth springing up before you know it.

Going back into the prophecy of the East rising up to retaliate against the West, when I first heard this prophecy, I asked the Guides what it meant in human terms, and how was it likely to play out. The answer I received surprised me but when I started to look around my immediate world, their words of wisdom started to make more sense to me.

The East is most certainly crashing into the West on the economic front. Walk into any store and look at the label of origin and you will find names like China, India, Vietnam, Japan, etc. Most of the goods and services we purchase here in the West are created in the East and shipped to the West. We pay our taxes to our state and federal governments but our taxes do not pay for the services. The taxes Americans pay go toward the interest the US owes its lenders, our biggest being China. The average American citizen, like many other citizens of other countries, has been lulled into believing that the US is autonomous, but it is not. I won't even go into the subject of the West's dependency on oil and natural gas because it's such an obvious creation cycle. Not only are we all so interconnected through games of global commerce on so many levels, but we will continue to move through the more ingrained cycles until we have transformed control through world dominance into global stewardship.

This part of our earth game is played out in the myriad of souls who have come to the aide of humanity time and time again. We have come here so often that many of us have become a part of the problem instead of working toward the solution. But, as we awaken from our slumber, we are seeing that the game can be played out quite differently. We are not here to change the game of power dominance but to transcend it entirely by becoming global stewards of our own lives.

How does this apply to us? By first liberating our selves from complacency. Many of us operate on the illusion that our appointed or elected leaders are making choices in our collective best interest. It's an illusion but a convenient one as long as their choices don't infringe upon our lives. But that is where complacency factors in.

The first step to transforming world dominance is to begin taking total responsibility for your life choices. Become aware and awakened to the choices that you make and make them wisely. Apply this feeling of being a global steward as you make choices as a part of your daily activities. Do so by becoming a conscious consumer, by caring about what happens to waste as much as growth. Hold the energy of all as one and use this as a filter for all the choices you make each day.

In our highest probability, by early 2009, enough of the world's population is awakened and begins the process of transcending the paradigm of world dominance. There is no need for bombs or retaliation as we accomplish this shift. As a part of the third probability, this revolution of heart happens by people everywhere holding to the higher frequencies of light. This activates the energy centers of those who are still asleep. Between the later part of 2008 and late-2012, we experience a build up of energy that will at some point in our conscious awareness feel like a big bubble that is about to pop. But in actuality, it is the collective consciousness of light beings waking up.

During the time of the quickening of consciousness that will be felt around the world, the masses will begin to awaken to another way to create within the context of humanity. To my knowing, it feels like nothing short of a modern-day miracle. Even in saying this, we are seeing the power of the individual swiftly sweep into a collective adjoining by accessing global consciousness through the power of the Internet. Our modern world is becoming smaller and more inter-connected by the day. Through streaming images, e-blogs, forums, and pod casts, greater numbers are witnessing both the atrocities and the solutions to issues of global significance.

Through our own eyes and ears, we can see that what affects one truly influences all. By staying alert, it becomes obvious that it is not the role of one power, one human force, to control and to manipulate the masses. It's up to each of us to take control of our own lives by commanding respect and by showing respect for others.

Now is the time, more than at any time in humanity's evolution, to challenge old paradigms by speaking your truth. By doing so, you will be helping the few to save many from death and further destruction. To this end, you are bound to witness a plethora of altruistic acts as new paradigm leaders make their way to the forefront of our collective awareness. And it so simple to do your part: When you are called to speak your truth, do so without reservation. As you do, have confidence that your voice will be heard over the din of those insisting that everything stay the same. Don't get discouraged. Just proceed with knowing that all is well.

The Guides say it this way: "There will come a time that many will tell you that you're crazy; that you are to back down and away from your positioning of light (that of honoring of the self) but you are to remain steady. You are to be creating in the oneness of heart and know that all is well.

"We will be there with you to help, to guide, to direct your inner knowing. Your sight will be blocked for a time but you are not to worry at all. You are to remember the oath you took before your arrival on the planet that you would be ready to take action, to follow through when it was time to totally trust your heart.

"You, as a race of nations, are ready to co-create in this manner. We are here with you to create in the vibration of oneness. The stories of old will be washed away. You will create in the oneness that will guide you. You are not to worry about getting it right. You are always right. You are always in the right place at the right time.

"Follow the flowing of your heart, and know that all is well. We will help you to shift the energy of the planet of light you call home. We will help you to see what you have not wanted to see up until now. You are a grand being of light and we are now ready to show you the truth of who you truly are. Be well my child and know that all is well.

"There will be four waves of sadness moving across the face of your human family. You are not to worry. You are not to doubt. You are to be ready to help where there will be great need of compassion. Know that as you are determining your fate as a being of light that you are to know that all is well.

"As we usher in tremendous feelings of joy, know that we are causing the fear vibrations to accelerate in their release. The human race will attempt to self-annihilate by late-2008 but you are not to worry at all. You will see many changes to the human structural way of creating by then as many light beings are focusing their conscious attention on evolving the paradigm of love.

"By early 2009, the perceived danger will have been averted and the creations of old will fall by the wayside. Many reforms and retributions will take the place of retaliations. You will begin to see the many beings of light step forward and offer differing ways of creating the new. You will be moving through cycles of hatred and malice for another 27 years but to a much lesser extent. You will experience pockets of failure, but you are not to be concerned. These pockets will fall into equilibrium as the players of the game realize there is no other way but to surrender to the light of love within.

"You will know your part in all of this because you will be ready. You will be ready to create, and you will be ready to realize that you are part of the new paradigm of leadership that will sweep the land. Know that as you open your heart and realize that your path is clear to love one another, that all is well."

Unconditional love transcends the anti-Christ
(powerlessness)

The energetic seed of the anti-Christ has already been planted in mass consciousness and will be played out in a crescendo-like fashion in early 2024 through 2027. As beings of light, we are here to dispel all notions of this dynamic by serving as channels for grace to others in all we are called to do.

The social aspects of powerlessness will be played out by

humanity as she works through grand games of innovation by then. But right now, people everywhere are coalescing into a collective consciousness around old familiar patterns of fear. It's like humanity is standing in a pool of water that is no longer refreshing. She has already had enough of being barraged with the many fear-based innuendoes. She has recognized that it is time to move into a clearing of fresh water, a new vitality that flows with life and innovation.

You might say that water is water, and it's not what it is but what you do with it, how you experience it: cold, stagnant, warm, murky, clear, still, moving. Of course I am using the metaphor of water to describe the state of human emotion. In this particular instance, the pool of mass consciousness has become stagnant with fear. Fear is the emotion of choice by governments and industries wishing to push particular controlled-based agendas and to subjugate huge populations into mental boxes and obliterate rights of freedom of expression, movement and privacy to name just a few.

We have an inherent right to experience and to express freedom. We, as light beings, have come here to awaken the others who have already surrendered their light to fear. The awakening can be found within a set of triggers imbedded deep within the subconscious mind. It's just a simple matter of teaching others, by example, what it looks like and feels like to allow grace to supersede the controlling, terrorizing nature of fear. Even as these fear tactics play out, the voices for joy are getting louder and bolder in their calling to be free. It is not a fight the world consciousness is involved in. It's more like a wave of joy crashing into fear. Fear has been with us for so long that many have lost their way. But with deeper, richer voices over-riding the drone of fear messages, people are starting to wake-up and say *I have had enough.* It's important in the process not to get discouraged.

Government entities and their compatriots, especially in the West where world dominance schemes and themes will continue to play out through 2017, will try to push the paradigm of fear into a mass state of apathy. Many people today have already surrendered to outside controlling forces and are moving into life circumstances that affect others merely by their choosing to do nothing but surrender their sense of self to the perception of an outside authority who promises to keep them safe from perceived threats. This is the continued playing out of an old paradigm. As the individual feels powerless against something greater, outside the self, an all-knowing, all-powerful force that affects change by wielding a powerful sword will come in with an agenda of controlling others. Little do they know that this form of control is actually in play to be swung back into balance, but it will first be swung back to the very person sitting in support of this dynamic.

We are witnessing the pendulum swinging now as many feel powerless to change the direction of plans, reforms or persuasions that have gone awry, which by now are clearly recognized as having been built on lies, deceit or errors in judgment. We have seen this in our own country as governments of the people and by the people have wielded great transgressions against the collective self in the name of righteousness. But in actuality, the consciousness that fuels this trend is blatantly inflicting violence against the self, and will be remembered as raping, burning and pillaging other families, communities, and countries.

As many sit back in horror and witness complacency at its heightened state of awareness, awakened light beings are making different choices. But by the time the pendulum swings back to a state of equilibrium, the tiger will have already escaped from the zoo and wreaked havoc on every one, including her zookeepers. But we will be off playing in the woods, exploring the fields totally unaware of the mayhem. This will be the time where the two rivers of consciousness will be so split that the lower will be playing out in full form while the higher is exponentially increasing.

As more and more will eventually realize, the only clear path to transcending powerlessness is to wake-up and reclaim our power in all areas of our lives. Invoke unconditional love in all that you are and everything you are called to do. *Love all, serve all,* is the motto for transcending this collective consciousness, which will sometimes take on values that on the surface will seem quite counter to the feel good feelings of unconditional love. But like all actions that are rooted in love, the outcome will be the proof that is needed to fully merge with your inner knowing.

Powerless has become such a prevailing part of humanity's reality that many of us have become complacent about our own right to claim and honor who we are. Pay attention to the finer nuances of powerlessness when it comes to your life. You are not part of a group, like cattle moving to market. You are a divine being of light and you get to choose.

The stories of people taking back their power are almost too many to remember now, but the more dramatic ones are those who have endured untold acts of violence only to wake-up and embrace the very essence of who they are. Rather than succumb to the circumstances that brought them so much hardship, they instead, make the choice for love. These are the most courageous and powerful people I have ever met. Many of us have heard the more publicized stories of those who have endured horrible conditions like Nelson Mandela and his years in prison. Hatred never solves anything. The people who have come through the eye of the storm of hatred and malice, and have forgiven others and themselves are remarkable people because they inherently understand who they truly are.

This example is a composite of three people but I have

reframed the common learning pattern into one: Dawn is a petite, physically beautiful woman with a gentle, quiet nature. The very first time I spoke to her, she announced in a very matter of fact manner that she was going to leave the planet. It didn't matter that her time was not yet up. She was going to *make* it happen. She had planned it all out and just wanted to see what the angels had to say about her decision. She had lived a rotten life thus far. She was sick and just wanted to put an end to it all.

When I went inside the channel, there was an unbelievable amount of joy and reverence all around her. The Guides told her that would certainly be okay but it wasn't her time yet. If she'd just wait a few years, she would be given the opportunity to leave then. But first she was to heal her physical body.

I couldn't help but to be awed by such a presence looking back at me. The Guides reminded me, after we parted, that she was one of the ascended masters who had come to earth at this time to offer aide to humanity. By doing so, she had taken on an enormous weight of oppression and it had taken its toll. I had no idea what her choice would be but felt that all was well.

I spoke with her on a few more occasions, and each time, I noticed optimism, a joy about her. The last time I spoke with her, she had developed an advanced form of cancer. She told me that she was fine with whatever happened, but now had just a glimmer of wanting to hang around to see what life offered next, and to heal the body. She was actually starting to have fun.

The last time I asked about her, she had accomplished the first part of her soul's mission. She was cancer-free, and was doing just fine. When I heard this, I was elated and heard the words *she is now free*. Even when I think about her now, I am in awe of her incredible will power to overcome the feelings of powerlessness that have plagued her throughout life, and to call forth unconditional love on all levels of awareness.

For her, no matter what she decides from here on out — to stay or to go — she has already gained her ultimate liberation from the body-mind continuum. The next leg of her journey as a soul having a human experience will come about, not by life happening to her, but by what she consciously chooses.

Healthcare transforms into light technologies

In all three probable futures the role of healthcare plays out a large factor in social, political and economic fronts. In the dualistic scenario of our lower probable future, people will use the health and well-being industry to continue to control people by using them as pawns in an economic power game. But it doesn't have to be that way. In our higher probable future, there is a very different outcome. For many of us who hold an understanding of energetic healing, this third probability, like the example above, is a current day reality. But for most in the world who feel that someone else has more power over them to heal the body, they will be moving more slowly to work through their beliefs around health and well-being. Like any power dynamic, you can choose to be a part of the play or step out and create a new paradigm game.

As more of us exponentially wake-up and take total responsibility for our health and well-being, by as early as 2024, allopathic medicine will be virtually seen as last resort or for emergencies only. In its place will return technologies (crystal technologies, energetic healing, herbology and vibrational medicine) for not only returning the body to full health but to include tune-ups for adjusting to environmental changes.

The very nature of health care will continue to evolve, to such an extent, that energetic healing will become the first thing a person thinks to do because the individual will understand the nature of vibration and the power to heal. Deeper levels of focus will be given to shamans, healers, and light bearers for the witnessing of the individual transgressions being healed and transformed by the self.

Survival of the fittest, as emphasized in today's society, will be replaced by the mindset that we are a soul living as human. Entire civilizations will rely upon their healers to minister to the sick. The sick will rely upon themselves to puzzle-solve by asking their own bodies to report back, to speak loudly, to tell, to share, and to transform.

A side note on specific diseases: The Guides have shared that leukemia will be the first of many forms of cancer to be transmuted to the higher vibrations through the practice of energetic medicine in our lifetime. Even today, there are many new light technologies to help human kind realize the power of presence of love in all forms. Those of us who have been called to practice energetic healing know the total sense of peace that comes from transmuting any malady into higher frequencies of light. Once we become practiced at breaking the code of fear, the rest is a flow toward perfect health and well-being. I have met a few extraordinary people whose specific purpose is to bring these new technologies into the planet. They are actively teaching others how to do the same. Many star beings are helping them as well. They work with their brothers and sisters who are serving others. Once they receive, each person they work with or teach receives the same trans-ference of energy and passes it right on along to everyone they meet.

I still laugh out loud about receiving the gift of healing, taught by a gifted Chiropractor. A friend had attended his training classes. She was so enamored with the energy that she regularly stopped people in the grocery store or on the street to give them the gift of an energy transference. After she gave the same to me, for months on end, whenever I was doing a session for someone in particular, my hands and arms would go free floating in mid-air. At first I thought it was hilariously funny to feel my arms go this way and that, but weirder things have happened.

I later asked the Guides why this energetic frequency came through for some but not others. They told me that it's the people who were originally from the star culture Sirius that are most likely to be open to receive the frequency. Many of these beings are here to help specific soul groups, and this particular wavelength is for healing of all kinds. Through the channel, I was transferring the energy to the healers.

We are entering a time when artists discover new inventions that only scientists have traditionally tackled. The same is true for healing. In the new paradigm, a healer may very well be that office worker sitting right next you. Your ability to embrace new ideas will help you to regain your power in this area of health and well-being.

When it comes to health and well-being, vibration will be front and center in our ability to maintain total equilibrium. This especially applies to the world's food sources. Within all three probable futures our ability to keep our bodies attuned to the higher frequencies will be instrumental in our ability to remain focused and in the stillness. By paying attention to what the body needs, we'll find that we'll be shifting our focus away from the societal norm and begin selecting foods by color and vibration.

Herbology is also on the rise and for good reason. The potency of vibration found in herbs will be far more effective than an artificial means of supporting the body's functionality. Our body is complex in the way that it assimilates the higher frequencies, especially if we are holding onto old soul-level memories or traumas of any kind. And this will only become more of an issue as we continue to take in more light.

For those who are attuning to the energetic shifts, we will

find that the source of our central sun plays a key role in our body's ability to keep up with elevated levels of light. The best time to attune and balance the body is by aligning with the frequencies that come into the earth's atmosphere in the early morning hours and at dusk.

The power of the individual forms a new paradigm of leadership

We are living during an unprecedented time in our journey as souls having a human experience. Many of us have lived through the harsher cycles of hate and malice during times when we have been led to follow a dominating leader. But now it's different. The Cultural Revolution that occurred in the 1960's was just the icing on the top of a very big cake.

We have been working through the deeper levels of oppression, and now we have come to recognize the power of the individual to affect vast global change. This knowing of our power is what is prompting humanity toward realizing a much brighter future. The new paradigm of leadership is to first become the change we so desire for the world, then by doing so, lead others. This all sounds great, but how are we to accomplish this kind of soul-level change? What are the steps?

The very beginning of this human revolution is to recognize who we are and believe in ourselves. If we do just these two things alone, life will open up in ways that we are only now imagining into creation. The individual is the dynamic that moves and drives the group creations and it's the power of the individual who ultimately global change into motion. Gone are the days when we follow a single leader. We are the leaders in this revolution of consciousness. It is the power of the individual, the power of the heart that will open and liberate humanity from her self-imposed constrictions.

As fully empowered light beings, we are to become ground in the body to be present in our lives. We are here to serve as catalysts for shifting the group consciousness. The energy of love fuels our hearts and powers up the group. Never underestimate the power of the heart to open doors, to move mountains even if they are comprised of solid stone. Love is the most powerful dynamic change agent in the universe of light because that is who we are. When we take responsibility for who we are and for how we show up in the world, we make the world a better place. As love is set into motion from one individual to the next, the magnification of love grows into a force of light that all beings of light recognize as unconditional acceptance of self and others.

This simple act of recognition once set into motion and put out into the world as an identity is the key property that changes the direction and the eventual outcome of all actions. Never underestimate the power of the heart to transform the most hardened of creations. I have seen it and experienced it myself. Love is more powerful than hate and malice any day of the year.

Once we are totally reconnected to who we are and have reset our identity of what is inside of us instead of what others think we are, then we begin to call forth our unique gifts. There's no stopping a light being that is set on sharing her gifts with the world. She is empowered and impassioned by the love that fuels even the tiniest of efforts. She'll work night and day to get it just right, whatever that is, to share her gifts with the world.

Beings of light are no slouches. They take their tasks very seriously in a joyful kind of way, and that is what is needed in this time and day. Passion. Many of us, as we move through the next few years, are going to find ourselves pushed and pulled by our communities if we are not careful to remember who we are at all times.

So, it's not what you are called to do, it's how you go about doing what is in your heart that matters most. If you go after social change, for instance, and you are angry or you have to right a wrong, think again. There's one thing about pursuing something with passion but it's another to go after change because you are angry or vengeful. When you put your passion into the steps you take, just be sure that it is the joy of the chase or the challenge of the puzzle that moves and drives you to the pursuit, and not the one-upmanship that so many can get caught up in.

We are here to transform the paradigm of fear into love, so just remember that as you are embracing the change, do so with peace in your heart.

Passion drives the change

This kind of power is the underpinnings of a new global consciousness. You can see evidence of joyful abandon even in some of the direst of living conditions, or the shambles of disaster. You can find it anywhere there is passion for change, or making something better through art, invention, planting crops or growing a new flower bulb to bloom in early spring.

We are social creatures by choice and find ourselves in relationship to members of our human family wherever we turn. But being with a light being is quite a different experience. The vibrations run high like a racehorse at the start of a race. You can feel the high-octane energy between the two of you when you are conversing, or playing, watching, or sensing. The communication that takes place on a nonverbal level is off the charts as one speaks volumes to the other in energy exchanges that feel more like informational downloads than the chatter or din of mundane conversation. And this way of relating and conversing will only become more pronounced, especially over the next few years as learning dynamics of oppression are played out. Much of humanity will be playing out the game of follow the leader. Discernment will be the key factor that will guide most to make choices on which leader to follow and which one to stay away from.

Whole societies will be faced with choices that will determine the path of entire populations for many years to come. The power of the individual will be felt in the mix of all this learning, but as light beings having already gone through these tougher lessons of subjugation of the self, we will be less affected by humanity's choice. We will be less affected, even as the masses begin to play out patterns and behaviors that suppress our individual expression. It will take a few years to play out as two separate streams of consciousness; one as total freedom of self-expression and the other being watched by big brother or sister at every turn. But eventually the two forms, just like in all the other dynamics, will eventually find new balance.

Here, again from the Guides viewpoint: "Allow your heart to fully guide you into the collective consciousness of love and joyousness, because many of your outward collected manifestations will begin to feel as though the world has gone mad. Many individuals will begin to doubt their frame of reference to society and that is quite all right. The period of chaos and disorientation felt by so many will serve its purpose of shaking up static beliefs that are rooted in patriarchal stamps of approval. The individual will be challenged on all fronts to claim victory over the human nature aspects of self."

The Guides tell us, "We are here with you. There is never a time to determine outcomes in a way that belies the true nature of a spiritual being of light. You can behave or pretend that you are human, but when the frequencies of joy begin to shift, begin to shake the human species out of complacency, the light beings that you are will be called forth to fully awaken from your slumber.

"From early 2008 through the latter part of 2012, there will be many in society who will want to escape the wrath of human suffering, but you are not to worry at all. There will be many who will come to you to discover the ways of old."

Star children, the leaders of tomorrow

As we continue to step into our power to affect change in all areas of our lives, we are also becoming mothers and fathers, aunts and uncles of star children. Over the last generation or so, we have been birthing children who already know who they are and are actively working to change the old paradigm of fear in all areas of society by just being who they are. The world is already experiencing their contribution.

Many children born from 2001 on have, as a part of their genetic make-up, what we would consider super genes. They have been called star seedlings because their DNA is very different than the rest. These children represent the next evolution of what it means to be human, and are, therefore, setting off energy firings within their families of origin. They are the teachers of tomorrow, the healers who are anchoring their light to help humanity to flip the old paradigm.

The precursors to these star children are the Indigos, now young adults who are currently in their twenties and fully aware of their light, their ability to affect change in society. We will find that as much as the world is bound to dive straight into the chaos over the next half-dozen years, that these kids will be like ocean waters calming the deep blue sea. They know who they are, and what they have come here to do.

Just as we have come into the planet along with our particular soul group, the children of today, particularly those who started coming in as late as 2001, have come to adjoin with theirs. Many are coming from strong earth alignments, other planets that have already played out these lower probable futures in their own way. For the most part, they have full recall of who they are and where they have come from. Most of these same children have been planted as star seeds on five separate continents to amplify their light, as a collective consciousness, within the grid of humanity.

Their caregivers are very special in their own right, and they will need to be held in the energy of deep appreciation to help these children blossom. They instinctually know who they are and thrive on love and appreciation. Their teachers are awakening now, or have been building entire light centers, houses, schools and communities to handle their needs today. These special leaders are also busy creating entire networks of light filled with nurturers and caregivers for greater numbers of these children. In the coming years ahead, especially beyond 2010, they will need to be surrounded with individuals who can openly accept their higher knowledge of situations, people and circumstances.

I have met and worked with many of these gifted individuals. They are driven by unconditional love for all children and have deeply connected with the visions of nurturing communities of caregivers freely offering their gifts to these special children. Or have come into the knowing that peace is to lead the way. In my work with people who are diligently coming together to form new community structures to buoy these children, the Guides have told them to expect their work to be fully activated by as early as 2010. For the first five to seven years, it will look more like disaster relief than care-giving and teaching, but take heart. Their work with children, and the adults who care for the children, will be a most pressing task as entire populations of children are displaced.

PART 4:

NAVIGATING THE WATERS OF CHANGE

Like a sailboat on the ocean of change, we too, can set our course even as we learn to navigate the high winds and rains. We know where we are going, so let's have some fun getting there.

9: CHAOS AND THE NATURE OF ENTRAINMENT

Mustering the courage to honor the self

When I ask event participants to tune into the timeframes of 2010, 2017, 2024 and 2037, all pivotal years in our call to shift global consciousness, I have been amazed to hear how similar the stories are as participants share their visions with one another. In all instances, 2010 and 2017 are times of profound choice for most. Participants report receiving an internal prompt to walk away, to leave the lives they have been living. Many are called to go to the mountains, which can simply be a metaphor for higher wisdom or be taken literally as a call to get up and go. We are being prepared to accept this inner call now by letting go of our attachments to fear-based ideas and perceptions of who we think we are; to let go of fear so that we can be a part of the solution and not get caught up in the chaos. In any new situation or development, each of us must make a choice to continue down the path of self-destruction or to make a different choice.

On a personal level, you can understand this in the context of your own life, but how does making a choice for joy, to begin flowing your life differently, change anything else? This singular heartfelt choice changes everything about your world and most sense it clearly, once they get a taste of it. And that's where most get stuck. Right there on the fence. Stuck in fear, the fear of change.

Once participants see for themselves what their lives will look like, feel like and have the comparison of others to help them bounce their disbelief off of their backs, the next question someone invariably asks is, "What do we do now to prepare for the change and to transform our future into a higher probable reality?"

This chapter is designed to answer this question and also provide you with an idea of how chaos factors into these key choice-points (2010, 2017, 20124 and 2037). It will also address what you can do to transform or transcend whatever dynamic you discover is playing out in your life right now. As I have come to ask, why wait?

Within the context of our human experience, especially as we are moving through the next two to three years, chaos is bound to play a significant role in our lives. For starters, setting our intention and learning to live each moment as peace will go a long way to navigating through the waters of change. For instance, there is destined to be peace in the Middle East fully realized as a part of our probable future but it is not a physical reality in our present moment. However, we can live in the present moment as though there already is peace, and not just in the Middle East either. By intoning peace within us, we are becoming that reality every moment. I realize this is a challenge, but by living in the present moment we are setting the energy of peace into motion. This one conscious action does more to solve conflict on every level of society and it all starts with you.

For many light beings, from early to mid-2006, we were called to make internal changes by dropping any heaviness about our lives, and to become very clear about our purpose. We were also called to pass out of those areas of our lives where we were not being true to ourselves, and to take a deeper look at what brings us joy. It was a time to come into alignment with our hearts about who we are and to take the time to discover our higher purpose.

Summer of 2007 set this awakened wave of light beings into full forward motion, and in their collective resolve, they put into play an even bigger wave that struck at the heart of complacency by the fall of 2008. What causes this motion of consciousness to rise and fall like the waves of an ocean crashing to shore? It first starts off as awareness. Once we realize that we are not alone in our newfound awareness, we seek out or simply gravitate toward others who are also awakening to new ideas, new understandings. Before you know it we find ourselves sitting on the edge, or right smack in the middle of an aligned consciousness with others.

Knowing that the soul loves movement, we put this newfound awareness into motion and begin creating waves in our physical world. When we come together around these physical creations, we have tremendous power to affect change. Our task is to pay attention to both the movement and stillness. As we move through the first of those four energetic gateways, we'll feel the energetic movement in the context of our communities well before the physical creations begin to play out. We'll feel a shifting, like we are walking on sand. This is the energetic movement of the group creation. From our now moment forward, this shifting will be all about economics—how we seek out fairness and align with righteousness. The economic structures and how we look at fair trade, for instance, are going to be in the mix of things.

Even the way that we create as a group is shifting, changing. As you have just read, there are many cities that are going to go by the wayside. There are those who will hold an understanding around the upheaval and light the way for others, and there are others who are going to be very confused and get stuck in the chaos. Confusion will play out as we experience a lot of death and destruction in various parts of the world.

Some people ask me, why does it have to be this way? The answer that shoots back from the higher realms is that it doesn't have to be that way at all. Humanity can choose to shift differently if she simply wakes up. She can make changes the easy way or the hard way. But many of her social, political and economic structures are built on the foundation of control and manipulation. Therefore, these foundations are to be broken down and rebuilt on the foundation of a reality of all as One.

Humanity has been working toward this time of rebuilding for a very long time. South Africa was the very first in a chain of events designed to bring about a very strong evolvement of soul. From an energetic viewpoint, this region was where the very first race of nations from the ancient world that was able to rise above the strife — one race having been pitted against another. Now that is not to say that all is perfect in South Africa, but it was the turmoil that was resolved in that area of the world that is serving as a model for the rest.

The strife-ridden tendencies of the warring factions of the Middle East would not fully be there, without the intensity of the globalization of the leaders of the western world trying to come in and create one world power. The Guides say that they are trying to do so by the capturing of people's minds. The powers that are interfering in others' affairs don't understand that it will be the hearts of the people who will govern the group creations not an outside force pushing in. New order will only come about when all rise above the strife by rising above the mind. Only then will we begin to see peace in this part of the world.

Riding the wave of chaos

The later part of 2007 marked the beginning of an incremental shift in consciousness and the time when chaos began to settle into the collective consciousness. The events that unfold from this time forward were designed to push or to pull us through an inner passageway that takes us from the old paradigm into the new. Complacency is part of the old paradigm and by the fall of 2008, this learning pattern will play out in our world to bring us all back into balance.

No matter when you are pushed into the feeling of being

out of balance, you will feel the affects of the chaos as your belief in duality is challenged in any area of your life where you are holding yourself and others to a double standard. Energetically, the very first part of chaos feels like a rise and fall (falling from grace on high to plummet to the floor of despair) but in actuality it is more of a spiral. Sometimes when we are spiraling up, it feels like we are going back and revisiting earlier dramas in our lives but we are actually moving up in vibration.

As our creations play out, given where we are in regard to the collective consciousness, humanity will experience a tremendous amount of internal and external chaos. For those of us who will have already gone through the first three energetic gateways, we will experience everything that is occurring within the collective as pulling sensations on our emotional and physical bodies, and to a much lesser degree on our physical manifestations.

Even before the great quickening of light in 2012, two separate levels or layers of consciousness have already emerged. Both rivers move through the same metamorphous but one moves us through a period of reorganization that spans from cathartic chaos to less dramatic levels of reorganization, while the other part of humanity's consciousness experiences stillness. This parallel living that first starts out as almost an imperceptible difference between the two is all for good. But by September of 2007, the two rivers began to radically divide. There's purpose in that. The more that we remain in the stillness and very focused, the chaos of the other will become more dramatic more quickly — the more dramatic the chaos, the more profound the polarization. This kind of polarization is not a byproduct of duality but a magnetic pulling against systems dividing as duality separates out from oneness consciousness. The wider we realize the gap between the two between now and 2012, the more quickly we move through the process of socially, politically, economically and environmentally coalescing into systems, new order.

We are not to be concerned about the chaos, or to buy into the strife. It's important to understand that we are actually the ones that are serving as the catalysts for the current playing out of the more dramatic displays of violence in the world today. We are the ones who are causing the polarization to occur. Just remember as you learn to witness events play out around the world that there must be chaos before a new order is realized. If you are called to jump in and serve in whatever capacity, it is the peace, the stillness of your heart that is to be your guide, not misguided compassion. That will only serve to create more hardship in the long run not less.

Most of us have experienced a reshuffling of our lives in one form or another. You might have endured a particularly fearful time in your life or learned new things very rapidly. But once you have come through that initial period of chaos, you will likely sense a peace about the confusion and gain new understanding. Once this occurs, you are bound to experience a new order to your life. That is what the quickening of the chaos within the context of the group creation is all about as well.

S   *haos as movement*

have always enjoyed chaos because chaos is
ement, and yet the kind of chaos that is coming to
plane in our present future will not feel that way
ho are still experiencing the lower echelons of fear.
there are legions of higher vibrational beings trying
to understand that chaos is a really great thing to be
ced when we maintain an inner focus. When we are
ed in the feeling nature of the heart and are immersed

in oneness, we feel great movement that is both deeply peaceful and at the same time exhilarating. It's the movement of consciousness that makes it so.

The kind of chaos our human natures thinks of is harsh like sharp metal. Our human nature does not like movement. We have labeled change as bad because we have associated it with someone making us do something we may not want to do. Like a child being pushed to go out and play when wanting to stay inside, no one likes to be pushed. We don't like change unless we are choosing it. We have been so programmed to move as a group in a tribal way that we begin to feel the movement only when the people around us are moving. Only then do we feel safe to navigate through the movement. Yet, chaos is literally the movement of the soul having a human experience.

Chaos only comes into an outward uncomfortable expression when we're not allowing the flow that the soul so desires. When the soul says, "yes, indeed. It is getting time for you to pick up and move across the country," you are actually feeling the inward prompt to make a change. You don't know what is truly coming your way or how it will unfold. It doesn't make sense to you, but it doesn't matter. The heart is sending you a strong signal that it time to redirect the flow of your life.

This feeling comes complete with mental pictures and is activated by your hopes, dreams and desires. You may feel the love of your life coming to you or your spouse getting ready to leave the earthen plane. There, inside, you might say, "I know that because I can sense that. I can feel it." That sensing, knowing is the language of the heart. That is the heart telling you that all is well. It's time to flow in a different way now. It's time for movement. It's time to make a leap of faith. It's time to shift gears. It's time to ascend further up the spiral. Chaos comes about, not from striving, not from pushing, and not from fear: Chaos stems from the soul's desire for movement.

The chaos that ensues is actually felt as the atamatine

particles, the very smallest increment of consciousness, are triggered by the soul. The soul's signal to the body consciousness first starts with a change in the body's electro-magnetic field. Our higher nature gets the signal that life is about to shift. Life is about to change, so get ready. Be on the lookout. Because life is exhilarating, joyful, a grand adventure. It's a really good thing to shift, to change, and to grow. But the lower nature, the human nature, sees change as fearful unless everyone in the pack is moving the same way.

When we feel that chaotic feeling inside of us, our life is already reorganizing around new ideas, new soul patterns. We might start to put labels on what we are feeling, especially if we are holding on to beliefs that counter our intuition. If we are really skittish about things, fear might set in and we might ignore the signals or put our head in the sand. But that's not necessary. It's only necessary to listen, to listen to the movement, to listen to the heart, and to go with the flowing of joy, of peace, that brings us the feeling of impending growth and expansion. If we remain centered and aware of our heart, we will even feel a deep measure of safety and security knowing that we are where we need to be. This kind of movement, even as mass chaos becomes a part of our global culture, does not have to be experienced as difficult, defeating, bad or scary. The quickening of mass consciousness can be felt as tremendously joyful, innovative and cathartic in a blessed way as exponentially more people wake-up and begin to say "yes" to joy.

The more that you let go and follow the prompting from the pulses that your soul is sending to you, you will create a very wonderful life expression. You've got to believe what your heart tells you to do because the soul is all about growth, understanding, love, compassion, and selflessness. It doesn't matter what the learning is to be. There is a way to navigate through the chaos that is a breeze. That makes the change or the transformation feel like the grand adventure that it already is.

Experiencing chaos on two levels

On the global level, we are all on a journey through the energetic gateways that were set up in 1952 and 1992. A lot of these gateways were triggered by light beings that were able to spiral up in vibration and pull the others along with them. Another shift came in 1999 and carried us through 2001. From 2001 to the fall of 2008, we experienced an opening where our lives took on patterns of reorganization and pushed us to let go of long-held resistance to change. Many of us discovered our life-purpose during this time and began teaching, healing, and serving humanity in myriad ways. As exponentially more people wake-up and make it through the gateways, we'll find that each one builds on the next. So it takes the culmination of these earlier gateways to create this next shift. By 2010, the feeling nature of the next shift in consciousness will be a thousand fold from what we have experienced from these past three incremental shifts combined. Needless to say, this next opening will be exponential.

For those who have been energetically spiraling up all along, this shift will be like we are leaves dancing along the water. It won't matter if this next shift in consciousness creates a rushing river or comes in as a trickle. The likelihood of us feeling the shift will be determined by how immersed we are in joy. We'll continue to dance along the water no matter how fast or turbulent the energetic push may be. For those of us who are acting like a sinking rock (those who like to go deep and submerge the self) the rush of this next shift is going to have a dramatic impact on our lives. Even the rocks on the bottom are going to be pushed or pulled along by the energetic flow.

On a personal level, any areas of our lives that are not in

alignment with the heart will be played out in a dramatic way. There will be no ignoring the white elephants in our living rooms. From early 2006 through 2008, a lot of this kind of emotional clearing became commonplace. It doesn't necessarily feel good, but as we tune into the heart, we can understand that we are preparing for what is on its way. The clearing is internal. It can be very chaotic. You can be at peace one moment and in turmoil the very next. But like a radio station broadcasting its message, this kind of clearing widens our bandwidth of light.

Stepped down versions of chaos

Another aspect of chaos is the stepped-down versions of change. Not all of us are leaves dancing along the water. In some parts of our lives, we are, but in other parts we are not. In other parts of our lives we have attachment to what we like and what we have been creating. We like the feeling of our creations. Or we feel we have to wait it out. We have to wait for someone to catch up to us, or we have to wait out a situation because we have to play it out until the very bitter end. We have to see something through, or we have assumed an identity in our lives that makes us feel important, makes us feel special and powerful—especially power. Power can be very heady. Power plays an important learning in our lives. For instance, the need to be needed is a very powerful position to be in. It makes us feel very powerful. Being a victim is a very powerful position. Most of us do not like giving up the role of a victim because it feels so good. We get all that attention however negative it may feel at the time.

These are all backward ways of learning. But none the less, we have all been through these cycles where we have learned it the hard way—and because we have, we are holding on to fear that keep us in cyclical or circular forms of creations.

As we wake-up, we are learning through life experience

that it is so much easier to navigate through the chaos being the leaf, by allowing, by moving through life with our heart guiding the way that we want to, to take a different tack. But again, we get stuck.

It's simple to know if you are stuck because you feel your life to be very satisfying, joyful or you don't. You're doing what you love to do, or you are not. Life does not have to be black or white. There are many nuances of joy even when life gets really hard.

But what happens if you don't even know what the higher echelons of joy look or feel like because you have been in the middle ground for so long that you can't recognize the higher vibration? What happens if you have never experienced the higher before? What then?

Go find a model of someone or something that reminds you of joy. Go see what Mother Nature is doing. Go see if the birds are worrying. Go see if the flowers are afraid they are not going to get their sunshine. Go find a model. Find the feeling of good — good like a high-dose of euphoria. When you do, let that be your guide. You decide what that is because everyone has that feeling. Everyone has that particular feeling that is unique to him or her. No one else has that particular feeling that makes you feel special.

As beings of light, we know that we are special. We know that we are souls here to have a human experience. We know who we are. Even those who have been beaten down by life — they really do know who they are. That is where courage comes in. This is not a challenge for the weak-hearted.

Navigating through chaos, especially as you are coming through some of an orientation of hurt, pain and confusion, is not easy. It's not easy to pull yourself together and declare, "I'm not doing this any more" because we get to the point where we know what we don't want to do, but sometimes we forget. We forget what we really do want for ourselves. We forget that we really do want to be joyful and that we deserve it. That it's actually our birthright.

Use chaos as a navigational tool. When first learning any new skill, it takes practice. My suggestion is that you take one area of your life or one situation that you are not particularly happy with or could be better and just start asking your heart, "Show me the open doorway. Show me what I need to do to improve my life in this area."

What you are going to get is the process in concrete steps. First you'll get it in a feeling then you'll be shown or presented with situations that will force you to make a choice. You'll be presented with a life-choice to say, "yes I will, or no I won't, or I won't make a choice." Refusing to make a choice is as valid a choice as any other but sets you up for experiencing greater degrees of resistance even as you are calling forth positive change.

If you choose to ignore your heart you are virtually saying to yourself and the universe *I am not ready yet, I can't do this*. You are siding with the mind and don't want to make a change no matter what you say, your attitude and beliefs are still running your life. You are essentially saying, *I want to stay right where I am*.

I see lots and lots of people do this, (and I am not exempting myself from this stance at times either), until they are finally ready to create a different kind of movement. Sometimes life has to get so hard, that we finally forces to change our thinking in order to release ourselves from the log-jam that we have created for ourselves.

If any of this is ringing true for you, know that it is a typical stance of hiding out. After enough of feeling stuck, it will become obvious what you need to do to shift your perspective and by doing so, make a different choice.

Needless to say, what I am describing here is the difference between being motivated to change out of fear of failure as contrasted by the joy of the grand adventure. The fear motivator is familiar for most but does not feel good at all. We don't like pain so we move. We want to get away from it. But the human part of us wants to endure, to stand right smack in front of the fire in hopes that it will all go away so we put our hands over our face, and say to ourselves, it's not really hot here. My face will not get burned. It's not really hot so we ignore as long as we possibly can until we can no longer deny the inferno. So it is this process of choice-making that propels us to take action, to make the choice to move, and making choice is a continual process.

When you are in that first stage of making choice deliberately, it can sometimes feel very dramatic or even traumatic because you have been stuck for so long that it feels like your life is going to come to an end. But in actuality you are moving now, letting go of things that held you down, and everything starts moving. Then you will realize that the fear of what the change may transform into difficult, harsh or perhaps an angry, resentful state of mind. You'll go through a full range of emotions but at least it's better than simply feeling stuck. As you start to flush through those lower emotions, you'll start to go more with the flow, and the chaos of your life will take a very different course. You'll begin to see the evidence all around you that life is no longer happening to you, and you will see how your choice is affecting your movement. Once you've gotten that down, and can really see how your choice affects your movement then you can start to see that you are moving up the spiral.

In the global view of this same process, the more that we do this the more that humanity will do the same. The more of us who move into the higher echelons of joy, the more dramatic the global shift will be. We owe it to ourselves to get the greatest benefit and the deepest joy out of this lifetime because that is what we have come here to do. We've come here to ride the wave of change with joyousness in our heart.

Twelve tools for transforming or transcending chaos

There are some very simple tools that you can employ for navigating through chaos. By incorporating these practices into your daily routine, you will be able to solve any puzzle with ease and grace.

1. **Listen to your heart.** By tuning in to what you are feeling, you'll know when your decision feels right because your heart will experience an open sense of light-hearted peace, stillness, or even excitement when it *is* right. No matter where you are, you can be the leaf on the water and simply bob along in that flow of oneness that comes with living from your heart. You are making the choice every day about being in oneness consciousness, to flow with this special feeling you, the soul having a human experience, or not. If you are in your mind, you are going to feel thwarted, tripped up or confined by your choices.

2. **Remove the identities, all labels from what you are feeling.** If you put a label on what you are experiencing, you're going to run into trouble because your mind will want to run away and hide or defend against the identity. The mind has to understand everything from a logistical viewpoint but the heart doesn't work that way. The heart is the navigational guide for oneness. As you remain in the feeling nature of the heart and let go of any preconceived notions of what your life is suppose be like, that's when you start to let go of allowing the outside world to disturb you. That does not mean that you stop working, loving and growing or co-creating with others. When you tune into your heart without expectation, you will be guided to flow step up your vibration and thereby will

naturally be drawn into the flow of the upward spiral.

3. **Be willing to look at even the hardest stuff.** When life is not working, whatever may be bothering you, become willing to look at it. That doesn't mean that you run away and hide. If you find yourself being pushed or pulled into someone else's drama, stop and wait one moment. Feel into what is occurring in your life then come back to center, come back into stillness. Get quiet and listen to your heart. Find out what your heart wants you to do. By getting into the space of quiet, you will reposition yourself as a part of the solution. When you are in the space of distrust or uncertainty then you are actually becoming a part of the problem. The problem is allowing yourself to be pulled into the deeper levels of chaos.

4. **Speak your truth.** Gain confidence in what your heart is telling you enough to speak your truth, and when you do practice full-disclosure, full transparency. Hold to the resolve to follow your heart no matter what. When called to speak your truth, speak about how you feel without any finger pointing (projecting your fears onto the other) and leave nothing out: No shape shifting in your viewpoint to please or placate the other. If your heart tells you to remain still, perhaps, when everyone is telling you to go, then stay even if everyone else is dong otherwise. The feeling nature of how your heart is speaking to you will only get more pronounced that way. Just remember that the center of your universe is your heart not your head. Once you fully understand that by keeping your focus on your heart the feeling of chaos will become very joyful, and the feeling of movement will satisfy your soul's calling to be free within each moment-to-moment experience.

5. **Do no harm.** Even as you are a part of humanity you are only to witness for the others. As a light being having a human experience and you are here to transcend the lower vibrations of chaos. Not a single one of us wants to see another person killed or maimed or tortured or raped on this planet. We have experienced so much of that behavior that it is familiar. When you bring in more love, joy and peace into your body by following your heart you will bring more joy into the planet. Others who are currently stuck in the lower octaves of chaos will try to pull you in, but by remaining steady, understand that aligning with joy is the very best help that you can provide anyone. This is the truest form of compassion.

6. **Embrace the clearing process.** Clearing process lower vibration from the body-mind continuum is an integral part of moving up the evolutionary spiral. It's a constant process of recognizing the soul's desire for movement by releasing what no longer serves your greater good. As you grab onto a new concept or ideal, you will feel new energy come into your life. When you do, in will come a new rush of joy. Suddenly you may feel grumpy, weepy, and vulnerable. If you are not careful, you'll think that something is wrong until you realize that everything is right because you have brought a new wave of high vibration into the body. Embrace this part of the process as much as any other aspect of your life, and you will create even more movement in your life.

7. **See the beauty in everything.** Know that the very thing that your soul asked to do within this very pivotal moment on the planet is calling to you to remember. Know that everything you need to know, need to learn is within you. You need only ask for help and assistance

then pay attention to how life presents itself to you.

8. **Listen to and learn from the people in your life.** At any given moment you can look around and see where people are in their learning by how they relate. Listen to their language, their attitudes. You can tell a lot by how they talk about their day or how they react to their spouses, children or job, for instance. If they are complaining, they are not taking responsibility for their own happiness. They might be working on issues of empowerment, courage, safety or security, or are simply confused. Listening with discernment will help you gain insight into your own learning pattern.

The people we associate with are mirroring our own behavior, attitudes and beliefs to varying degrees. Learn to listen with an ear to paying attention to what they are bringing to the quality of your life experience. If you find yourself jumping in to commiserate or to share your own complaint, stop and pay attention. The inner chatter has become so loud inside that your lower mind has taken over. Use this as a clear signal that some where back there you stopped listening to your heart. You decided that, for whatever reason, you had to do something, had to stay, or persevere. But that's actually not the truth.

The truth is that your heart never wants you to suffer. Your soul is never looking for you to feel thwarted. But everything you have and are experiencing in your life is because of some choice you have already made. Change your very next moment by making a choice to align with the stillness and that will help you make best choices for aligning your light with others.

9. **Learn to spot yearning.** When you are embroiled in inner chaos, you are stuck. When you are embroiled in creation

that pushes you into chaos, you are immersed in yearning. The yearning only leads to more and can get very big. Whether you are yearning for a beloved or yearning for a car, yearning for a job to come your way, yearning for a different place to live, it's all the same. If you are yearning for anything or anyone, know that you are allowing your human nature to rule your life. You have turned away from the heart and let the follower (the mind) is dictating the terms of your reality. But if you tune back in, you'll find that the heart is absolutely in charge, you just were not listening. Your heart is always present and on the ready to give you the correct answer. If you are not getting an answer but are feeling peace, you can say, *Alright I am at peace. I am not enduring; I am at peace. I have what I need. I'm where I need to be. I see the blessings all around me.* Then you'll know that all is well, and yearning is not ruling your life.

10. **Look for the blessings in your life.** Blessings are everywhere. Blessings are those nuggets, great and small, that are showing us that we are headed in the right direction. A blessing is not necessarily for the kudos of a job well done, but may simply be the understanding you gain from learning.

11. **Let go of fear with ease and grace.** Everything is moving. In any aspect of your life, you may think that all the cards on the table may have been dealt but there may very well be more coming. More players in your world may yet play their hand. This is where a lot of people become off kilter, and dive into the lower echelons of chaos. They feel that they are getting lost but are actually in the middle of their creation cycle. When they can't see, can't feel, they start questioning. If you feel that you are getting lost

because you are in mid-cycle (where what you have been guided to do has not yet fully materialized) just go into the stillness. In the stillness, you'll become more awakened to the current in which you are flowing. And with this awareness, riding out the cycle becomes an easier ride. Let go of any fear that may be lurking behind to trip you up

When you get scared and start questioning or start doubting that you're not going to realize what your heart has guided you to create, that's when you take a job offer, for instance, that's not meant for your highest expression. It's only one that is in process, in flow, but you haven't yet arrived. But you say, *Well I have to take this one right here because I'm scared I might not get my highest expression.* You start doubting your heart, the flow of grace in your life. When you can take the time, instead of doubting, go back and check in, you'll feel that you are still in process. You can feel if something is best and right. If you feel joy, a sense of exhilaration and anticipation then you are in the flow.

12. **Discern the movement through the filter of your heart's desire.** You may have received your inner direction and following it to the letter when one of these opportunities presents itself. You become aware that what is presenting and what is presenting are not an exact match. There are times when your soul calls you to a place along the way to shift the energy of something before moving on. That does not mean that you are stuck. It simply means that you are aware that your calling to pause is a part of the overall plan, and does not signal to you that you are stuck. So what is the difference in knowing which is which? Letting go of any attachment to outcome is the key. As a new opportunity presents itself, discern if you feel resistance

about it. If you do, let it go. Let it all go. If you do not, ask Spirit to show you what is yours to do. Use the tools in this list to discern best and right, then go for it!

The point of all these tools is to give you an operational framework for making any choice with your heart not your head. That's the foundational and underlying principle tool right there. It's a confusing world out there to say the least, but if you are paying attention and put to practice even a few of the tools above, then you'll find just about any answer to any question at any given time in your life to pull you out of chaos. You'll even find that by using even one of the above tools, even if you are thrown off-balance, you'll quickly get right back into the flow.

I'll share with you just a brief example to illustrate my point. This is a composite picture of about a dozen profiles of people who fit this same basic scenario: A spiritual man who has been put off making a choice to marry, in what he described, as the woman of his dreams. He absolutely loves this person. In his words, "she is the best thing that has ever happened to me." He's experienced different kinds of romantic love, but this person understands him on a soul level. This feeling when he is physically near her is precious to him. But there's one thing that is not a fit: The more earth-bound variety of love is not a fit. What does he do? Does he throw the relationship out and start all over or compromise a valued part of his life expression? What does he do?

This profile has come up so often that I had to include it. What the Guides would have said about this is to go back and look at his belief. The tool for this is straight out of number two: Identity – *remove all labels*. If he is holding onto an identity that said he can't have it all: He can't have both a soul-level and romantic relationship all rolled into one then his mind will push his buttons until he separates himself from her.

The remedy to any division is to practice full disclosure about how he is feeling and what he desires. Again, right out of Tool number four - *speak your truth*. He is then challenged to let go of expectations that come with that identity, and let go of his yearning for life to be different. By stating his desire, and accepting his partner as she is, enough movement will be created by their dialog, that he'll begin to see whether there is a desire by both to co-create or not.

Just by clearing the air and resetting the alignment with his heart is enough to bring his deepest desire to him. As you can imagine, these are not easy choices. But as he continues to practice full-disclosure with compassion for self and his partner, the answer will reveal itself to both.

As you put these tools into practice, when you find yourself in the midst of chaos, you will be more likely to say *thank you soul, thank you God for bringing this new opportunity to grow into my life*. Rather than wasting it by feeling miserable because your life is changing, you will use it by tuning in to the heart and realize that change in the mix; change is coming. With any stepped-up vibration, you can feel it because you can sense an air of excitement in the wind. You know that it is coming. You'll be on the lookout. When we are in that way of seeing and feeling then we can see that chaos is absolutely bringing to us an opportunity to transform.

The role of entrainment in shifting social consciousness

The power of the individual fuels the creation, and it is our contribution that we make to any group energy that we consciously adjoin with that transforms the paradigm of fear. This world is physically a very big place, but energetically we are all connected. We are quickly approaching a time when this feeling of connection is not only felt within our heart but is experienced as a physical sensation. Many of us are already aware of group energy but have not equated it with what is happening around the block or around the world. We think that everything that has to do with the "little I" is only about that, but in reality, what happens to the other is actually happening to us as well. And many of us are feeling the affects of the shift in consciousness physically.

We are becoming, and will only continue to become, more keenly aware of many different levels of consciousness and cycles of group creations in the years ahead. We are already aware of the energetic pulling sensations when the group is activated. Beyond 2009, this pulling will become a conscious part of our daily lives. With more and more people becoming aware of the grid, we will begin to feel not just a quickening, but a kind of implosion that will take place within us. This feeling will, at first, feel like we are in one density then suddenly, we are in another. To use a metaphor, implosion is much like the experience of going up a fast-moving elevator. When you get in and push the button, as the elevator begins to rush upward, you suddenly feel very heavy then light. Once you come to a sudden stop, you feel very heavy again. Now amplify that feeling by one thousand and that is what the body will experience.

This implosive energy is going to intensify to such an extent that something that was not even a bother yesterday, by next week or months from now will seem like a proverbial elephant sitting in the middle of our conscious awareness. That is another reason why it is so very important to let go of fear-based beliefs and perceptions about the stories of our lives now. As the intensity of the energy of the planet is stepped up vibrationally, what used to be a minor annoyance will suddenly become unbearable and cause us huge problems, or even physical death.

It's easier to clear these vibrations now, as they come into our conscious awareness than to hold onto the past only to face them once again, but under more stressful circumstances. As we do, we will become very still, very present, and clear about the energetic of who we are. The clearer we become, the better we are able to sense the energy shifts, in many cases, before they create an issue in the body. With an ever increased sensitivity to the energy shifts, we will more accurately assess when we need to get involved in the group dynamic and when we need to step back and away to allow whatever is going on in the world to clear out before re-engaging our energy.

What we are doing, as we practice this kind of energy surfing, is actually a form of entrainment that occurs when like-minded people come together. We do it all the time but are not consciously aware that we are doing it. Like attracts like for sure, but this level of attraction is the foundational process for shifting consciousness. Entrainment is when one vibration begins to sync up or harmonize with another. Singers and musicians make a practice of doing this, and animals have their heightened instinctual sense as they attune to a variety of frequencies to help them navigate their world.

Entrainment is a physical property and a part of life. Whole communities are formed this way, starting with the like attracts like coming together of lovers, business partners, playmates, and schoolmates. We travel in packs or tribes and tune into what needs doing based on our fear of survival, or what brings us joy. We watch and we wait or take action based on what our heart tells us to do.

This way of matching up happens when we are in sync with the vibration that feels good to us and others join in. We don't even have to be present to tune into someone else's vibe. It's an automatic happening as we tune in or simply hold a thought of that person in our heart and mind. They think of us, we think of them, and voila! We're connected. One will drag the other down or buoy the other up. Friends do this for one another all the time. Families are famous for instinctually knowing what's up even when the norm is to hold secrets and pretend something different is happening when it is really not.

Take this basic structure and apply the law of resonance out to the group. From the microcosm to the macrocosm, we are all connected. Imagine taking this form of group movement through vibration and begin to consciously flow the energy into a collective consciousness and suddenly we have enormous power to affect change. But then again, that is where knowing and trusting the self is essential to this formula of a relative few very powerful beings of light affecting the collective. Entrainment is a powerful tool for transformation, and is the energetic engine that can exponentially shift the grid.

The grid-like patterns that form when like-minded people come together provides an opening for larger numbers of individuals to step into the feeling of oneness. This realization that we are all one stands outside our current system of leadership where the powerful few are in charge of protecting the meek. We are seeing evidence of systems based on oppression and control being over-powered by self-empowerment happening everywhere, especially in systems that are designed to serve the community.

In current governance structures, leaders in positions of power are more likely to exploit their positions for the sake of holding onto broken structures long after it becomes clear to those they serve that change is needed. Just know that this is a fact of life and learn to use your knowing of entrainment to guide you through life. Feel your way into the vibration of what is actually occurring then make your choice to step back and away from anything that pulls you into drama.

Even as we witness structures crumble, listen to your inner voice to see what if anything you are to do. In many cases, it will be a matter of simply witnessing the fall of the old while stepping back and away, and blessing everyone on board.

Polarization occurs as a part of the continuum

Growing numbers of people are stepping up to shift the paradigm within the context of their community and this is what is causing a polarization with the vibrational spectrum. Polarization is entirely necessary and is a part of the process of moving quickly through chaos before a new order is realized. With group creations, people shift viewpoints, become disillusioned and then grope for new answers to old issues. People are turning away from leaders that no longer listen to them or flagrantly exploit their power. People are seeking self-empowerment and are thereby coming together with others who are establishing a basic common of self-respect.

We will see more of this kind of social reorganizing take place as greater numbers realize that more and more of the old paradigm structures are no longer serving them. Polarization speaks to the dynamic that one group wants change and the other does not. Since oppression is what most of us are working to transform, power feels good, and when a few have it they don't want to surrender to anything that might take it away. As humanity moves through the many processes of reorganizing around higher vibrational creations that dispel oppression in all areas of our lives, chaos will be a very necessary part of the transformational process.

Our ability to hold to the highest vibrational expression is what will dramatically shift the entire human matrix. If we get hooked into the pain or swayed by fear, we become a part of the problem. Holding the light, as the Guides say, is the most important aspect of being on the planet today. Many group creations are moving through very dramatic polarization cycles now and will continue to do so until a new order is realized. We are to stay out of the fray, even as we are called to serve. Know that this cycle of being pulled into the chaos through these polarized creation cycles is not ours to do. By holding the very high frequencies of light intact so that the others can shift, everyone who aligns with the grace that flowing through us will realize oneness.

The regions currently most dramatically affected by this kind of monumental shift in consciousness are South Africa, the Middle East and Eastern Europe. Surprisingly, the United States is currently not a part of the entrainment even if she would like to believe otherwise. She is exercising her power over other countries through the filter of her own self-interests. But as a government of the people by the people, she is complacent about her role in the many activities she has sanctioned. A very big part of the self is still asleep, complacent, about how she is creating and why. Therefore, the United States, as a collective consciousness, is still flowing in the river of fear. Like all creation cycles that are out of balance, the pendulum will eventually swing back to bring her into balance. The more exaggerated the imbalance becomes, the more dramatic the adjustment needed to bring something back into balance.

Complacency: As humanity plays this learning dynamic out, she will experience new waves of sadness as Mother Nature makes the appropriate adjustment. This adjustment will come in the form of rain on many areas that are not accustomed to receiving such downpours. Stepped up patterns of hate and violence will bring more extreme weather patterns of cold and hot as she does her part to restore balance and harmony.

The United States, like the rest of humanity, on some level, is so focused on her mind that she is missing the message of her heart entirely. Her continued stance of control and manipulation of others will trigger a period of natural catastrophes that will play out on the surface of our beloved blue planet to bring her back into balance. However, in her collective higher probable future, she is to wake-up now and become consciously aware of what she is doing and where she is going.

Starting in 2003, as an example of the role of Mother Nature in my home country, she started stepping up her wake-up call by slamming the land-masses that define the United States and points south along the gulf of Mexico. The results of human strife sent a ripple of discontent into the hearts of those who were still asleep. This wave of change was implemented as a result of our entrenched thought patterns that coincided with the dawning of the Industrial Revolution. With high winds and flooding rains, many, including the southern regions along the gulf and points south were inundated with destructive weather patterns. These wake-up calls will only become more pronounced until humanity has aligned with her true nature.

It is not necessary to belabor the point and counter point of creation where Mother Nature is concerned. She can be just as volatile as any social uprising gone awry. What's more important is to understand the power of the individual to shift the group that is turning the entire creation away from the path of self-destruction.

All group thought flows through the heart of love that we are into the creative knowing of all there is. As we connect with this energetic flowing within our soul groupings, we become the change we so desire as a region. Regions energetically connect with countries and countries connect with global alliances. It's all a chain of events that begin with the individual. As we determine each physical or emotional change that is needed to correct any imbalance, we realize that we are not alone in this monumental effort. We realize that there are legions of light beings prepared to carve out vast areas of light for the ascension of humanity. They are here to hold the space for her to shift into higher vibratory rates as a collective consciousness, and thereby add power to the process itself. This measure of entrainment is the help that we are all seeking in order to reset humanity and put her back on the road toward oneness.

Trust is the key

Once you have moved past the point of doubting whether any or all of this method of knowing is true, you are almost home free. The rest is just a matter of trusting in your ability to affect incremental change in your own life. As you practice these very basic principles it will not take you long at all to gain confidence. The fun part is residing in the stillness of heart and seeing the patterns of thought unfold around you. Be quiet and listen. Feel the power of the group creation, and decide where you want to be. You really can be a part of any energy, any formation at any time.

Discernment is a key factor in the entrainment process because as you will discover that the greater the focus you place on your own ability to affect change, the more present the energy becomes. By maintaining a quiet centered focus on the grid, you will see, hear and feel where you are to be at any given moment. As you listen, you are seeking to align with a feeling of timeless freedom, the kind of freedom that comes with the deeper states of joy.

Love takes on a very different quality when the inner conflicts are gone. Without conflict there is only stillness: Oneness. Tune into the group and find your way there with others. That's what it is all about. Find your place with your brothers and sisters of the light, and you will find your life to be quite the adventure into joy, and a continual self-discovery of everyone living and working as one in action.

It goes without saying that the power of the individual cannot be realized without a deep knowing of who you are. If you believe that you have no power as an individual to affect positive change in your world, then you have none. If you believe that you are a powerful being of light who has come here to shine your light, to share your wisdom, to heal the sick, to shake up old paradigms then that is what you will do. Belief in who and what you are is what determines your experience in the world.

The Guides say it this way, again speaking to us as a singular expression of humanity: "We are here with you to determine your fate as a collective consciousness. As you suspend your belief in human form, you will find an entirely different reality creation before you: one that supports you, and aligns you with a heart-centered framework for walking through your physical world with different seeing eyes. As you witness the many forms of God of worship, for instance, you are at once struck with the power and beauty of all paths leading to one heart. These varying paths are born from one Source. The outward practices are merely a way to allow the still voice of love to shine through the inner heart of hearts.

"We are all here with you, each and every one of you. Even though you may not relate to these words, we are still with you. There is never a good time to suspend belief in your human experience. We can say, though, that there are myriad ways to connect to the divine essence of who you truly are, and to also create life in perfect balance and harmony with what you have come to the earth plane to do."

10: GOING WITH THE FLOW

*Keeping your head above water while moving
with the current of change*

It is a particularly exciting time to be incarnate on the planet today. The gateways that have already been opened by a collaborative formation of souls, of light beings, working together to bring about profound change to the human experience is already an exhilarating ride, and there is so much more to unfold. Knowing that the individual is key to the transformation of the group, we must not worry or belabor the points of lights that have not been activated within the grid. If we follow our heart in all manners of being, and allow our heart to guide us in our effort, fear will fall away. By doing so we'll become aware of our feelings on any given matter. We will find that the transgressions against the collective self—as individualized by each of us holding onto fear from previous incarnations—will eventually give way to unconditional love. As we do so, we are doing our individual part to transform humanity and help the planet to incrementally step up her vibration.

There are many light beings who will tell us that we are to create within the timelessness, the awakened state entirely, but at present moment, as a soul group, we are not fully asleep nor have we completely awakened to claim full and complete victory over our human nature. As we work through the next five to seven years especially, just remembering our souls inner quality of oneness will be enough. By doing so, it will serve to keep us in the world but not get caught up in the drama. We cannot fully escape our intertwined history with humanity, not just yet. Until we do, we are to work toward transforming our human beliefs and perceptions into new qualities of higher awareness.

We have all moved through a long series of earthbound incarnations, and with these learning experiences, we have picked up human qualities that are rooted in our need to be needed. We tend to create within a particular wave of consciousness that is familiar to us because we have done this together so many times before. However this time is different. We are not here to prove or to disprove any theory that is set in stone by what humanity holds dear. We are simply to awaken to our own unique way of seeing and remember that the way has already been paved by other soul groupings that have come before us. Our job is simply to pay attention as we work to carve out a wider energetic swath of freedom.

Some of us were a part of these earlier efforts to break through the harsher dense realities of oppression so there is a part of our energetic makeup that remembers that we have done this before. These earlier efforts were valiant but many of us interpreted our leaving the body before we completed the task as failure and have therefore stored this belief in our subconscious mind. By listening only to the stillness, we will hear the tones of victory and feelings of a job well done and will be encouraged. Anyone who is fully aligned with the oneness can see that we will not fail. The awareness of one as all guides us in our creations of heart. All beings of light who have awakened from their slumber — those who have entered into the doorways of this deeper understanding and have already united through this feeling with their brethren — understand what is needed to create this global shift in consciousness.

The realization of a new-world consciousness will come about as the power of the individual is fully realized which will take us through some of the deepest levels of societal upheaval that we have ever seen. In our present moment, people are experiencing their darkest hour as their brethren are being slaughtered all around them, or their homes are lost to storms, sudden earthquakes, or death through starvation or disease.

We are also seeing evidence of this today as millions of people take to the streets and fan out into communities to rebuild, regroup, clean up, educate and develop new processes, new ways of taking care of basic human needs. Compassion for one's fellow man is what is fueling this effort on the physical level and a strong knowing that we are all one, as the family of humanity.

Events that unfold in our world are designed to trigger us into action, and it is the actions of many united in a spirit of cooperation that is in direct alignment with social, political and governmental change. The environment will be the last to be addressed because the human race is totally focused on issues of hatred and will continue to work through the fall out of this dense energy for generations to come.

Change does not have to come with crisis. Unfortunately, that is the way that we, as a part of humanity's collective consciousness, learn how to make different choices. When we are doing something that is so totally out of alignment with our heart that life smacks us in the face and tells us to wake-up, then we do. But most in this world have grown so accustomed to fear that we will do anything to keep life the same even when we claim that we want freedom. A classic example is that of a battered spouse repeatedly returning to his or her abuser.

Even as we live out our lives on earth, we are being prompted to wake-up and listen to our inner voice, to begin creating our lives that vary from the norm. Our families will not necessarily understand us for following this voice, or for choosing our path, but that is okay. We are to keep our focus on the flow of our life force.

Don't expect anyone to come and tell you that you are

right. Reside within the stillness, and allow your heart to speak to you about your inner direction. We are not to be influenced by the choices of others in our world. We are to be quiet and to listen to the stillness within us, and to create within the reality creations of our own knowing.

This message may seem redundant by now, but it is a constant reminder being sent from the angelic realms to me, to repeat to others, time and time again. In the angels' way of seeing, it cannot be repeated enough. Why? Because we forget. We forget that we are light beings in a human body, and therefore we repeatedly fall into the deeper waters of fear. When we do, our worldly happenings disrupt our peace of mind and push us in to confusion.

Being in a human body while remembering who we are is very challenging for many. This earth plane is dense and for some it is very difficult to maintain harmony without getting swept into the misguided creations of others. In the spirit world and in other galaxies, the group play is a very open, light hearted game of learning, but here on the planet, lower vibrations from humanity's belief in duality can cause us to become disoriented. Many of us are not used to the backward way of creating, so we step into environments that catch us off balance and before you know it we are enmeshed in a deep layer of unknowing that takes us, sometimes, a lifetime or two to spiral out of. Many of us continue to hold to this unknowing embedded deep within our psyche.

I hear the stories all the time. The fears that my brothers and sisters hold are rooted in their memories of other lifetimes, other fears that have nothing at all to do with who they are now, but still these memories and soul patterns plague them. These fears are a force to be reckoned with but as we re-center, re-align ourselves with our heart, the mindful way of creating will fall away, and our awareness of our inner light will begin to guide us once again. Following our joy keeps us in the flow, and makes it easier to find our way into our higher vibrational creations.

Keep your focus on oneness.

The Guides tell us that there is never a best or right time to be free. Each of us has our own inner rhythm and timing for this total sense of expression and we will know when the time has come just by our continual focus on the feeling of oneness that is deep within us. As we are guided to our own particular feeling of freedom, we are to understand the inner drive for realizing freedom is fueled by letting go of our egoic ways, and allow, as the Guides say, "the divine right-action to guide you to create within the inner heart of God."

Again, from their perspective: "There are many pathways to God, finding your way back to the great central sun, but only one destination. This inner pathway that brings you to the clearing of deeper feelings of the Divine that knows no bounds where love flowing through your inner heart is concerned. You may not allow the voice of reason to dictate your earliest beginnings, but you will know the voice because it speaks to you about your feeling of oneness of beingness. It speaks to you about the integrity of your heart. It speaks to you about your energetic place in a world of light. You are not to be focused on the eternal trappings of the mind. You are to be aware of the many feelings of love rejoicing inside your very own heart.

"How can you determine your voice if you are forever questioning your heart's inward direction? You are to understand from the very beginning of time itself that there was a feeling inside of you that set off a signal that tells you that you are loved. Love is the very essence of universal life force coursing through your human veins. Now is the time for you to consider your earthly beginnings in a way that will not only set the trappings of the mind free, but will also help you to create your reality in a different way altogether.

"You will find that as your create again and again within the confines of the mind that you will grow tired of your creations. As you experience the pain and suffering of your human expression, you will find your way through the maze of confusion and see where you are to begin anew. The mind is quite circular in this fashion. It is always wishing to create in a way that is both familiar and comforting. Yes, comforting. You might say that sitting in the misery of confusion brings no comfort to the soul, but think again. The soul knows no bounds where the trappings of the mind are concerned. Before you arrive on the earthen plane, you have already determined your version of 'best and right', reverently 'right' not as in right and wrong, but as a form of 'righteousness.'"

Make choices deliberately.
In the more pragmatic view of our lives, as we allow our soul's calling to be free to guide us through the maze of our lives, we begin to recognize the many energetic pathways (some may say potential destiny lines) that are there to guide us back to Source. You might not think that freedom and destiny belong in the same linear thought pattern, but they do. To get a mental picture of this way of learning, you may wish to look as far back as your own childhood. For instance, put yourself back to age two to three years old. There is something in the mix of that time in your life that has recognizable determining factors, especially on an emotional level, that resulted in your current day circumstances.

Of course, there are many such instances or times in your life that have pushed you into making those pivotal choices that have shaped your life direction, but you don't know how they will play out later in life. That's the magic of the learning in the physical world. It's like playing a game of tag with your eyes shut. All you know to do is to keep putting one foot in front of the other and follow the feeling that guides you in the direction that feels most joyful.

As you keep doing so, you will find that you can easily look back and give thanks for the choices you made, or you might even wallow in self-pity for a time and feel sorry for yourself. Or perhaps you might sit in blame or guilt for awhile over what you thought you should have done differently. All are valid ways of learning to listen and to pay attention to your heart.

Forgiveness, while still in the physical body, has always been the most effective way to clear these lower vibrations from our energy fields. Now, forgiveness of everyone and everything is more pressing than ever. By practicing a simple act of forgiveness, we can be a part of the change that causes the quickening of mass consciousness. In the end, we will discover that our willingness to let go of remorse and regret is, at the end of our time on the planet, our greatest gift to humanity, let alone to ourselves.

The benefit to doing so now is that you will step back into the joy that lets you know that you are in the flow. By doing so, you will move more quickly toward that open, blue-sky feeling that guides each of us to freedom.

You may find that as you learn to recognize your life choices that they will serve to point you in a different or vibrationally stepped-up direction, and help you to go with the feeling nature of any given heart-based choice. With practice, the mind will push less confusion into the mix.

Intermixed in the hum of our day-to-day realities are major crossroad choices. These choices are made as we go about taking care of the details of our daily lives. With so many things to grab our attention, it can sometimes be easy to do just what we need to, or to take action out of familiarity without even giving that *something* another thought. But there, within us, is a feeling that stops us in our tracks if we are listening.

Just remember that the mind is always focused on the trappings of the world and will tell you anything that you yearn to hear. On the other hand, your heart's natural desire is to always flow her creations freely. It is your job to pay attention, to trust in the knowing of your own heart, even when the outside world reflects back to you a different mirrored image, but therein lies the magic of shifting the paradigm, one choice at a time.

I love the example that one person shared with me following a teaching on alchemy. Here is what she discovered about choice in her world: "I've been working on the heart verses mind as you know. I've found some vibrational crumbs, which have led me to some tools that I'm now working with. My particular focus is work related. I am currently intending to see only the beauty and what is good about my work environment verses observing the potholes because I only want to feel good. I've learned and know that the potholes don't make me feel good. Funny thing is that lately and ever more so, I find that my workday is improved. Things are not as bad as I once thought and felt and people are much nicer. I take it there has been a shift in my vibration. I am also turning a great many things over to Source to deal with. Right now I can discern good feelings and not good feelings. I guess the finer discernment of the degrees between the two will come."

Align with integrity to find your center.

There are many cast and characters that will come into your life. These are the ones who will try to convince you that you're just like them but you will know the difference. No matter how hard you might try to conform to a human nature way of being it's just not possible to become someone whom you are not.

As you clearly see the truth of where you are headed, you will be led to create within the realms of the unknown, the untouched, the unmistakable feeling of oneness. This feeling, once you have surrendered to your true nature, will serve as an inner beacon to guide you home toward freedom. No longer are you to surrender your light to others but to awaken to the true nature of a light being having a human experience. As you have already learned, there are two worlds or two realities getting ready to merge as one. By paying attention and not allowing others to sway you off course, you will reach your final destination.

The Guides tell us not to be dissuaded by the agenda of others: "As you begin to fully settle into the body, you will find that the perspective of your life experiences will shift and change according to your day-to-day activities. There are many who will tell you that there is no need to pause or to halt, but we are here to tell you that as you quiet the mind, and begin to create the reality of your heart's desire, you will go into the silence of your own knowing.

"You are never to be dissuaded by those who will not want to come back to the core of their creation. They will want to help you to see something or a viewpoint that has nothing at all to do with who you are and what you have come to do.

"There are many who will want to share their way of being to sway you, who will try to persuade you to discover your sense of self their way. There is never a good time to be dissuaded to determine your fate as a being of light. You can see that as you become the change you so desire for the world that you begin to see, hear and feel the transgressions fall away.

"Many beings of light are allowing others to determine their fate. We cannot assume that you are not aware of your light. You are to be quiet in the light of God that you are. There will be many who can begin to prepare their way and create a way to understand the world as it will be created so that mass consciousness can begin to move into a different formation of light.

"You will see what you will begin to create. Creation, in and of itself, will begin to shift and move in dimensionality. You cannot remember who you are if you continually allow others to dictate your creations, to distort your light to please the other. As you can remember to see, hear and feel the movement around you, allow the members of your family to come to you."

When the Guides are speaking, I usually see the corresponding mental pictures to show me the more detailed pictures. During the passage above, I was seeing a lot of other light beings, beings from other galaxies now incarnate coming to us and trying to persuade us to bend our light in ways that will only steer us off course. Going back to the antibiotic metaphor used in chapter one, we have a particular mission. We are looking for other star beings that have their own mission. Therefore, we cannot assume that everyone who comes into our lives are showing up to lend us a helping hand. Some come to adjoin with us to learn, others to take or to suppress our light out of fear.

Our only task at the point that we are feeling the difference in vibration is to bless and release these individuals from our lives as we wish them the very best. We are not to interfere with their mission, and we are not to go out of our way to evangelize about who we are either. We are only to practice kindness and compassion to all those cross our paths.

There will be cloak and dagger games playing out in our world (especially when this next period of earth-timed chaos is in full swing), but we are to stay out of the fray and move into the higher streams of consciousness. These two streams will feel very differently later, but for now they may continue to be a challenge to fully discern the difference between the two until we have gained enough practice at releasing the heavier vibrations from our own systems. In the grand sea of choice, there are many influences that sway our decision to shift away from becoming our true human story. Fear of change is the most predominant one. Some of us have such a fear that we unconsciously give our power away and therefore take what we get rather than what we desire to create in our lives. This applies not only to our life situations but to other energies, other beings, as well.

Here is a basic tool that you can use to get yourself back to center: Once you realize that you are feeling off-center, go into the quiet of your heart, and simply scan your body. Find out where you are feeling any discomfort. If you are finding yourself in a state of anger or sadness, take a few deep cleansing breaths and close your eyes for just a moment to tune into that area of your body that is responding to the lower emotion. Once you locate the area and the emotional quality of what is bringing you distress; start moving the energy out of your body by thanking the body for feeling this way. Tell the body that you understand it now, and that you are releasing the energy from your body. Keep breathing deeply and repeat this form of prayer of thanks as you release anything at all that does not feel peaceful.

What I have just outlined here is a very simple process for detecting anything in our energy field that holds us down. I will never forget the time that I was walking on the streets of New York City in 1991 with a friend when a drunken man uttered something to me as he staggered past me. When he did, I doubled over in pain and suddenly felt very disoriented. It took me a long time to recover. Once back in my home environment, I asked one of my spiritual teachers what had happened? He told me that because I was so open (I had just come from spending two solid days in the presence of an Indian Saint) that it was like I had allowed someone to urinate into my energy field. Needless to say, I was appalled at the thought, but his advice definitely got my attention. I came to understand that we most certainly are all one, but we don't have to open our fields when we are in the midst of lower vibrational environments.

Many people walking the streets of major cities inter-mix with lower vibrations or lower vibrational beings all the time. These energies are attracted to individuals who have overloaded minds, who are sitting in fear everyday of their lives. These are the people who are working over-stressed, boring jobs. They are carrying the burden of over-committed debt loads, and often times find themselves in dead-end relationships with no way out. In general people who are plagued by depression, who are demoralized, are often magnets for lower vibrational interference from other people, as well as from other non-physical beings.

The urban areas of the world are full of lower octane frequencies especially in areas lacking trees and green spaces. This statement does not mean to imply that lower vibration cannot be found in mid- to small size towns. They most certainly can. Anywhere you find people, you will find this vibration. All I'm saying is that in environments that induce fear, you'll find stress, and stress is a killer to the heart.

Why does this occur? Because the subconscious part of our selves, that part of our human nature tied into tribe, creates out of fear and like attracts like. It's that simple. As we begin waking up to realize that what we really want to create in our lives is joy not misery then we will begin to make changes. But only if we are willing to see through the societal mind traps and become courageous about taking the steps to get what we want. And what most of us want is freedom. Some are willing to take concrete steps in small slices and be satisfied. Others get a taste and want more. Whatever you choose is really what you'll sooner or later get, so choose wisely.

Clear soul fragments.

Since many of us are still working in these high-rise, high-tech environments and not paying close attention to what truly brings us joy, we will literally leave our bodies as a way of not dealing with the day-to-day stresses of life. We are multi-dimensional beings of light so it is very easy to check out for a while and come back into the now moment anytime we so desire. But do enough of this—escape the pain and anguish of self-inflicted choices—and we find ourselves in a perpetual state of not being present, not showing up in life. If you take this basic concept and apply it to the totality of what has brought you pain and anguish, you can imagine how difficult it is for some of us to remain totally in the body 100 percent of the time. It's a challenge to say the least, but that is exactly what we are called to do.

The Guides once told me that in order for me to stay, I had to come back into the body and play. At the time, I was spending most of my time outside the body, and was not grounded at all. It took me quite a few years to understand that taking flight is not the thing to do if I am to show up and be fully present in my life. Most of us are carrying around deep scars from former incarnational experiences, which drove us to live these over-stressed lives of ours. We haven't learned yet, that it doesn't have to be that way.

It's important now, especially as the energy of the planet is intensifying, to look inside ourselves and see what's missing then begin to call back to us all those soul fragments that have been missing all along. These are the fragmented memories that are tied to the deepest most cherished part of us. Most hide or tuck these fragments somewhere inside of us or literally send them away to a place of safe-keeping until we know that we are safe. If you can imagine doing this over lifetimes, many of us are living on soul fumes and doing only what we have to get by. Just tuning in to how over-stressed, unfocused or unsettled, lonely and vacant, for instance, is enough to get our attention and challenges us to bring more passion back into our lives.

When you decide that you are ready to bring these fragments back together again it's just a simple matter of recognizing those parts of your life that are lacking in joy. Pay attention to the details of what you are feeling. Take an internal inventory of any areas of your life that feel incomplete or unbalanced. Look at the part of your self that is still crying out for change and sit with the emotion of what that feels like. Then forgive yourself and call this most precious part of yourself back in.

It is within this recognition phase of healing that you will become aware of inner stirrings that will perk you up and surprise you with things that you haven't thought about in ages. You will surprise yourself with the inspiration that will come to you in a flash, or wave of emotion. It's all quite fun to rediscover those parts of ourselves that we have tucked away for safekeeping. Just remember that it is a process and one that, once it gets started, you will not want to stop. And there's always more to discover about the self. Don't ever give up.

You might fear a major life change as you continue, but that is actually what you are headed toward. As we have explored, the human part of the self does not like change. We don't like it even when we are sitting in total misery. This kind of dread is so familiar that it literally becomes us. Many of the people that I encounter have become so enamored with being stuck that when I point out their particular brand of "being stuck"; they laugh out loud at how completely ridiculous their manifestations have become.

This ability to call back in the fragments of our soul can only occur when we have awakened enough to separate out from the stories that we have created. As we remember to accept the pain we have created within ourselves, and let it go, we will begin to look around at the life situations we are actually sitting in. By doing so, we recognize that the life-choices made through the filter of self-denial is in direct contrast to what the soul recognizes as its natural state of joy. Sometimes this kind of awakening causes a dramatic shock to the energetic system. Shocks may take form as processing deep sadness for no reason at all, body stresses such as headaches that come and go, disconnected dreams of other times, other places, or perhaps electrical charges that feel like an internal lightening storm moving through your body. There is sometimes little or no explanation that makes any logical sense as to what you are experiencing, but you will learn to discern the difference between actual ill-health and these kinds of energy jolts. By learning to listen to the body, you will learn what is needed to restore balance to the body.

Maintain balance and harmony.

The very nature of being human dictates a very different sort of life flow. The human body remains a part of Mother Nature while the body consciousness struggles to gain a sense of balance and equilibrium in a world set for self-destruction. As light beings, we are also a part and parcel of our physical environment.

Like any amorphous process, we may find it difficult at times to maintain our sense of balance and equilibrium. But we are not to worry. Regaining balance requires us to get quiet and go within the inner sanctum of the heart to understand what is truly before us. In your own experience, you may find that as you do, there will be many challenges waiting to disturb your piece of mind.

The Guides offer us help in this way: "We, as your teachers, are not here to dissuade you from any action or thought pattern. We are here to help, to move your awareness into a balanced state of readiness. As you find your heart moving into the depths of your very own self, you will find us there to guide you home to us.

"There are many different creative forces but there is only one heart, one awareness of freedom. Be always in this awareness and you will allow lowered expectations of life to pass before you. You will allow the awareness of love, of oneness to come into your inner sanctum. As you do, know that no harm will ever come to you. It is not possible.

"You will also experience the essence of many teachers, many traditions, coming into your conscious awareness. Love them; honor them; bless them; release them. We are to be birthing the new age of collective consciousness that sees, feels, and hears no boundaries of heart: Only oneness of being reigns high.

"All paths truly lead to one feeling for all. One source reigns high. You will find that at as you intone this feeling in all that you are called to do that others will be attracted to the oneness as well.

"Remember, my dear one, we are near and dear to your heart as you embrace this oneness of beingness that you are. Remember to feel the feeling of your very own soul. You are not to worry, or to doubt your resolve to create within this native state of being. Know that as you do, all is truly well."

Make conscious choices that bring focus to life.

We can all rest assured that our soul is well in charge of our experiences here on earth. There are many people who will tell us that it is in our collective interest to repent, to renounce any beliefs or perceptions that prompt us to act on the impulses of loving and honoring of the self. There are many individuals in our human experience who will tell us that we are all condemned to suffer through life as best we can, and that true freedom will not be realized in our lifetime, or even within the next two to three generations at best.

This form of argument is rooted in a view of looking backward and judging the now moment based on past outcomes. Buying into this belief thwarts any future projection of the higher self by truncating one's understanding of manifestation. Most like to stay exactly where they are in time even though they do not like where they are. Comfort of knowing is more important than feeling the body, mind and heart move into alignment with joy.

Instant pleasures come into form to bring about the activity that solves boredom, washes away pain, settles the mind. But in the very next moment there is movement toward the Divine. We feel the feelings of the divine spark of love and joyousness swelling from deep within us. But most of us, by the time we were six or seven years of age, began to determine whether or not we felt safe or if we were accepted for who we are. Most of the people that I find myself working with deemed that it was not safe for them to fully express as the divine being so they hid or revolted against their families of origin to one degree or another. Whatever the choice, they were afraid that they would not be loved.

As children, once this feeling was in our minds, many of us began to shut down. This form of shutting down took us outside our experience as love. Acting out of fear of survival, we shifted our focus to the mind. It happened to the best of us, and is continually being played out by souls incarnating today.

We are not to run away from this more mind-oriented way of being, but to understand it for it is—*a choice*. Choosing to experience our lives as human was a critical juncture point in our early life and took on twists and turns as we matured. Choice dictates our ability to wake-up to the truth of who we truly are even after we have navigated through the waters of our early learning. Depending on just how deep we have dived into the waters of the mind, the inner prompting of our heart puts us in direct contrast to when and how we are to awaken.

Once you awaken to your own version of your life, you may invariably find your way back into your choice, the point where you started, and begin to put a new perspective on your childhood experiences. We are each called to rewrite the story that we had become as we reconstruct the old with a renewed understanding of the truth. Life in the physical is that way, always reconstructing our lives to rewind and see where we have made a turn in the road or twist in the bend of life. Everything about what we do is all choice-oriented. Once you get past the old paradigm of sitting in stances of victim or martyr (that no one is at fault for anything that you have experienced in your life), you are almost home free. This revelation will help you to piece your life experiences back together and realize the beauty in the creation of one energetic stream of consciousness. As you reconnect the dots of your life, you will eventually see the poetic justice in the lessons you have learned and how far you have come to this point of recognition. You may even realize that if you had, in fact, changed one thing, just one, one event, one choice, one fear, one hurt, then you might not have awakened at all. Now, that is the sign of true freedom.

After reading the above passage, you might say, "Stop right here. I could have awakened sooner. I could have avoided this pain. I would have realized this or that." I am here as your witness to affirm that without every choice, no matter how painful or challenging at the time, you would not be reading this book. You would not be thinking your same thoughts. You might not even be here, right here, today.

When we look back, we realize that everything is truly perfect. We realize that our lives have been perfectly orchestrated for this very moment in time. With this deeper knowing, we now know that we are here to affect vast global change. We are the thinkers and the doers of creating in a new global consciousness.

As you fully awaken to the tapestry of so much coming together to create within the oneness, you will find others who are also wishing to create differently. They will come to you, and expect profound changes to be made for them. As you encounter these individuals, you are to bless them, honor them, and then release them from your path. As light beings, we are to allow the light of God within us to witness the light flowing through others to create in a way that sets their heart free as well. We are not to interfere with the human experience. We are to co-create with the others who have also recognized their choice to awaken.

As you have just read, as more and more align with the energetic frequencies of love and loving of self, unconditionally, this kind of inner shift will affect a change in the other.

We're also not to be dissuaded by outcomes. We are to understand who we are at all times and remember who we are not. We're not the stories that we have created. We are here to liberate ourselves from the self-imposed limitations that we have been taught to put on ourselves as we continue to play human.

Once you have fully awakened to who you truly are, you are ready to liberate yourself from limiting beliefs that may have held you captive to the inner ways of creating from the flowing of your inner most heart's desire. Many people find this difficult at first because they have operated through the filter of the mind for so long, but once they get a taste of what true freedom feels like there is no going back.

Once you have moved through the process of re-centering yourself in the knowing of who you are, the flow of light draws you into new experiences, new expressions of thought.

This deeper knowing will fuel the flow and manifest through your every thought. Continuing to flow your life into great rivers of love will lead you to realize the higher perspective of your world which will shift your awareness away from struggle and move you toward deeper levels of inner stillness. Inside this inner stillness is the heart of your ability to tune into a growing awareness of the grid. Combined with your innate knowledge of universal law, you will eventually, or surprisingly, realize that anything is possible. As you dream your reality, especially as you begin to coalesce with other beings of light who are also dreaming their realities of oneness, your imaginings will be magnified by the collective.

11: THE RIDE TOWARD FREEDOM

Applying what you've learned to life

By now, you have read that oneness is not only who you are but also it is actually where we are all headed. It is the stillness that only comes when we are free from fear. Right about now you may be asking how you can identify with the oneness that comes with such a feeling of joy, and how will your own special brand of joy manifest in your life?

The feeling of oneness is different for everyone. We can feel it by the way our body relaxes and our emotions settle into a feeling of *all is well* that comes with the knowing that we have the tools to rise above chaos. The feeling underneath all creation, when we are in the stillness is that all is well. All is well within the little us, and everyone and everything. Oneness includes the big picture as much as it involves the tiniest of details.

You may only feel the deeper levels as a flicker of peace in a sea of confusion but you will recognize it because this sense of well-being is in stark contrast to where you have been.

As you begin to understand this inner feeling and connect with it on a daily basis, inner strife begins to fall away. Everything that is in misalignment with this particular frequency of light must fall away. Wherever you put your focus, there you are. The kind of focus I am speaking of employs the body, mind and soul. We can begin with our emotional body, for instance, or the mind but in the end we are to focus our heart and the mind on what we so desire.

You will know if you are, or if you are not, by simply tuning into the mind's inner chatter. If you are worried about what others think or are stressed over a relationship or focused on how much money you don't have, that is exactly what you will get: unpopularity, turbulent relationships and insecurity about your sense of safety and well-being.

Turn all inner struggles around by focusing on the feeling of well-being. It may take some time as you break down the steps and focus on creating the feeling, but keep at it until you are convinced that you are that. Every time you catch yourself feeling insecure, counter this lower thought by telling yourself how very blessed you are. Keep at it until feeling blessed is the prevailing thought that floats around your head.

Or you may wish to focus your feeling of oneness on those you most love and care about giving thanks for all the love you feel inside. As you focus on one area of your life to anchor in this feeling of oneness with all three, your heart will begin to expand out into other areas of your life. This expansion process is a life-long flowing of your thoughts, feelings and perceptions into all areas of your life. As you do, you will eventually become more and more aligned with the oneness because you are becoming the living embodiment of who you are.

Many people ask me at this stage of the awakening process, "How do I overcome fear of change when the rest of the world doesn't live this way?" The answer is quite simple. It doesn't matter what others are doing; it only matters what you are doing.

Transformational practices for flowing into oneness

Affirmations combined with the practice of meditation are the most powerful tools we have for calling forth our highest expression. Whenever I am having a hard time figuring out what is disturbing my peace of mind I get quiet and allow the flow of light to work through me. My most often used affirmation calls forth my highest expression. It goes like this, "Make me an instrument of God's love and peace. I am a divine being of light. I am free (free to love, to allow, to express, to be in joy)."

By recognizing the truth of who you are and by invoking a

feeling of oneness in all you are called to do, issues of separation have less of an opportunity to arise. If anything at all interferes with your peace of mind, stop and get quiet. You may wish to ask yourself three questions: 1. Am I at peace? If not why? 2. Am I where I need to be according to how my heart is speaking to me? 3. Is my current expression bringing me joy? If not, why not? If you have found yourself answering no to any one of these three questions, you may wish to invoke some of the transformational tools that I have outlined below. All these methods have been used in both my personal life and in my practice and taught to others. The most important point here is to find what works for a continual process of creating more joy in your life.

Release fear.

- If you are experiencing any hardship experienced as frustration, resentment and depression, for instance, remember to take step away from the feeling by witnessing it as a movie passing before your eyes. Do not dive into the creation. Simply witness as you intone peace. If you find yourself falling into the emotional quality of the manifested creation, step back if even just for a moment to get yourself re-centered. Allow your mind and your emotional body to settle. Take a deep breath and move on. As you do, you will find that the fire of the experience will move through you and begin to clear.
- When you notice your mind moving into your story, and can feel the nagging emotion just beneath the surface, state your intention for healing then allow yourself time to process as the metaphors behind the emotion flood into your conscious awareness. Don't get attached to your story, just allow yourself to grieve the loss of sadness. Yes! Grieve the loss of sadness.
- Inwardly ask what might be deeply hidden from you by

stating the following: "I release (fill in the blanks...worry about, fear of...anger about...resentment of...). Keep stating what bothers you until you have completely run out of things to release. Keep coming back to the intention to release when you feel bothered, or have lost your focus of joy.

Practice meditation, use of the breath.
- Breathing meditations are great for taking a proactive approach. Pick one method that resonates with you and make it a part of your practice. Of course, there is always Mother Nature there to provide us with such amazing balance and harmony every time we wish to partake.

Quiet the mind, go inside and listen.
- Quiet your mind and know that all is well. The next time your emotions pull you into a feeling of heaviness, stop, get quiet and ask your heart to lead the way. Once your heart shares its guidance, step back and allow your mind to receive its inner guidance. Once you have received the inner guidance, then muster the courage to speak your truth, take that action, or change that direction. Even though you may not understand the logic of this heart-based choice at the time, trust it, and just take the leap of faith.
- Stop, get quiet and listen. Listen to your inner feeling of peace. Invoke peace and clarity as you realize the truth of your inner knowing. Allow this inner vision to be your guide. As your heart prompts you to shift your viewpoint or to change your outward direction, trust your inner guidance no matter what the circumstances in your life may look like. Give thanks for this inner vision, your inner knowing, and realize that all is well.
- When you sense the mind pushing into your creations, feel your way back into the heart of stillness, and patiently wait

to receive the gift of joy.
- Listen to your intuition for creating joy and more joy!!

Affirm who you are.
- Remember now, and every day, who you are becoming. Call this feeling of who you are forth by saying, and feeling, "I am [your word here] Peace, Joy, Freedom, and I am so very happy with everything I am creating. I am God incarnate in the physical. I am that which I am calling forward. So be it. It is done."
- Embrace your heart's desire; release the constraints of the body and say, "Yes, I am ready to be free!"
- Know that you are an integral part of the source of life that sent you here.
- Love God with all your heart as you love each and everyone else.

Choose joy.
- Claim victory over your fear of change by intending your desire to change aspects of your life that no longer feel joyful. Affirm the truth of who you are by outwardly moving toward that feeling by doing what your heart has already prompted you to do. Rejoice in your courage to embrace your heart's desire to be free.
- Identify your joy then take action accordingly within every moment of every hour, every day, until this knowing of joy becomes you.
- All is well. Choose peace by being peace. Allow your mind, your heart and your inner feeling to come into balance and harmony.

Engage your imagination.
- Imagine the world as a golden ball of light where there is only love, and you are in the middle of this ball resonating

as the vibration of peace. Each time you find yourself reacting to the latest round of news or sensationalism, stop and remember that there is only love.

- Imagine the world as you wish to see, hear and feel it all around you. Create that reality within the feeling that you hold deep within you. As you hold this feeling, make a wish for your own desire within the inner realm of your very own heart. Then toss it to the winds of change and know that your creation is now complete. Allow your imagination to be your guide. Dream big, and with feeling. See, hear, and feel the reality of your heart's desire manifest in your life.

- Accept where you are in life and love everything and everyone who crosses your path, deliberately. Deliberately bless and release all past hurts, slights and inner struggles. Deliberately let go and forgive. Deliberately embrace the love that you are, the love that you give and the love that you receive. So be it.

- Know that you are God incarnate. Identify your joy then take action accordingly within every moment of every hour, every day until this knowingness becomes you.

Take total responsibility for your own personal peace and happiness, and allow others the opportunity to do the same.

As you continue your practice of reclaiming your power as a spiritual being of light, you'll also begin to discover that your personal peace and happiness will dramatically increase. Not only you will you realize a major shift in your awareness, but the power you invoke to change your life will become instrumental in shifting any group dynamic. This deeper awareness of the self takes you away from maintaining a stance of life happening to you and transforms your awareness into a total knowing that everything that you create in your world begins with you.

No one has the right to change anyone else, to make a choice for any other person. Our job, as light beings, is to stay focused on what brings us joy then simply pay attention to who shows up in our world. As you adopt this practice, you get to make new choices about how you feel about what you are creating. It goes without saying that when your perspective changes so too does your focus and maintaining your focus is the key to opening your heart.

I often hear back from people who tell me that they really understand this feeling of oneness but are experiencing a difficult time maintaining peace in all aspects of their lives. When I follow the energetic lines back into their creations, I find that they lost their focus at some point, and allowed misguided beliefs or perceptions (lack of trust, self-deception and self-loathing etc.) to creep back into their lives. You can be sure that if you are not happy with a particular aspect of your life it is because there is a hidden belief, I call it an unconscious program, at work. However, with these tools, you can find and clear just about anything that is disrupting your life.

As I share what I see, I usually hear laughter on the other end of the line or a sigh of relief, which tells me they got it! With this essential life-skill under their belt, they set a newly corrected course and give thanks for the learning. If you are open to adopting this perspective on your life, that you are always learning, and your life is always about you and not the people in your life, then you will refine your skill sets and become prepared for tackling complex life issues in a very simple way.

Just remember feeling is the key, not who said what, but what the feeling nature is trying to tell you. If you are feeling frustrated, go find faith. If you are angry, take note that you are not taking responsibility for your own life. Resentment breeds contempt of self. Look inside and there you will find exactly what ails you. Knowing and understanding are the keys to transforming all lower vibrational thought.

The ultimate task of taking responsibility for your creations is to reside in the stillness. When you feel off-balance, just remind yourself to stop, get quiet. Find your center then set out again. If you get really lost or confused about what you should do to take corrective action, just ask your spiritual helpers, the Guides, for help. You will invariably get the answer in a mental picture, a dream or a clear signal that will point you in the right direction.

You have an endless sea of help but you are the one who is to be moving and driving the creations of your world. As you take ten steps toward your goal of awakening to joy, your angelic helpers and guides will take ten times ten steps toward you to help your achieve your goals. Just remember to ask with confidence that you will receive your answer promptly.

Accept change as a part of life.

The long and short of it is that the steps required to create a life worth living is one that takes courage, and the call to change offers us the biggest challenge of all. Many of us, in our human expression, sit and weather the storm. The storm, of course, has occurred because we have resisted the prompting to follow the inner guidance of our heart.

We have all been reminded of people in times of impending demise who refuse to leave to seek out safe shelter. Some live to tell about their adventures later. Others pay the ultimate sacrifice for not heeding their own inner advice.

Human nature abhors change and resists it with every breath even when it is literally killing us. We witness many dramatic examples of weathering the storm. I believe they provide us with clear examples of heart verses mind choices. One might suggest that we are much smarter or wiser than someone getting caught in a storm that had been given advance notice to leave. But I have personally witnessed a plethora of instances where very smart people refuse to make a change because that is simply what they have always done. They sit and wait for life to change around them, or for others to make a choice that only they can make. Our human nature wants us to sit in the state of non-movement no matter how miserable it makes us. That's our fear of survival mentality at work, which is often counter to its own programming.

Fear of survival tells us that we all have to stick together in order to make it in the world, but the world herself is changing. The energy, as I have mentioned has already shifted from fear to joy, and it will only become more intensified in the coming years ahead. If you are sitting in fear, and feel that it is just a matter of weathering the storm, you might want to think again. This upcoming storm is not a hurricane, but a full-blown change in frequency.

As you create your world by following your heart, you will find that once you realize your heart is always there to guide you, then it's just a matter of maintaining your focus. When you find yourself resisting inwardly guided change, focus on the feeling of joyousness, the kind of deep inner stillness that floods into your heart when you are following the prompting from your soul.

Once you are fully seated in your intention for flowing the stillness through all your worldly creations, and once you let go of the mind's way of emotional boundaries, you will delightfully discover that you are always in the right place at the right time. You are never wrong, and always right. Right for you. As you more fully identify with the joy that you are, you will realize that change is happening every day, every hour, every second. So that means that you can change anything about your creations at any time. There are no wrong choices, but you must choose. I have often been told by those that I work with, "but I didn't have a choice, or I didn't choose that."

Sitting in your stuff and making no choice is actually making a very loud announcement to the universe that you are staying right where you are. But how many times have you done just that with your behavior and attitude about life? We are all prone to loosing our perspective from time to time. Like anything in our physical world, the first step is always the most challenging. Once you take the first, the second is usually close behind. Then before you know it you are not even looking back over your shoulder. As you may eventually discover, your job in this lifetime is simply to follow your bliss.

Expand the flow into all areas of your life.

After you have become practiced at making choices that bring a smile to your heart, you will find that living life in the flow is ultimately best and the only way to create in a way that makes your heart sing. When we are outside the body, this is an easy thing to accomplish because we have no resistance, but in the body it's a very different learning dynamic. As we have just explored, the biggest roadblock to living in the flow is the mind or emotional body.

As you are relating to your life, see everything as movement. This will help you to allow your emotional body to release its hold over you and prompt you to listen to your heart. Once you do, you will find that Spirit will nudge you this way or that for the mere purpose of positioning you in life to receive enormous blessings. As you move as you are prompted, the happenings in your life will take on delightful synchronicities that cannot begin to be orchestrated by the mind. Your heart is totally connected to the grid and knows where you are to be for you to realize your highest expression at all times. Learn to trust this timeless feeling of oneness as it envelops you. This feeling is letting you know that you are in the right place at the right time, and that all is well.

We can often feel the difference between pushing our way through life and flow. Flow feels so much better. It's easy, joyful, and playful. Just ask anyone who has experienced both and see what they have to say about it. Most will tell you that once you have experienced the difference there is no going back.

I speak to many people who have accomplished this way of living in one aspect of their lives but seem to get stuck in another. Yes, it is possible to straddle the two reality creations but it is very difficult to shift back and forth without getting frustrated or feeling demoralized at times. However, one level of creation leads to another. If you're finding that all is well on the work front but your beloved never seems to materialize, you are in the flow in one arena but not in the other. What blocks you is your attachment to a perceived outcome.

Most people are in one of these two categories. They are totally lost or frustrated with where they are in their learning, overwhelmed even, or they have gained a measure of flow and are working to create a wider bandwidth of love through all facets of their creations. It is not that they are consciously allowing transgressions against the self to enter into their heart, but just the same, they are allowing self-limiting beliefs and perceptions to rule their awareness.

If we are asleep, we are in our human nature. If we are in the flow, then we are awake and flowing with life with no attachment to outcome. As you feel the difference between when you are listening to your heart and when you are allowing the mind to push you off balance, begin to see that flow is just that. A flow. Our human nature way of creating always feels like a push or pull.

As you practice bringing more flow into your life, your creations will take on twists and turns but that's all right. As you listen to your heart and go into a deeper stillness, your dreams will tell you where and how you are to be. Many will tell you that you are crazy, or try to hold you back from pursuing your dreams, but you are not to listen to the nay-sayers, the doubters. Move into your heart and know that all is well.

The role of surrender in attaining flow

There is never a good time to say goodbye to an aspect of your life that has given you so much love and enjoyment. But therein lies the very act of surrender. Surrender is the key to flow. As you listen to the still voice within you, you'll discern the only clear choice is to follow that awakened part of you. It's that deeper river of stillness that knows all is well, even in the most turbulent of emotional waters. Once you have discovered that deeper calm, your inner world will open up to reveal your higher vibrational path.

Lack of trust is a most human trait. We've all heard about the battle of the sexes but I believe the struggle between the heart and mind is the war to win in today's word. It supersedes any other struggle because it is the key to merging the human nature with our divine nature.

With or without outside intervention, that is where we are headed—toward the evolution of a super race of humanity, a global family, that finally wakes up and realizes that she can't keep killing herself, or taking from others because she is frightened of her divinity.

As a part of this collective consciousness, here we are in the midst of life serving as the basic building blocks for teaching others how this works. Your heart may already be speaking clearly to you but how often do you do get stuck right at that point, that precipice of surrender, and hang or hover there until that golden opportunity has passed you by? Or you have managed to convince yourself that it's just not worth the risk, and back down the proverbial clift or shape shift your way back into a familiar comfort zone? Sometimes, you may finally experience the act of surrender out of pure exhaustion—bringing only willingness to the table. Surrender this way, seems like you have lost every hope, and are simply giving up. But it's actually the struggle that you are letting go of, nothing more.

Surrender is the conscious choice to allow—allowing you to take orders from your soul having the human experience. These orders are all about creating joyful, expansive realities. Some will say that this way of living is impossible; that it's not logical; it's not the way the real world works. I say that it's the *only* way to fully realize freedom, the kind of freedom that makes your heart sing.

Have you ever wondered what it would feel like to flow your life with joy, without any stops? The Guides speak to the notion of allowing. "Allow, allow, allow", they say. I have come to understand this mantra of allow to mean, allowing the love that we are to flow unimpeded out into the world; to get out of our own way.

As you listen with the sure promise of following your heart, you'll know exactly what to do when you feel the knowing that comes with surrendering to allow for this most amazing flow of grace that permeates our entire spectrum of reality. Without trust, faith and knowing, surrender would not be possible. As you adjust your perspective on life to include surrender as a moment-to-moment inner positioning in life, you'll be amazed at the direction your life will take. Just the inner peace, alone, is worth listening to the soul's perspective on who you are.

The time-space continuum

Linear time was created, and continues to be perpetuated, by the mind. It's a choice we make. Linear time was first set up by the creators of this third-dimensional world to help us to maintain our perspective. Like setting up a series of markers to delineate what we were learning. However, linear time was never created as a holding tank for everything we have ever done, or for some, to use as a selective way of remembering. Once we have learned a particular lesson, we are to let it go. When we do, we loosen the grip that linear time has over us. Linear time is anchored in our emotional body and is a part of our human nature.

You will find that as you move through the key gateways that time is not metered at all but a place, a dimension. But for us here on earth, we can enter nonlinear time through the feeling of timelessness, or a state of no time. There are many passageways through the linear concepts in order to gain entry into the time-space continuum known as nonlinear time. Each passageway has its own unique property. Within each of the parallel happenings, synchronicities create a different variation on the same life theme. As creators of these life-path probabilities, we choose our direction from the feeling that guides us. And it is the feeling that takes us into the dimension of non-linear time. As we create in the third-dimensional world, others in our world respond to us exactly as we first felt it into being. But because we live in a backwards world, as the Guides say, we project our focus outward and forget that we are the one who set the creation into motion.

How often we are surprised at what we get back depends upon our orientation to our inner world and how locked in we are to our third-dimensional belief patterns. These patterns are ingrained in our subconscious choices but nonetheless, we are creating as the totality of our life experiences.

The key to both creating and dismantling any part of our reality is to move back into nonlinear time, into the place where all thought resides and transform the feeling that fuels the creation that is causing us to react to others in our world. It sounds simple and it is but it takes a matter of getting used to looking at our world through a different set of eyes, a different filter. As you keep getting clearer about what signals you are putting out into the world through feeling, then you will gain real power in creating what you so desire. You will also not get hung up on what is happening to you or feel thwarted by life. That's how it works for one. Now let's take a look at how powerful we are in the midst of a group creation. Stepping into nonlinear time to transform anything at all into a higher vibrational creation works the same way for one as much as it does for an entire population.

As we look around our immediate world, we can see the very basis of our life's awakenings. But as we look beyond the confines of our natural world into the reality creations of larger social-cosmic systems, which may take a back seat to our creations, we may say that we have no affect on changing these systems. We say this because we can sometimes feel that we are only one, small insignificant part of the whole — we assume that we cannot possibly shift the dynamic of the group. But no part of the whole is insignificant — small has been moving mountains forever.

There are those of us who have been called forth to do just that — shift an entire structure, whether it is social, political, economic, etc. It does not matter. What matters is that we follow our heart and go with the flow of the frequency that brings us so much love and joy. As we do, we find ourselves immersed in nonlinear time. This feeling of timelessness, when we are doing something that makes our heart sing, creates vast changes within these lower vibrational systems. We are reaching into the very heart of the creation and transforming it.

We remind ourselves that we are not the body and we are not the energetic of the changes that are being made. We are divine beings of light of the highest order and we have been called to shift into higher states of joy, even as we witness those around us who are feeling so much pain and suffering.

12: ONENESS

Leaves dancing upon the water

There is power in numbers but only if we, as a group presence, are clear in purpose about our ultimate resolve for peace. This kind of work is not for those who are unsure of their place in the world. There are forces of nature (human nature) that push anything that feels like a threat to remain in the dark (ignorance), and unravel the power dynamics of human suffering into a deeper state of darkness. Humanity has long identified with suffering even as she has been pulled or pushed toward a different state of being, from time to time, that might prove detrimental to her sense of safety and stability. To bring humanity to the light too quickly, for some, may send them right back into the darkness — the Guides tell us that everything is light. Even the darkness is light. Darkness is light inverted. To cloak one self in darkness seems pretty preposterous looking at it from the viewpoint that everything is light, but remaining in the vibration of the familiar is comfortable even when it is killing us.

And herein lies the dilemma for all light beings. We have no right, no purpose, in pulling humanity to safety. After all, whether light being or human, we are all endowed with certain inalienable rights, and free choice is one of them; even when humanity perceives that she has no choice at all. With this being said, what is our individual and collective choice then if we are, indeed, here to affect vast global change on every level, and layer of consciousness?

Our choice is for freedom, because that is who we are. There is no other choice that liberates global consciousness than to totally liberate the self. In this call to take back our power, personal peace and happiness pushes the dynamic of change. The doing part is simple because it is a natural out-flowing of who we are. Liberation, the way that our souls have been programmed to remember, is to merge with the divine light of God that we are, then to enter into communion with all as one.

Like a fire that is lit from within, all those who come near feel our warmth. Our passion for life, of course, is the fuel that ignites great deeds, small and large. We are to realize the change through joyous acts of service. The condition of human suffering has long been acknowledged as a poverty of spirit first, material second, so we are here to reverse that trend, to balance out the sleight, to make it right by being both happy and prosperous in all areas of our lives.

Show me a wealthy person who is truly happy and I'll show you a poor one who understands life in its most basic form. We, in the West, know how to build material wealth but have forgotten what spiritual well-being feels like. It is not surprising that lack of self-love is running rampant in suburbia and cities alike. We are so busy chasing after material wealth that many of us have forgotten how to be happy, truly happy. We have forgotten. We have forgotten the internal connection and look outward to fill the void.

Once we are reseated in this inner connection to the divine light that we are, then everything we do becomes an extension of this feeling. Connection to the Divine fuels a connection to humanity herself, and to the planet. Our sense of well-being will lead us to open up and feel free again. This new found freedom will help us to find new balance and realize that both material and spiritual well-being is possible.

All as One

There will soon come a time when we will look back and realize that humanity has built her life on a foundation of self-destruction. And we will find that there is redemption in knowing that we tried our very best. As you awaken to your divine presence and purpose, you will rediscover both the inherent sadness of not being human mixed in with a profound sense of love.

Loving and honoring the truth of who we are is an essential right of passage to becoming a being of light experiencing and expressing as freedom. This concept of freedom is meant to be realized by vast reaches of social, political, and economic openings within our human family, and is also an inner feeling of oneness fully realized, and without emotional filters, societal roadblocks, or fear of one another.

"We know that this may seem like an impossible task," the angels say, "but you are ready. You are ready to shift the consciousness of the planet in ways that you can only begin to imagine now. You may think that your fate is left up to the very few, the powerful who hold sway over many in the worldly way of creating, but we say to you that you are much more powerful than all the mighty power brokers, landowners, and soil-depleters, commanders of vast armies. You, my dear ones, are much more powerful than all these trivial pursuits put together.

"The power of love always transcends the illusion of duality any day or hour of self discovery. We see that as you ascend and begin to discover who you truly are, you will be quite amazed, surprised really, at your power to wield vast armies of a different kind. These armies are fueled by the love of humanity, grounded in one's own resolve to be free.

"We say to you, that it is now time to accept the challenge, to rise above the strife. See all of humanity's creation for what it is, as you claim victory over your human nature. As you do, you will witness atrocities committed by your human family. You will see horrors, and steadfast ignorance played out before you, but you are to hold fast to your ascension as you claim victory over your human nature.

Freedom comes with a price to pay. In all realms of light, there are many forces pushing back away from the creation cycles of oneness. Power begets power. Once a worldly force has garnered, or shored up, one's power-base there is no giving back. The fortress is built and defended at all costs. Fighting to the death of an illusionary force is not uncommon. But once the illusion is identified the rest is easy."

Like a fast approaching mirage, as we come into a greater degree of understanding, the circumstances change, viewpoints come into focus, and the bigger picture is realized. All parties agree to split, and multiply. There is no longer any need to procreate the illusion. Freedom brings great expansion for all concerned.

The forces of nature will try to dissuade these kinds of group ascensions so they fall apart in order to perpetuate the feeling of separation, but we are not to turn back. How will these scenarios play out in worldly terms? We will see many people tell us that our world is to be shaped in a particular fashion but we are not to listen. We are to go within, to focus on the oneness. This reminds me of the images I have seen around the issues of mass migration.

If we allow ourselves to be used as pawns in the culture of self-protectionism that is bound to play out as global cultural upheaval begins, then we will need to pull back and see that all is well. By early 2009, there will be more than the race of nations in Africa and Middle East on the move. We will begin to see many other cultures moving into new territories thus disrupting the social order of people already established. But this is just the precursor for the kind of mass exoduses about to occur. If we get caught up in the debates, we'll lose the overall point. From one heart to another is to be the focus.

If you find that you are pushed or challenged to accept the lower road in these kinds of life choices, you might want to inwardly ask for clarity. Ask for the reality of oneness to be revealed to you. As you take a step back away from confusion, you will find that your heart will speak loudly to you. As you listen to the stillness, therein, you will find your inner direction. As you take action based upon what you have been given, your heart will soar. You will begin to shift your creation, and will begin to contribute to the absolving of any group distortion that may be present.

This way of transcending distortion takes courage and conviction to follow your heart over the roar of the mind, and requires us to continually call forth our highest life expression in any given situation.

In one sense, you might say that it doesn't matter what is happening in the rest of the world, as long as your piece of the world is working for you. But even as you make these choices that are rooted in oneness in your world, just know that you are totally connected to what is happening everywhere.

We truly are all one—one light, one energetic field or grid of consciousness. What happens to one is felt by all (on the conscious level and more subtly). We are all tied together as one organic, growing, changing, field of light. As we turn our lives over to the oneness, we are fueled by a different motivation. Some choose to be quiet, some to serve their communities. Others become motivated to shift a group dynamic, to enter into a helping mode or assume leadership roles by teaching and facilitating. For as many self-expressions as can be imagined, there are many who will tell you that your role in this particular moment in time is not valued for who you are, only for what you do.

Our angels and Guides are merely here to stand witness, to prompt us from time to time. We are simply to be quiet, to listen like a child listening to the heartbeat of her mother. Be quiet; be still. Listen to the heart of your own knowing. As you do, you will find that, truly, all is well.

Acting from the wisdom of one's heart is always a magical, mesmerizing mode of reality creation. We are here to

248

determine our life choices by the way this inner knowing guides us. If we are clearly aligned with our heart, and have made peace with our former choices, then surrendering to a higher path becomes self-evident. If you find that you are mid-stream between these two modes of creation, then the play between the mind and heart can become a real challenge. No matter where you are in the process of honoring your heart, know that it is a process and be patient with yourself, but focused on your goal.

PART 5:

SPIRITUAL ACTIVISM

New paradigm leaders know who they are because they are at peace with the life they have chosen. They understand that they are here to follow their bliss by choosing what brings them joy. You can spot new paradigm leaders by the sparkle of passion in their gaze or the sweetness of their smile.

13: THE ROLES WE PLAY

What we have come here to do

Within the context of the grid, a global mosaic has emerged right along side the probable futures. This mosaic represents light beings of every configuration imaginable, and the growing light of humanity. The roles that have emerged represent a collective group of people who are selflessly serving humanity. They are courageously following their heart, and by doing so are changing the world. These descriptions and accompany examples represent composite profiles from conversations I have had the privilege of having with people from all walks of life. They reside in the Continental United States, Europe, Australia and parts of Asia. As you read through the descriptions, you may wish to stop after each and ask yourself inwardly, does this role apply to me? And to aid you in your process of self-discovery, I have also added an abbreviated list at the end of the narratives to help you to decide how these roles may fit your own unique life-path.

Our more worldly roles, the ones that we are accustomed to relating to, represent only the surface of what we are doing. The 3D roles have names like mother, father, brother, sister or office worker, president, accountant or perhaps shopkeeper, massage therapist, or radio talk show host. These are the roles that we can easily relate to and help us to bring order to our lives. They are designed to create a common language to communicate our basic function to the rest of the world, and are based on an elaborate hierarchy of labels that identify us in the context of the game we, as a group consciousness, choose to play.

But just under the surface of these 3D roles is where the work of the soul, the light being having the human experience, is taking place. The roles, outlined in the following passages, have more to do with how we, as light beings, use the human energy matrix to do what we've come here to do — to go about the work of awakening our brothers and sisters of the light.

The roles as light beings in human bodies is more along the lines of how we are best suited for channeling light into the human matrix. In short, the roles outlined as follows represent how we have chosen to serve as that shot in the arm of grace into our ailing human family.

By learning more about the role you have come here to play, you will become more effective and offer up less worry and doubt about your purpose and how you are to best create in fulfillment of your highest expression.

What you will also discover is that some of the roles will feel like a perfect fit or there may be elements of one that is more *comfortable* than another. However that feeling of comfort is not necessarily your *primary* role this time around. I'll give you a "for instance": One may feel at home serving as a gatekeeper, someone who transforms others by taking stating the obvious or simply holding the gate open for others to pass through, but whose role in this lifetime is to be an activator. An activator, as you are about to learn, is someone who activates others by *doing*, and it's their joy when doing the doing that opens the doorway of the heart. Many entertainers, artists and musicians are activators. My favorite example of an activator is a school principle (a classic gatekeeper) by day, and dynamic, irreverent singer-songwriter by night. He is totally immersed in his joy and feels liberated when sharing his gift with others to the delight of everyone around him. It is obvious that he just loves the thrill of performing beautiful music.

So here we go:

Way-Shower

Way-showers are new paradigm leaders. To one degree or another, light beings are all way-showers once they awaken. And once we do, we begin to understand that our role is to walk our talk. We stop making excuses for our lives and the way we were brought up or why we are not experiencing in life what we feel inside. Many of us have come through the fire of deep disconnect but have finally reconnected the dots: We are the ones who are to pick ourselves up and create what we so desire. The rest of the world may or may not understand who we are or what we are all about, but that is okay.

We are way-showers because we are the first to create the first steps where others may later follow. Not that there have not been others who have come before us, but in this time, this day and age, the energy coming into the planet has never been here before, and the state of humanity is quite different than it has been in the past.

On the surface of life, we inherently can see right through someone who is totally disingenuous — people who consciously shape shift to manipulate outcomes, usually from a motivation of greed or power and control.

Way-showers are the leaders of a new-world consciousness. These are individuals who have given up on following an oppressive style of leadership and inherently understand that the only real person that one can lead is oneself. This new paradigm way of leading offers us a flattened social structure model, and challenges us to live our lives by what we feel is right for us. Being true to the self is the model of deliberate choice making. Way-showers know that the only person they can truly please is themselves so they stop trying to fit in to structures that are no longer working for them, and instead, join with others to create the new.

They don't get involved in shape-shifting (setting up hidden agendas or hiding behind a mask) because they are motivated by their alignment with truth. These are individuals who are caring, sensitive and considerate of others. I do not mean to imply that old paradigm leaders are not also compassionate human-beings. But way-showers do not allow the pain and anguish of others to dissuade them from realizing their own sense of inner stillness.

Way-showers also come in all sizes, shapes, nationalities and ages. There is no one set parameter or prerequisite for becoming a way-shower outside of living life by one's own standard of behavior. Their behavior is realized by listening to the inner stillness that guides them. That is it!

Transformer

I have met many way-showers but very few transformers. They are a unique breed. They know who they are intuitively but they are not necessarily aware of what they are doing, or when or why they are doing it. They just know that they are divinely guided, and can go anywhere without feeling a need to prove their worth or to be needed. Transformers are rare in number because they have incarnated during particular times in humanity's history when the bridge between the great divide between ignorance (unconscious choosing) and enlightenment has become so wide that on the surface of life one would think that there is no hope of change.

These unique beings are fearless. Their courage has been honed by thousands of lifetimes living in the pit of human despair. Nothing truly bothers them and nothing at all surprises them. They are also some of the most loving, compassionate people that I have ever met. A few have become so enamored with not wanting to be on the planet that they have become consumed with self-righteousness. But they are in the minority.

Transformers take on roles that no one else would want. They are aware of the deepest levels of self-hatred and the highest forms of love. They are here to hold the sacred space for others and have learned to tread lightly around those who would call them by name. Therefore, they shy away from jobs that bring them fame and fortune in favor of more ground-level societal roles that allow them to be more autonomous to move about freely in society.

They usually hold down positions of great power in the higher light kingdoms but choose strikingly ordinary, household kinds of positions in third-dimensional life to avail themselves to others who are engaged in unconscious behavior. The mere presence of their light transforms any given situation. In their day to day lives they are homemakers, mothers, fathers and industry workers. They are Mother Theresa types enmeshed in the outer trappings of making a living working, going to school and dreaming of traveling the world when life eases up.

For those who are rudely awakened to their role as a way-shower, they are often called to drop what they are doing and walk away from down-trodden existences that have become so familiar to them that they have taken on the role of *stepped-on* as an identity. Because many of them have lived in the lower bowels of human emotions for so long, some get lost in the sea of confusion, but do eventually find their way to the light. When they do, depending on just how buried they have gotten, they are often called to stop and re-evaluate their lives. In doing so, most are incredibly clear in their recognition of who they are and are called to walk away from these lower vibra-tional identities that have held them hostage for so long.

For those with whom I have witnessed such a metamor-phosis in their before and after-lives have all been dramatic, to say the least. True to the profile of a transformer, once they shift, they adopt life paths that place them squarely on the path as major transformers of other people's lives. A perfect example of a powerful transformer is that of a young man and

256

the gift he passed along to his family, particularly his father. He was killed while serving with his country.

At the funeral, his family members were overwhelmed by the sea of people pouring their love and affection out to the family of this remarkable young man. They were not there to honor him as a fallen soldier as much as someone who personally touched their lives. He was remembered by young and old alike as someone who was kind, compassionate, and open-hearted to everyone he met. Most were struck by his deep and abiding faith in God. He never met a stranger.

This outpouring of love for his son so profoundly affected his father that he decided to keep the spirit of his son alive by giving-back to the community. By doing so, he began to open his heart and is actively finding ways to enrich others' lives. Transformers are like that: Once awakened, their mere presence and their kindness of heart transforms the lives of others.

Awakener/Activator

I have grouped awakeners and activators together because they are essentially the same with one big difference: Being verses doing. We are all here to affect change and some of us decide to do so by just *being* who we are. Awakeners are like that. They are here just for the joy of living. In their unconscious state, they are often depressed, isolated or feel confused about their path. But once awakeners understand that their role is to serve by simply being (joyful, peaceful, compassionate, etc.), their lives will often transform very quickly.

On the other hand, activators take that same being nature and go out and do. I have met many activators who are at first striving to awaken. In the less conscious state, they feel that they must prove themselves, and do so by fervently striving to awaken others. But after they realize that they have nothing to prove, they are inwardly motivated to take that wondrous being nature that they bring to the world and share their often times stellar creative gifts with others just for the pure joy of it.

Many way-showers are like the activator when they are becoming more conscious. Because they feel such a rush of joy when first opening, they will often feel compelled to share their joy and their new-found wisdom with enthusiasm. However, awakeners and activators do not to do so by waving their flag of choice and telling the others how to (or even to) *follow me*. Their role in the grand awakening of humanity is to live their joy. Virtually every single person that I have met, minus a few lost souls, serves in part as an awakener. But those who are called to this role are particularly focused on the personal play aspect of life—and life supports them to do just that.

The role of awakeners and activators are designed to place beings of light in visible yet, from a 3D power structure viewpoint, very invisible life situations. I have met awakeners that, given their position in the higher realms of light, are huge beings of light that are here to bring down entire old paradigm structures, and by doing so play the role of janitor, company tech rep, or roving sales person. The traditional roles place us inside structures to allow us to bring more light into the planet in our own unique way.

Many of the awakeners that I have met change physical positions frequently, which is why many are motivated by jobs that take them in and out of a variety of locations, and industries. Many are single, and have never been married. Some are long-time, stay in one place kind of folks with people who seem to find them wherever they are. A great example of an awakener is one of my very favorite people, a nurse who works in a school system. Even though she is there to administer to the needs of school children, her office and her home is always buzzing with activity as her colleagues and friends find her company and her deep wisdom comforting and encouraging. Another many are familiar with is Oprah. You might not think that her primary role is as an awakener because she is such a doer. But no matter what new project she is rolling out, it's her joyful being-ness that is transforming her world.

Activators affect change by purposefully doing what they do to activate, to cause upset, change, or a shift in others. Unconsciously, both awakeners and activators (in early life) were trouble-makers or lost souls, who were born into troubled households, families steeped in dysfunction or chaos. In their higher nature they are deliberate about their role of being joyful and stand away from chaos but are not bothered by it because they understand it so well. They share their own special brand of joy with the world. Activators live high-impact high profile lives, like the example of the school principle - dynamic singer-songwriter, they are called into the doing. Many choose professions or life-situations where they are highly visible, and are called to take action to create high-impact awakenings in others.

Bridge Builder

Just like the name implies, the role of bridge builder is to bridge the gap between the great divide. They often come from very abusive backgrounds and have seen it all, but many of them, at least initially, are in denial about how badly their heart has taken a hit. Instead most have become over-achievers in life and have become very successful at what they do. Surprisingly enough, many that fit this category have made quite a name for themselves, but when the denial catches up to them their lives take a turn and fall apart to greater or lesser degrees.

This is usually where I intersect with their lives. They choose not to seek out traditional forms of therapy because they intuitively know that they are not actually mortally wounded by their beginnings or recent turn of events. Most believe that they can outrun the denial or see the change as a positive step in the right direction. Therefore, my work with these often times brilliant, hardheaded individuals is to get them to understand their role as a light being. Once they really *get it*: that their early lives were propulsions for ambition, and the ambition was what was needed to get them into key positions of power, then the rest is simple.

After an initial period of reorienting to their version of their new world, most soar. A few get stuck on what should have been or what should be but most recognize it as the mind and quickly allow their fears to fall away. Once on track, these individuals go out into the world much the same way that they did before but now they are on fire with a desire to serve. The skills they have honed to carve out their niche in the physical world is then applied to solving problems — global warming, inequality in the school system, economic inequity, housing, urban sprawl, efficient energy usage, etc.

They are living life *their* way, and doing what they love to do, which is to connect with others for the sharing of new ideas and creating new systems, deeper levels of connection but most of all problem-solving. Many of the bridge builders that I know are on fire to create a new world consciousness and have no fear about the new because many of them are entrepreneurs or totally understand enterprise as a way of life. They are risk-takers, if you are looking from the outside in, but to them they are simply following their joy.

An example of a bridge builder is a woman who owns her own manufacturing business and is involved in her community through a variety of philanthropic activities. She is also working to bridge the gap between the East and the West by co-authoring a book to help US companies better understand how to do business with China.

Wisdom Keeper

I've met fewer wisdom keepers than bridge builders, but when I do, I am struck by their innate ability to discern the Truth. Their ability to track any distortion by following one's speech pattern is quite amazing. Most wisdom keepers, when I first meet them, have so buried themselves in issues of unworthiness that it is sometimes very difficult for them to accept the truth of who they are. Many are intuitively off the charts but do not use their skills for helping others. But even in their "wounded healer" state, people naturally gravitate toward them and seek out their advice and counsel.

They have learned to use their intuitive skills (most are empathic) to keep themselves safe and out of harms way. Many have witnessed much violence both in their former lifetimes and also as a product of their current lives for the purpose of higher learning. Many in this category remember long stretches of being tortured, maimed or ostracized in some way for speaking up in other lifetimes. Or carry a very deep sense of remorse or responsibility for not being able to follow through on a mass ascension in another time. Some remember the time of the crusades, others Egypt or Lemuria or Atlantis. Some drop in later during the turn of the nineteenth century. Therefore, they have a tendency to be very timid about speaking up now.

Most are unfazed by fame and fortune and can see right through a get-rich-quick scheme or if someone is trying to tell them something that simply is not true. Few will actually speak up and challenge the untruth. Most will hold their tongue and simply witness what is happening.

Wisdom keepers hold great knowledge that they have gained through the ages. Many are coming from other star galaxies and are here to tell the stories to the others to help them to remember the truth of who they are. They are the storytellers, the poets, and the writers among us. They are also the timid, the meek in physical and powerful in their inner knowing.

Through my work, I have met wisdom keepers from all walks of life but most are here to witness these next few years and allow the images that they receive to pass through them. They are witnessing the global prophecies pass before them. Some are witnessing the atrocities of humanity inflict pain upon her collective self. Some are watching as the plant and animal kingdoms fall into disreputable hands. Others are here to witness the earth changes take place before they actually do. But in witnessing, all understand their power to heal by the very fact that they do not jump into the story that is playing out before them, but simply to intone love into the creations thereby forever changing them.

Many will be called to witness these changes in the coming years ahead but it is the wisdom keepers who hold the flame of love where others cannot.

I once met a woman who told me that she did not understand why she was so disturbed by the violence happening in the world today. She did not have to know what was actually happening. She could feel the harshness before it even played out, usually one to two months before it actually occurred. Once she recognized what was happening, that she was stepping into the creations rather than witnessing them, she was able to make the energetic adjustment. Once she did, she realized that her job was to transmute the lower energy just by tuning in to what was about to occur and thereby change the outcome. In some cases, she reported that it didn't change the outcome but did change the level of harshness she saw as opposed to what actually played out. This knowledge greatly enhanced her ability to maintain her focus on what was most important — to hold to the love that flowed through her and let everything else go.

Seer/Intuitive

I am actively working with seers and intuitives all the time because that is my primary role. I love meeting other intuitives. Seers are fewer in number but when we meet it's like old home week. Our combined energy is like getting to go home without ever having to go anywhere. Put a bunch of intuitives in the same room and the conversations fly all over the place without ever having to say a word, which is pure joyousness. I fully believe that that is actually where we are going. We are transitioning into an age where words are already becoming secondary. Fuller levels of communication are realized by tapping into and recognizing vibration. It's time. With the world coming to an end in ways that we cannot even begin to imagine in our present moment, our communication skill sets are moving in this direction for a reason.

The very nature of being a seer is to help others see what they cannot. But the very virtue of having inner sight does not guarantee wisdom. Most seers, however, are aware of the worlds and universes of light that influence and change our perspective, as we play human. Some are attuned to the level of the afterworld, like a John Edward. These gifted souls are here to help bring focus and awareness of life on the other side of our physical reality creations. We are truly not alone and seers are here to help others discover their way into their life path with ease and grace. The seer in all things unseen helps others to understand the energy of what is occurring so that we can make our way into our life path in a way that puts us at the right place at the right time for change to take place.

There's another kind of seer; someone who can see into the soul and spot an energetic block then trace it back to its root cause. I have met a few intuitives that are very gifted this way. They can see right through a learning pattern all the way back the point when it was created. Most seers that are gifted in identifying a root cause also serve as awakeners or healers.

The path of a seer is similar to an intuitive but I surmise that we are all intuitive. Some, though, are here to help the others realize this very gift within them by demonstrating what they see, and what they feel or sense about them. This telling nature of serving as an intuitive will soon come to a close, as the veil will soon be lifted for all. Intuitives are quickly being transitioned into teachers and by doing so are providing a wonderful and needed service to show the way to help others learn to open and navigate the world with an inner sight that will take them far deeper into the heart.

My all time favorite story is of a very dear friend who is a seer, and a very gifted one at that. She used to extol the virtues of the gifts that I had been given, then in the very next breath downplay her own intuition. Then she would move into sharing the most amazing insights about the world as it was, is and will be. It was always so clear to me that even though we might try to hide from who we are, it is impossible.

I hold high regard for intuitives. It takes courage and conviction to speak to another about what one sees. Like any great advice giver, those who do not freely call forth higher knowing but wait until they are asked, are the ones to pay the closest attention to. I have witnessed many such individuals give of themselves this way and to be on the receiving end of their wisdom is quite a gift.

Healer
The Guides have said from the very beginning of my work with others that we are all healers. Everyone who holds pure intention to help another without regard for receiving anything in return, other than to be of service, is a healer. When our hearts are open to receive, and we give to another, miracles really do happen. Of course, we will look back at our lives and realize that those who have stepped forward to help us, even in the tiniest gesture of love, have helped us to heal

the sickness of fear inside of us.

Needless to say there are many different types of healers but the basic foundational frequency is the same. In fact, the very act of healing is to witness, to hold forth the perfection in the other. Some choose to learn mental processes and procedures, a set of technical skills to become healers. These are the technicians, and many who practice modern day medicine are skilled technicians, but they are not healers in the new paradigm sense of the word. In the new paradigm people will come to understand the very nature of medicine as love, unconditional love, and learn how to love themselves enough to heal the breech between the emotional trauma and the physical malady, or to see the untruth in any given situation. Instead, they will see themselves as perfect, whole and complete.

In today's world, we seek outside help to bring the body, mind and spirit back into balance but in tomorrow's world, we will seek out healers to witness our own innate knowing of who we are. There is, of course, power in numbers, so with each malady, there will be healers who are gathered around particular issues of health and well-being, and hold the higher frequencies thus allowing the shift in the other to take place.

Healers are selfless servers but this does not mean that they are unpaid, or under-appreciated members of the new paradigm society. There will be more healers per capita in our future communities than there are accountants or autoworkers today. Many will specialize in vibrational healing and schools will be spawned from the study of whole system anatomy. Body, mind and spirit will be a part of any given school curriculum because we will have learned to treat the soul having a human experience and build on our successes.

One such example of a gifted healer is a woman I recently met who is a walk-in. She came into the body in the early 1990s for the purpose of bringing a new-light technology to the planet. Her role is to awaken other healers by teaching what she knows to others. The Guides have said that in just a few short years, the medicines and ways of working will no longer be effective for the general population. New energetic modalities will be taught to those who are ready to receive the higher vibrational frequencies, and to learn new ways of aligning the body with health and wellness.

Waterbearer

Waterbearers are here to teach us how to manifest our heart's desire. They hold the very life-blood or life force in their hands and hearts. Today's water bearers are fortune-tellers of grief and sadness. They can pick out the underbelly of emotion where the other is unconsciously moving through life. Most waterbearers are born incredibly empathic and stay that way throughout life. They have learned to survive by testing the waters of fate and living by going deep into the other to weigh and measure their steps to anticipate another's impending action.

Most waterbearers today will be the bearers of truth tomorrow. But for now most are grasping with issues of how to stay alive in a sea of others who do not know or understand who they are. Once water bearers step back and away from their first evolutionary cycle of survival in a hostile world, they will begin to call forth the emotional qualities needed to bring peace to warring nations. They will want to hand over all the goods of the castle to those in power, but they will think again. They are future problem solvers, at heart, but for now, they will continue to evolve their incredibly sensitive psyches into a form of way-shower for the emotions.

Once we have transitioned into a society of accepting energy rather than pushing with the mind, waterbearers will be there to teach us how to manifest water out of air, food out of spoil. We will need their ability to lead the way. Like Jesus showing others how to fish in times of famine, waterbearers understand the innate laws of the universe better than anyone. They are directly tied into not only the natural kingdom but also the finer vibrations that govern the very structure of life.

We are seeing more and more waterbearers flip away from pain and anguish by moving into the acceptance of who they are. They are learning that what they are made of is not a curse but a blessed event in the life of a soul having a human experience. A wonderful example of waterbearer is a warm-hearted, intelligent woman in her fifties. She has been empathic since birth and has felt the emotional bodies of others for so long that she has had extreme difficulty pulling herself out and away from this dynamic of merging her energy fields with others. Now, she is teaching young children how to shift their perspective when adults crash their way uncon-sciously into their fragile emotional bodies. She is, by her teaching, teaching a new generation of enlightened beings how to be true to the self.

Visioner

While a wisdom keeper remains steady, a visioner is someone who is actively engaged in the creation of new reality paradigms. In the coming years ahead visioners will become formalized roles but for now, we witness visioners as they are called to envision our collective future, or they witness the change prior to the time of it's actual manifestation. Visioners are very different from seers or intuitives. While seers are guiding others by watching the path ahead, visioners are envisioning the path ahead. They see what is and vision what will be, not just for themselves but for others, and not just for their own self-interests.

Visioners are very kind, wise people who know who they are. They have very compassionate natures, but are also attuned to the natural order of life. They can see right through the illusionary nature of chaos and are not dissuaded from their mission of visioning new order into reality. They are also not swayed by possible outcomes that may look great on the surface but just underneath the surface are fear-based creations. As they actively witness these self-centered schemes, they actively envision bringing balance to the whole.

These people are grandmothers, sisters, brothers and fathers. They are dairy farmers of old and high tech master creators of the new. They do not get ruffled over details because they see the bigger picture before everyone else does. These individuals come together to form a collective consciousness.

They represent the law and order of our future. Yes, our future will not be ruled or managed by power of the mind or muscle, but envisioned into being. Reform will come when we, as a collective consciousness, recognize that fear is no longer to rule our world. The world at large will undergo much change before the role of the visioner is formalized. Unfortunately, we will have to move through some very harsh lessons first. I have seen that by early to next millennium, we will realize an equitable way of managing fairness and reformation by the coming together in small groups that will vision outcomes.

We are doing so now, but the vast majority of our population would laugh us right off our thrones if we were to suggest that we empty out the prisons and vision our future societies as peaceful coalescence. In our present day moment we would rightfully consider ourselves off-balance, but in our future world, we will look back and realize that our system of gaining monetary value from the warehousing of human bodies was one of the most barbaric practices of our modern-day world.

Gatekeeper

I have seen gatekeepers in action. These are individuals who are very grounded. They definitely know who they are and have their feet firmly planted on the ground. They also have their heads in the clouds and are aware of the role they play in waking people up. These are the individuals who can usually point out the obvious that everyone else in a room has managed to overlook. They are very sensitive to the needs of others but know what they have to have in order to make life work. You'll find these people strategically positioned in corporations, families and communities. They serve quietly and effectively without much fanfare, but energetically their job is huge.

A gatekeeper is instinctually aware of what is needed at any given time to create movement, to release anger, judgment or to shift into higher forms of love. Group love is what most gatekeepers are attuned to but helping an individual who is here to play a key role in shifting the earth plane is always known as planting one's feet squarely at the root cause of most inner strife. Uprooting inner strife is a keen awareness that most gatekeepers hold but most do not interfere.

I have met many who do not interfere but do step into their roles seamlessly with ease and grace. They utilize their energetic positioning that reveals their strength as they come to the aid of others. It's interesting to note that some gatekeepers, at this time, do not recognize the profound role they are here to play, and do not always recognize one another because most are few and far between. Gatekeepers do not stick together by design. Like a farmer waiting at the gate to let in her sheep, there is only need for one gatekeeper for many.

Many gatekeepers are positioned in organizations to point out the obvious road to take or what needs rerouting. She might be the engineer that sees the weakness in the structure, the homemaker that spots the troublemaker on the playground, the teacher that sees the promise in the shy one over there and challenges her to speak up. Know that if you are a gatekeeper, you are to be surefooted about your steps and vocal about what you see.

Energetically, these rare birds are a gift to others who are open to receive. When the world comes into balance, the gatekeepers will step back into their lives and live out their days quite happily. Like soldiers going to war, the role one plays in a specific instance does not brand them for life. It is just a role and one that speaks volumes about their ability to become versatile when the time to step up and be counted draws near.

I remember a gatekeeper who is now living in the Northwest. He is a waiter by day, a healer by night. He moves about the city with ease and grace. Another is the mayor of a large city, yet another a janitor in the building of a large consulting firm, the incarnation of Thomas Jefferson's master slave. The roles we play today are not the roles we played before. It's all different now.

Balancer/Stabilizer

Just saying these two words makes me think of a wise father, or Rock of Gibraltar kind of person who understands what it means to be in chaos, but someone who has also walked through the fire of their own volatile environment and lived to tell about it. Balancers and stabalizers often are tuned into the energy of the group dynamic and play peacemaker or simply hold their presence to peace as they play along with the fun or chaos in the room.

Of course balancers and stabilizers are not confined to social or family settings. They make great relationship holders but most are found out in the world making things work. They are doers and keepers of the flame. They are very passionate people but are often quiet about the role they are actually playing. They may take what they do in life very seriously on the surface but underneath they have it all figured out.

In the lower echelon of vibration, balancers and stabilizers are worriers beyond belief. These are the nurturers who have not moved on into their higher expressions and are always worried about the very next bad thing that might happen. Of course, it never does so they move their energy or focus into seeking out the next thing that might go wrong, and they make sure that those around them know that is how they are thinking.

In the new paradigm society, that worrier nature will become virtually non-existent. This vibration will not hold up against the more powerful energies coming into the planet. Hate and malice will be reduced to total chaos in the coming years ahead by those balancers and stabilizers who see the writing on the wall, and help to maintain the higher vibratory patterns as humanity moves through chaos.

Even though the very name indicates non-movement, balancers and stabilizers are always in flux, always moving. They may be steady but their energy fields much like water-bearers who are often on the move. When I tune into a person who is here to serve as a balancer or stabilizer, her light body is reaching out in all directions but primarily oriented horizontally, forever reaching out like large spidery tentacles. She is someone who has her finger on the pulse of whatever group dynamic she is involved in.

A perfect example of a stabilizer is a young woman in her early forties who owns an international investment firm. She is an up and coming superstar in the financial arena. On the surface you might think that she is a way-shower, and she is. But to watch her move and create in the world, she is forever focused on balancing out the energies of the group to bring about deeper levels of peace of mind and prosperity to those that are moving and shaking up world systems. Monetary gain is just a front for her actual activity of spreading the vibration of balance and harmony to her part of the world.

Master Builder/Master Teacher

Master builders/master teachers are old souls who have been around the block so many times that they are war weary. They are totally in the know about who they are but most, at least when I first meet them, are frustrated, angry or sad about the current state of world affairs, and feel that we should be further along in our global efforts than we are. These gifted souls see what needs doing and are frustrated that they are not out on the front lines doing what they came here to do. Most are tired of the game of life as it is and just want to go home, or get on with getting on.

In the new world consciousness, these individuals are the ones leading the way by teaching what they know to others. They are the ones who have seen the visions of new world societies, new healing modalities, and creative strategies for realizing most if not all of the world's problems because they have played their part already in times past. Most claim remembrances from the time of Atlantis and its downfall. Most take total responsibility for having failed the first time by allowing ego to seep into their perfect world, and many remember how it all came down, and where they were when they struck out.

Many of these same souls have come back to try again, to see the transition through to a different outcome. Even though some are traumatized by past life remembrances, they are working diligently to both clear themselves and to teach others what they know. Many are healers, fine artists, and social scientists. Their modern day activities are played out as accountants, teachers, administrators and high-tech gurus but that is not who they are. Most have skill sets that are untapped, and they eventually let the world know about it.

In what seems like a moment's notice to their colleagues

they announce big plans and set their dreams into motion by opening up light centers or teaching about organic gardening, showing others how to see light through color and creativity, how to make and use floral essences for healing. The key word is how.

These master builders/master teachers are all about building — building new societies, new structures, new inventions, and new concepts. Therefore you will find them in every walk of life. The most obvious ones are those who create their version of a new something before everyone wakes up and is in need of what they have to offer. At the same time they are frustrated that the world has yet to awaken. But they are ready. They are ready to lead the way, to build the structures, to usher in the new paradigm, and to teach.

One of my favorite examples of a master teacher is a young divorced mother of three who works as a youth minister in a busy metropolitan area. She is also steeped in ancient spiritual traditions and invites others to come together under the guise of teaching world peace dances. When I first opened to see who she really is, I could see that she had been a high priest in ancient Lemuria. In her former life, she was quite removed from the day-to-day building of community. In today's world, she has brought all her wisdom with her, but this time she is actively engaged in the building of a model community where children are heard and respected. She has also brought all her knowledge of healing and energy balancing with her into this lifetime, and she'll need it in the coming years ahead. In short, rather than being aloof to those she serves, she has positioned herself on the ground floor of working collaboratively with others to build new educational environments for the star children.

How to know what my role is?
As you can see, you've probably spotted aspects of yourself in

most of the roles, but there is most likely one that serves as your primary and one or more that serve as your secondary. On the soul level, most of us have already played these roles, which is what makes it feel so comfortable to interchange one role for another, but in our third-dimensional world we are here to play a primary role at this pivotal time in history.

If you find, after having read the above descriptions that you still do not have a clue what role you are here to play, I invite you to ask yourself the following questions then scan the brief descriptions listed after that, or go back and read the synopsis.

Am I a loner who likes to create in my imagination?

Do I thrive on the midst of group activity?

Can I go for long periods of time and be perfectly content by myself?

Do I have to have a project going at all times?

Do I get weepy at the thought of someone hurting?

Do I worry about my loved ones when they are away?

Am I a person who has to know everyone's business, and that they are happy?

Do I gravitate to problem-solving other people's problems when I am in conversation?

Do people come to me for answers to their questions?

Do I feel people's hurts, worries and concerns?

Can I take my life and apply it to another's?

Do I empathize with another's plight?

Am I a goal setter?

Do I look at a problem and have to get it done regardless of what others may want?

After answering these yes/no questions, go back and take a look at the descriptions and life examples. Find the description(s) that are a *best* fit. If you are still confused about your role in forming and building in the new paradigm of world consciousness, take a look at some of the deeper motivations and patterns in your life that propel you do what brings you a deep sense of satisfaction, connection and ultimate joy. Pay less attention to the skill set and more on how you have threaded your life-force into the physical creations throughout your life, how you move through the world, what motivates you to move toward one form of relationship or another. These are all factors in how your soul is inter-weaving your light to activate the grid of humanity.

You may wish to consider keeping a journal of your self-discovery process, and as you explore your role, consider maintaining an inward focus. It's easy to be side-tracked by the functional roles of the world, but this about discovering how your soul is bringing light into the planet. The doing is an extension of your role but does in no way drive your role. Your role drives the creation: Where you create, how you choose to create, and with whom you choose.

Also as you become a clearer vibrational channel, and let go of the worldly way of picking up on identity, you'll find that clarity will come more quickly, especially as you let go of any expectation you might be holding onto of what you think you should be doing. Allow your heart to speak gently to you as you recognize your role in this grand play of activating the grid.

More on roles:

Way-Showers
- are new paradigm leaders,
- are continually called to move into charted terrain,
- are inwardly focused,
- understand that they are the creators creating from the inside out; and

- realize that we are all one and through this knowing, walk their talk.

Transformers
- are unassuming and nothing phases them;
- have lived many lifetimes in the pit of human despair; and are
- aware of the deepest levels of self-hatred because they've been there;
- are rudely awakened; and
- are called to drop whatever they are doing, and walk away from downtrodden lives.

Awakeners/Activators
Awakeners
- are be-ers of joy,
- don't wave a flag and say follow me; they live out their lives as an expression of joy;
- are often called to move around frequently or travel;
- go in and out of people's lives, but sometimes they are stationary with people coming to them.

Activators
- affect change by purposefully doing what they do to activate, to cause upset, change, or a shift in others;
- unconsciously, they (in early life) are trouble makers or lost souls who have been born into troubled households, families that are steeped in dysfunction, chaos;
- in their higher nature they are purposeful, and deliberate about their role of being joyful.
- Many choose professions or life-situations where they are highly visible, and taking action to create high-impact awakenings in others.

Bridge Builders

- bridge the great divide between unconscious and conscious behavior;
- see the whole picture of systems, organizations or structures before anyone else does.
- are connectors by desire;
- are born teachers, organizers, mediators, and facilitators of change;
- like to be in the mix of family, community, structure but are rebels at heart;
- are over-achievers and have mastered the old paradigm power structures but get burnt out by them; and
- once they connect with the new, they are on fire with passion and create from the ground up.

Wisdom Keepers

- have an innate ability to discern the truth and
- have buried the self in unworthiness;
- have used their empathic nature as a way to survive;
- carry a deep sense of remorse or regret for having messed it up the first time;
- are master teachers and healers but their primary path is to align with truth and to tell the story of truth through story, arts, and ritual to others; and
- are highly creative and often times very disorganized in day-to-day activities but once they connect with their passion of bringing light to community, they know exactly what to do, and allow others to come and play their individual part to create the greater whole.

Seers/Intuiters

- share the road ahead with those who cannot see, and
- help others to see what they cannot see for themselves;
- use their intuitive gifts to defend and protect themselves from perceived harm; and

- are initially fearful or shy away from self-expression out of fear of not being heard or understood.
- carry a deep-seated burden of responsibility; and
- become teachers, healers and mentors to others to shed light on the way ahead; and
- some focus on clearing the root cause of fear by looking back.

Healers:
- are conscious of their gift from birth but choose life paths, which deny their gifts;
- are focused on holding the sacred space for others;
- go where they are most needed without reservation; and
- serve others selflessly as a primary life path; and
- bring in new light technologies to transform the human condition.

Waterbearers:
- teach how to manifest one's heart's desire;
- today, they are fortune-tellers of grief and sadness, and tomorrow will be bearers of truth, and help others to go deep into the truth to manifest differently (teach how to manifest water from air).
- still carrying incarnational wounds are ruled by their emotions and are proverbial victims because they have lived so many lifetimes as the persecuted.
- in their awakened state, they are the peace makers and hold the key to manifesting miracles of tomorrow.

Visioners
- have many of the same qualities as seers/intuitives, and
- call forth the future and bring it back into the awareness of the now;
- establish peace councils of the future; and

- represent the world's future judicial system.

Gatekeepers
- are very grounded but have their head in the clouds;
- see what everyone has managed to overlook;
- realize the obvious;
- are instinctually aware of what is needed to shift the person or group; and
- know what the real deal is by seeing through the surface stuff.

Balancers/Stabalizers
- bring peace to volatility;
- are tuned-in to the energy of the group dynamic;
- make great relationship partners;
- bring about harmony and calm in times of chaos; and
- are the connectors in companies or families that keep everyone happy.

Master Builder/Master Teachers:
- have been there done that and know that they are here by choice.
- in their unconscious state, are always looking out for others but do not own their power;
- are always looking for a teacher until one day they stop and realize that they are the teacher they have been searching for;
- are here to bring in the energy and the knowledge of oneness consciousness;
- are here to do it right this time around; and
- are called to let go of all attachment to be the most effective.

In service to humanity: What *everyone* can do

As you can see, these roles represent the actual work that we have been called to do. You might be having a surface conversation, but as you become more aware of your role, you will open to the energy stream that causes the activation or opening that is occurring not only in yourself but in the other as well. Now the question you might be asking is, "How will I know what is mine to do?"

You have already read the overview of the group creation cycles that are in play, especially as the energetic doorways open, and generally how to flow your energy even as chaos begins to reshape the flow of our lives. But the question of "What is mine to do?" addresses the doing part of life.

For starters, if you have pre-cognitive abilities, you will want to witness the mass upheaval within systems of governance not get into the mix of it all. You are merely to witness and to intone (intone: know, feel, embody) peace. Your inner sight will be triggered this way to send internal impulses of light wave frequencies to the others who will then be triggered to take myriad actions.

If you are a healer, master teacher or activator, especially in times of great upheaval, you will find a very different kind of person coming to you. They will have no background in metaphysics but will begin to come to you out of physical and emotional complaints of disease. You are to speak to the heart of the matter, and allow your intuition to be your guide.

The inner gateways that are opening now are providing us an unprecedented opportunity to embrace higher vibrational light technologies for self-healing. We are here to transfer this inner knowing to the masses now. If you are teacher or healer, it is now time to share what you know with others.

If you are a transformer or bridge builder, know that your time for connecting to the many diverse social, economic, cultural, religious factions is also now upon you. Trust as your calling is activated that you are fully supported in your every selflessly motivated action.

Accept your gift of heart.

You may be aware of your role, but are afraid to take the next step. This first part of the next step is not really a step as much as an inner shift in your awareness and acceptance of self. It's a choice (to fully embrace and to accept yourself) that only you can make—accept the gift that you are bringing to the world. Spend a few minutes each day to reside in the stillness. As you do, you will feel your heart open, and with this opening you will realize that there is nothing to fear.

At some point in your time of quiet, once you connect with your heart, you will know when you are ready because you will feel the inner stirrings of joy and excitement, the kind of excitement that wells up from the soul. At some point, the inner feeling will prompt you to take that the second step, which again is an inner prompting: *I am ready to receive. I accept the gift of love and joyousness for me* is the feeling nature of this next step.

At some point in this process of opening, a name, a feeling, emotion, image or situation will likely pop into your awareness. As it does, stay with it. Instead of going deeper into the awareness, just observe it at first. Look at it then you decide. Acceptance of this knowing is the gift that your heart is giving to you.

Applying your gift of heart to transform your life and the world

Once you are feeling comfortable about what moves and motivates you to create and have become familiar with the feeling nature of the joy that comes with knowing when your heart is speaking you, you may wish to deepen your inner awareness of others. If you are asked to pray for another or are guided, hold them in this same heart space. Experience the person or situation through feeling, emotion and awareness as you continue to hold the other in a place of honor and appreciation. This same act of holding sacred space for one who is troubled is the same as holding sacred space for someone who makes your heart sing. As you are holding your focus on peace, you will feel an inner shift in consciousness. That will tell you that all is well, and the prayer is complete.

The power and presence of light amplifies as you adjoin with others.

If you would like to experience this same flow of grace amplified when two or more are gathered together as one, ask a friend to join you. Silent meditations are a great way to amplify grace out into the world, and by doing so you are opening your heart to receive a deeper, richer expression of your soul having a human experience. Coming together with others to sit in the quiet and reside in the knowing is powerful and transforming. As you go into the stillness, you will find others there with you who are consciously amplifying unconditional love out by embracing others and the world at-large. The ability to heal and transform this way is the most powerful tool that we have.

If you have a desire to adjoin with others to learn and to create deeper levels of connection, consider forming a sacred circle. Or consider joining one that is already established. A circle is for learning to speak truth and for channeling grace in an open, nonjudgmental setting. If your passion is for healing, then consider forming a circle group whose focus is on exploring energetic healing.

If you are ready to step it up from there, find your passion and go for it! This is the time to jump into the river and start flowing with the others who are wishing to come together and play.

14: GOING DEEPER INTO THE WATERS OF CHANGE

Transformational practices for staying in the flow

Once you better understand the role you are here to play, creating in the physical takes on a whole new dimension. Knowing your role provides you with a different operating system, a different perspective on, not only, what you are here to do, but how. By going deeper into your role, you'll find that it will be so much easier to stay in the flow. Without this underlying sense of what's really going on in your life, the transition into oneness consciousness can get pretty confusing at times.

In the old paradigm, we have been schooled to pay attention to what presents itself as logic, rule and order. But in the new paradigm, we are to look beneath the surface explanation and dive beneath the logic of the mind by paying close attention to our heart. We are to listen with our whole body, not just one aspect of self. By doing so, your inner senses will open up and with this, you'll find a deep and abiding wisdom there to guide you.

The physical world around us represents what we have already created; so in the coming times ahead, making choice from a place of knowing is the only way to realize your freedom. We are building those new paradigm structures now even as many of us are struggling to keep up with the shift in consciousness.

Regardless of the role you are here to play, most of us must first focus on breaking through myriad perceptions and expectations that are based on an elaborate construction of beliefs that defend and protect our identification with the third-dimensional world. You can liberate yourself by mentally and emotionally stepping back from your inner defenses, and by doing so take a different look at who you are, really.

We are new paradigm leaders and we are an evolution in process. Accept where you are and begin to make sense of your life in the context of this global happening. In this chapter, I will share with you the very same questions that others who are going through this same process of awakening. The questions are focused on helping you to make fundamental changes to the way you think and feel about your life. If you are like others that I have worked with, the shift in consciousness comes suddenly but, sometimes, only after you have asked that ten thousandth question, or read that last book, or heard someone tell their story just a little different than you have heard before. Then suddenly you shift; you wake-up, and you get it. So this is what this next section is all about, to give you the benefit of what others have asked for themselves. We'll start with some basic questions.

What is my purpose?
Who are my guides?
How do I connect to follow my heart?
How do I let go, get out of my head (and into my heart)?
How do I know when I have found my purpose?
How am I doing?
What comes next?
How do I fix, make better _____?
How do I find my passion?
How do I transform my relationship?
How do I find that best and right person for me?
Who is my soul mate?
Why do I not attract that person?
What's taking so long for _____?

The questions seem endless but over time, I have narrowed

most down into three main categories: mind verses heart, relationship, path and purpose. You will find that this section is reflective of the topics, with special sections on the new paradigm of prosperity, food and nutrition, new healing technologies and the environment among others.

The teachings help to make sense of your life in a way that not only bring greater clarity but offer a completely different perspective to what you might be experiencing. I have yet to meet a single person that does not want a life full of joy, but at the same time may be so stuck in misery that no amount of words will do it for them.

That's where experience comes in. No matter what another says, it's the experience aspect of learning that does it for us. That's why we have a physical body — to experience, and with experience comes knowing, wisdom. No amount of words will do that for us. That is why I am so enamoured with vibration. Vibration does not lie. It's not confusing. You can feel it. It's real to the senses and there is no doubting what reaction we are having when we experience it. Take the word vibration now; substitute it for emotion, and voila! What is complex is suddenly simple.

Even inside this paradigm of *simple*, you may have become so tied up the complexities of life that you, like others, feel the need for some specific steps to help you to gain clarity around the answers to the questions above. As simple as it may sound to be joyful — and it is — many of us are looking for a way out of the pain. And we are seeking help in finding our passion, our joy. So this is what this next section is all about — sharing with you, the process that I have gone through myself and shared with others. This next section breaks the teachings down into steps.

The emotional nature of learning

I love what a fellow student of Truth, Ravi Berg, had to say about the emotional nature of learning: "Change is what happens when the pain of staying the same is greater than the pain of changing." The long and short of this statement is that no one likes to feel emotional pain. But life is full of pain. I'm talking about the kind of pain that keeps us in relationships that stifle self-expression, the pain of over-eating to fill a void, or the pain that comes with engaging in addictive behavior to hide away. I could go on — poverty, greed, hatred, violence, confusion, resentment are all a part of the spectrum of emotional pain, and keeps us tied into our human nature.

Hiding our fear, our self-hatred behind *nice* or the face of denial is the worst. Not only are we feeling the lower vibrational tones but are hiding it from others, *we think*. We think what we are doing is playing the game of life smartly, but there are no secrets. As vibrational beings of light, there is no such thing as a secret. It's all out there. We are walking, talking, vibrational calling cards for everything we have experienced and every emotion that we are holding onto.

Once you begin to understand this in its most elemental form, you will begin to understand the true nature of change. As I have often found myself saying, *Let it all go. Let go of all the pain, the anguish, fear of not being good enough. Let it all go.*

But how?

Emotion plays such a major role in our ability to navigate the waters of change. Therefore understanding that you are not the stories you tell, even when you are suffering the consequences of your unconscious choosing, is essential. This unconscious behavior — of holding onto and repeating your story at nauseam — only perpetuates the pain you are sitting in. But worse: It causes you to lose your inner sense of self by keeping you focused elsewhere. Your focus is to be pointed inward toward you, the True you, not the one you have come to believe is you.

The human part of the self will always identify with the emotional body. But as the light being that you are, your emotional body is to part company from here on out. You are to learn how to witness that aspect of self and understand that you are not that. You are not the lineage of the mind-body continuum. You are a light being having a human experience.

Once this knowing fully settles into your own knowing, you will begin to learn things about yourself that you had no idea. Your history as a soul having a human experience will become crystal clear to you. And your awareness of yourself as human will reveal itself to you in a different way as well. Compassion will replace judgment, and unconditional love will heal the breech between the two vibrational expressions. You'll begin to realize that *that knowing* that you have had all your life will step up, vibrationally, and begin speaking to you. But only as you allow it. You are the one that gives that inner voice permission. No one else can do it for you, only you.

You'll discover that the more reactive part of the self is actually the mind-body continuum. That's the consciousness of your human nature. You might say that there are two of you, not one. One awareness is on the body-mind with a focus on survival. The other is the timeless aspect of self that sees the bigger picture, and feels the feelings of the self quite differently than the aspect that is residing as a permanent resident in the body. What brings the two together, as we have now explored, is the intertwining of the emotional bodies — light being and human.

When someone makes the statement that she wears her emotions on her sleeve, it's not far from the truth. This field literally hugs the skin. The middle field is more viscerally oriented to our emotions. It's the holder of trauma and incarnational life patterns. The third field or outer layer is our intuitive, feeling nature that is directly hard-wired in to our collective consciousness and can be accessed through intuition. The fourth and fifth layers are more attuned to the soul's way of communicating with higher beings and allows us to navigate the higher realms of light. This is where your ability to communicate telepathically emanates from. This lighter vibrational layer is also where the untangling of self is bound to occur.

What I have come to understand is that we are to disconnect from that part of our emotional body, the part that identifies itself as human. When I say disconnect, it does not mean go away, I am suggesting that you no longer sit inside this emotional body and participate in the continual loop of drama. But to step outside and be the watcher watching the story.

Some of us are so immersed in the reactive nature of our emotional bodies (and love the visceral feelings so much) that we become confused about our core identity as light being. It is difficult to be both the student and the observer at the same time. But just remember that we are here to transcend the body consciousness. This simply means that we are to stay clear about who we are and learn to live from our heart. (That more reactive, visceral reactive nature is our human nature, and a part of the mind-body continuum that is human.)

Clearing the emotional body

By clearing your emotional body of the old stories, you will open the way to realize a greater awareness of self. Like a snake shedding its outer skin to make room for new growth, we too, as a race of light beings, are preparing to experience freedom in a way that has yet to be realized on earth. We are separating out from that reactive, unconscious aspect of self and by doing so, are remembering who we truly are.

Below I have compiled a list of ways that I have personally used to clear the emotional body. To say that this process is finite is not accurate. As long as we are in a human body, we will continue to clear the emotional debris from what we have inherited as a human experience. Some of us have come into mind-body continuums that have long histories. Therefore, we have much work to do. Others are coming into the body for the very first time, and have selected incarnational stories that have fewer traumas attached. Whatever your personal situation, be kind to yourself and do what is necessary to help the human aspect of self feel safe and honored. Use this list as a start. Be creative, invent your own process, and stay open.

Maintaining the flow
- Meditation
- Journaling
- Processing out your dreams
- Witnessing the emotions, then inwardly asking what is behind the feeling
- Use of affirmations, mantras, singing
- Listen to heart-centered music
- Laughter
- Communion with like-minded people
- Immersion in Mother Nature
- Energy and body work

Unearthing the deeper emotional roots
- Body and energy work
- Color or light therapy
- Regression therapy
- Emotional freedom technique

For those who have attended Arayu events, they have first hand knowledge of what it feels like to take in huge amounts of high vibration. At first the body, mind and spirit feel so incredibly joyful. Then body aches and pains creep in or the auric body flares up. We think we are back in the old but we are not. Each time we take in huge amounts of higher vibration, profound knowing is realized on myriad levels so it's important as you assimilate the light into the body to refrain from pushing into the process with the mind. For most, that is the root cause of any discomfort after being so open to receive, and it is when the mind kicks into gear. This form of integration is only the precursor to the more intense periods of adjusting to vibration that is stepping up in intensity as we go; so find what works and keep opening to the integration process.

After a recent activation event in Washington, DC, my co-facilitator went straight into a deep level physical processing out. He experienced body aches, headaches, muscle tension, etc. I was flying high all week before crashing into an old emotional pattern then worked through it to clear it out of my system. Then back up the vibrational spiral I went, with the help of a friend and the benefit of tuning back in to the activation music Mark had played and recorded during the event. Just a few minutes of listening, put me right back into joy!

Mark and I have been through these kinds of dramatic shifts many times before so we have developed a process that helps us move through it a little more gracefully than when we first started doing this work. But for those who were moving through this intense period, many for the first time, I received a plethora of questions about what to do to get through the integration period more gracefully. This is just a precursor to what we will be adjusting to, so gaining insight into what helps your body to adjust is important. Most of what I have discovered causes the body to experience physical pain is a subconscious emotional block, and there are a variety of ways to bring the body, mind and emotional body back into balance.

To echo the list above, for deep-level body aches, take a hot salt bath or seek out a practitioner of choice: Cranial sacral, polarity therapy or energy work for balancing; massage for muscle tension. For headaches, especially migraines, suspect an early childhood emotional block. Or seek out the help of a medical professional where necessary.

If your emotions are on the surface but feel stuck, EFT (emotional freedom technique) is a great tool to use. I have found that when I am using EFT, the energy moves much faster when I witness the emotions even as I am releasing them through statements of affirmation. Bless and release any heaviness as it is leaving your body. Some of these patterns have been with us for a very long time, so the leaving process sometimes feels like pulling skin from skin.

When doing this kind of dramatic clearing, relationships suddenly become volatile! Why? Your overall vibration is stepping up and what was okay before is not all right now. As you move through these sometimes-challenging times, keep focused on your joy and with compassion speak your truth. Allow your heart, not your head, to be your guide.

The cure-all is to get out in Mother Nature. Move the body, clear the head. Practice meditation, yoga, Qigong, Tai Chi, dance, walk, and lots of it to move the energy through the body. Take hot salt baths and drink lots of water.

Keep a positive attitude and give thanks for this time in your life. Above all expect miracles to happen. As the old energy moves out to make room for more of who you truly are, know that you are moving up the spiral and new surprises await you. As your vision opens up, accept what is without trying to push to understand with your mind. If you are feeling vulnerable or are holding onto hurt feelings, let them go. Above all, encourage yourself during this time of integration that you are headed home to joy.

Mind verses heart

The role of our human mind in our creation cycles

The human mind is incredibly powerful and for good reason. The role of the mind has been to defend and protect the body, to stand guard over us and make sure that the species survives. At least that is what its role has always been. Now is the time that the heart says to the mind, "Now that's alright. You have done a very good job. Now it is time for you to listen to me."

I'm sure that we can both agree that these are very simplistic statements. In actuality, the mind is a deeply sophisticated part of our humanity and has invented all kinds of ways to recreate itself in physical terms, but no matter how smart it is, it can never know the higher road to ascension because it is a doer, not a decider.

It is that simple. Once we realize that our human nature, our mind, is the doer, and we, as the heart, are the deciders, it makes life super simple, in theory that is. We live in such a mind-centered culture that it is extremely difficult to derail the mind long enough that it actually gets quiet.

I actively studied meditation for a few years and made a practice of doing meditation twice a day, and once a week for an hour with friends. During those hour-long times of silence, it became almost predicable that my mind flashed into quiet mode just a few minutes or seconds before the hour was up. I was always amazed that it took that long, especially since I meditated daily, but that showed me just how powerful the mind is.

Quieting the mind is the most important skill that we, as beings of light, can learn. Without a quiet mind, we cannot hear the heart. The heart has quite a different rhythm and tone from the mind. The heart never pushes to be heard but gently waits for the mind to settle.

The deeper that we go into quieting the higher mind, the closer we get to discerning the difference in thought as wave patterns, and by doing so, we can then break through the barrier of the lower mind. The mind is the holding pattern of our history as playing human, and has a tendency to operate on a kind of automatic pilot. The lower mind picks up on the patterns that the stories have carved into our emotions and is constantly replaying the thoughts, perceptions and behaviors that are fueled by those emotions as background noise. No matter what we are doing or where we are going, the hum of the mind dictates the terms of our now moment choices, based on past programming from old behavioral patterns. Before you know it we are operating in auto-pilot and just doing what we have always done, because it's comfortable and conforming. Like grooves in the road, we blindly follow to where it goes we do not know, but it's familiar so that will do. It is not until the heart discerns the difference in feeling that we begin to wake-up to what is actually going on.

As I work with people, I find that most are looking for a qualified measure of happiness because they don't believe they can have something better. Most believe that they can experience only what has been given to them by life, and lack the understanding that they can realize whatever they so desire. When the Guides speak to their desire, the most common reaction is that no one could have pegged their inner most desire without having intimately knowing them. After either tears or a long pause they begin to ask the question, "But how? How do I make the changes in my life to do this or to make it all come about?" The answer is inherent in the question itself. Most of us are in touch with our heart's desire, but because we have for so long allowed our mind to dictate our behavior, we settle for less.

Along with getting locked into the mind, there is the fear of change. People tell me that they cannot open for this reason or that. My response is always that it takes courage to actualize the truth of who you are, but as you do, you will find that these very same people who doubted your resolve to open are the very same ones who honor you as you do. They may not understand your inner process but they will see, hear, and feel the difference within you. If you find yourself in this category of trying to break free from the mind, take heart. You may falter or stumble as you work your way to following your heart but be kind to yourself. Allow the very grace of God that you are to guide you, to protect you as you declare victory over your mind.

If you are by now practiced at listening to your heart, and are working on the finer nuances of discerning the difference between mind and heart, then you may find the list at the end of this section helpful.

Deep listening

I am often asked, "How do I know that I'm receiving guidance from my heart and not my head? I explain it this way: When your heart speaks to you, it feels like you are receiving a delightful gift, a pleasant surprise. The inner knowing seems to miraculously materialize out of thin air, because you are not seeking it out. Others have told me that it has felt like a very painful realization, but they also knew this feeling was their heart helping them to cross over from mind to heart.

Expectation is not a factor at all. On the other hand, when you are filtering your emotions through the mind, you will feel yourself pushing, thinking, searching, mulling over, and strategizing your way toward a perceived answer. From personal experience and from working with others, I must say that all choice acted on from the mind, predictably results in failure or less than optimum outcomes. On the other hand, choices acted on from the heart always feel like a flow, like receiving a wonderful gift that just keeps on giving.

The points listed below are consolidated from the many teachings I have received and relayed to others over time:

- We are not the body, and we are not the mind. We are souls, beings of light, having a human experience.
- We are not here to heal the human soul who is suffering from pain and anguish by being scared right along with that part of our human experience. We are here to transcend the fear by remembering who we are.
- We are to honor our sense of self at all times. We are timeless beings who resonate with peace, but who have also had many incarnations with that part of the self that resonates with being human. Our emotional bodies are intertwined with the human species. Therefore, we can become very disoriented at times, and actually believe that our demise is at hand, when in actuality, it is not.
- When we go into the knowing, we are in the flow of our heart. Our heart opens wide to receive the grace of God that we are. When we step outside that flow, we feel small, insignificant and without answers or direction. When we are in the flow, we are empowered because we can feel it.
- We are to remember the truth of who we are by remaining in an open, receptive state of being. We are to honor that feeling at all times, and know that that is our navigational system.
- We are not to back away from our inner direction if our heart tells us all is well. No matter what our outer world may look like, we are to pay attention to what we are feeling when we are deep in the knowing.
- Our imagination will lead the way.
- When we are in mind, we become confused and begin to push with the mind to go after an outcome. In heart, an outcome comes to us. Our most important part is to receive the revelation through our imagination then to do what it prompts us to do, then wait on the next clue or revelation to steer us in the direction of our heart's desire.
- We cannot live in the world through our mind and also be

living in our heart. It is not possible. The two ways are different, even worlds apart. Once we shift into the heart-centered way of creating there is no going back.

- Remember when you find yourself pushing with the mind, reset your center by going into the knowing for just a moment to remember. Then off you go again!

- There is never a right or wrong answer to any choice, decision or action. There is no such thing as a mistake, only learning. We learn by what feels right and true to our heart.

- Honor the self. Make the commitment to listen to and believe what your heart is telling you. Your heart is the direct link to your soul. When you shut out or cut away from your heart you are cutting yourself off from Source. Your mind is bound to logic, and will jump in to the mix and try to deter you from honoring yourself. Just know that all is well. When you get confused, go back into the feeling that you first had and reconnect. Let go of what is going on around you and go inside. Allow your heart to guide you in this way. Your heart feels open, free and unobstructed. Your mind is full of thoughts, strategies, reasons and doubts.

- Imagination flows from the heart, and the heart is directly tied in to the soul. Many people mistake visioning, which is a mindful activity with their imagination. An easy way to tell if you are truly receiving through your heart is that you'll know it because you are not doing anything but traveling, exploring, being shown like a tourist on vacation. One doesn't try to figure out where you are going; you just allow your tour guide to show you the sights. This is what it feels like when you are connecting with your imagination. If you are planning, doing, strategizing, seeing how to make life happen, then you are visioning and in your mind. Learn to spot the difference. It is sometimes tricky to feel the difference between the two, especially when you have an attachment to the outcome.

Our minds are very strong and easily steer us in the wrong direction but by allowing our heart to guide us, we will never go wrong. Stated in the most simplistic way, the use of terms right and wrong, in this context, is merely a navigational direction for fear verses joy.

It's all about relationship

Our lives, here in the land of duality, are all about relationship. Whether we are willing forth our highest expression in third-dimensional reality, or not, we are experiencing life in relationship to something or someone. As I work with individuals struggling with aspects of relationship that require them to make a choice, I find the Guides surprisingly devoid of the kind of human limitations or boundaries that are a part of our mutual societal moral code of conduct. They take a very simplistic view: If the relationship feels good, joyful, expansive, then we are to jump in and play; if it feels constrictive, confining, twisted, oppressive, painful, then we are to liberate ourselves from the relationship.

No matter what the nature of the relationship dynamic, the higher choice is always centered in the relationship to the self, first and foremost. The deeper the level of self-honor, the richer, the relationship we experience with others. Sometimes, this means that we are to stand up for ourselves and by doing so, surrender to a deeper level of self-love. This continual act of surrender, when it comes to making a choice around any issue of relationship, does not mean giving in to impulses from our past experiences, or going along with anything that does not bring us a total sense of peace or joyousness. Each relationship, each time or season, is different but the relationship to the self is a timeless one and the most sacred one of all. Honor the self and watch the world around you transform.

How to shift the pattern of relationship

When it comes to finding peace of mind about who we are to live and love with, or work and play with, the use of affirmations are always helpful, even when, or especially when, we are confused. Affirmations serve as a way to release ourselves from the kind of internal bondage that keeps us suspended in fear and inner struggle about any given choice. Affirmations serve to center our focus on what is really to be driving our choice. Like any great sound vibration, the rhythm and cadence of our own voice set to a new beat is healing and often transforms our inner view of ourselves. A typical affirmation that the Guides often impart, is this: "I love myself, my God self, with all my heart. All is well."

You wouldn't think that such a simple statement would be so powerful but it is because it speaks to the heart of the matter. Remembering that our world is a mirror image to our own soul, what we are experiencing in our world reflects back to us in reverse. All we have to do is watch and listen to what we are feeling. If you don't like how you feel as a result of who you are with or what you are pining for, change the vibration first, then take action as you muster the courage to do so.

And as much as we'd like to wish away many of the choices that we have made that have caused others and ourselves pain and anguish, the Guides remind us that we are to remember our true nature. We cannot wish away our human nature but we can offer a dose of compassion to ourselves as we remember that we are doing our very best. Looking back at choices is sometimes not a very pretty sight, but when we are seeing from the perspective of growth, there is real magic in the learning.

As you move through your own process of self-discovery around your particular issue of relationship, remember to be kind to yourself and know that the answer to your question is, "Yes and yes, and yes again."

Yes, you are loved beyond all humanly comprehension even when you are feeling dejected. Yes, you are a cherished being of light even when you feel small and insignificant. And yes, you are divinely protected and guided even when you feel that you have totally lost your way. Know that you are the light of God within your very soul. And all is well.

The most important thing that I can say about relationship is that no matter who you are co-creating with, the most important person in the equation is you. You are the protagonist in your own play. The relationship you are to continually nurture is with you. If you don't take care of you, then no one else will. In fact, that is not the other's job; it is yours. If you are nurturing the relationship to the self, then your relationships, as reflected back to you by others, will be as loving, kind, open, and expansive as you allow yourself to be. Contrary to popular opinion, no one is doing something to you that you are, on some level, not giving him or her permission to do. Discover what that might be so you can see if you are unconsciously attracting a particular behavior that brings you pain. The following life-scenarios are designed to help you see how others have figured these unconscious patterns out.

Fear of commitment

Many of us have a fear of commitment on some level of our conscious awareness, and most are running, what I call unconscious programs in our subconscious mind. Our subconscious holds all the patterns of thought that have brought us so much pain and anguish that we are just not ready to deal with yet, so we push the emotions down a little deeper until we have the time or the inclination to heal. But most of us are not that diligent. We move on in life and when we are feeling that life just can't get any better, these programs pop up and run interference or wreak havoc with our lives.

Fear of commitment is so common these days that it brings to light what we are here to clear within us. If we cannot make a commitment to ourselves, we cannot even begin to make a commitment to path and purpose with a free and open heart. The key to uncovering any fear of commitment issue is to take a look at what you are avoiding. The answer is often right there in front of you. Or if you are like many, you blame missed opportunities on others. But in actuality, it's your own fear that's moving and driving the creation. The hardest issues to figure out are the desires closest to your heart.

Here is just one example of someone who is working through her fear of commitment: Elana is a shy, radiant young woman in her early thirties. In our first session, I sensed a young single woman who seemed a bit ill at ease with herself. Inside the channel, the Guides spoke to her about her life path and purpose before telling her of her beloved. They described the feeling, the setting, the circumstances of their chance meeting and their future lives together. When I came out of the channel, after asking very few questions, she seemed ready to leave the session with a renewed sense of optimism.

Eight months later she was right back there, sitting directly facing me. But this time, her eyes were downcast, and without saying anything else, she wanted to know if she should move to New York, and almost as a side note, she asked me if I could tell her anything about the relationship.

As soon as I stepped into the channel, I found myself blurting out that her beloved was not in New York but in her immediate surroundings, in her life and in her heart now. I went on to tell her that she was currently in a relationship with him but she had turned away from his love.

Shaken and not expecting this answer, she told me that just as the Guides had said she would, she met this person exactly in the way they had described. She recognized him immediately. They quickly came together, but then a short time later, he very abruptly told her that he didn't love her. She was so devastated that she stopped all contact with him. It had been six weeks since she last saw him and he had been calling her every day but she'd been refusing his calls until the day before our meeting.

She reported that he had told her that he was sorry and wanted to come back together again. But she was so scared that he would turn away again that she didn't know what to do. She wasn't sure that she could ever trust him again. Her question put to the Guides: "If he was truly the one for me, why did he so abruptly back away, and will it happen again, or should I move to New York and just get away from it all?"

As she was asking this last question, I heard a very loud, clear voice in my left ear say, *fear of commitment*. I shared this inner speaking with her then was given the following metaphor for her to consider. To the best of my memory, it went like this: "There was a man standing at the ocean's edge. He was watching as the gentle waves came lapping in around his legs. Then one time when he was not looking, another gigantic wave crashed onto the shore and knocked him into the water. He regained his balance then began to feel the water around his body again. Feeling his way back into this push and pull of the ocean water as it crashed into him then onto the sandy shore, he adjusted to the new rhythm and cadence of each new wave.

Then the explanation came: The metaphor of the water represented her love, and the man standing in the water was her beloved. The teaching for her was to allow him time to adjust to the rushing waters of her love. The Guides told her that she was harboring a fear of commitment so what better way to bring this fear to light than to attract her mirror image. Their advice to her was to meet him in the way that he showed up. As he takes one step toward her, she was to mirror him and take one step toward him. Take it slow. Allow her heart to open, to feel safe and he would in return feel safe to do the same.

As I found out after this story was told, she had been badly hurt by the breakup of not one former marriage, but two. The second marriage ended abruptly when her former husband left her in the midst of raising their young children. She was understandably gun shy yet yearning for the love she so desired. He had also come from a broken marriage, so both were trying to find their equilibrium to allow their hearts to open to one another. As she left the session, I couldn't help but feel a deep measure of optimism because she seemed so at peace.

Fear of Loss, fear of not being good enough

When it comes to fear of loss or fear or not being good enough, I have heard the Guides share many variations of the butterfly alighting on one's hand, or the flower attracting the butterfly after a sun-soaked rain. Mother Nature provides us with so many wonderful metaphors for life if we are willing to listen, especially stories that sooth our fears.

I can't tell you how many people come to me with stories of the one that got away, or of being left behind because they just weren't good enough. Many do remind me of the big fish stories I heard as a child about my uncles and their adventures of catching the big one that got away time and again. But unlike not catching that all-elusive fish, these are real people with real stories of missed opportunities filled with hurt and pain.

The most common theme in relationship is fear of loss that is often fueled by the feeling of not being good enough, and plays out in a variety of ways. This learning dynamic plays out so many times that we are forced to stop and realize that we are sitting in a perpetual state of yearning, and yearning is directly tied to fear of loss.

Yearning may show up in a failed relationship or unrequited love. It can be identified in feelings of lack, which is a result of our holding onto trauma. Our past experiences and former incarnations are chock full of trauma so it is no wonder that fear of loss sometimes runs rampant in our subconscious mind when we think we are on to something good. Entire soul groups have come in to clear deep trauma of all kinds, so we attract our mirror image to us. But because we are so schooled to only look at the outside package, at least at first, we often will jump into a relationship with both feet, with full expectation of living out a fairytale life. Little do we know that what lurks beneath the surface is the sum total of our mind's memory of trauma. Once we open, we find there is more to our story than first meets the eye. Again, I use the example of a metaphor to demonstrate the dynamic of this learning pattern.

I worked with a brilliant young man, an American who was raised in an eastern culture, an Islamic religion. He deeply loved his family and would not do anything to dishonor them, and was devoted to his faith. Against this backdrop, he was also raised as an American. He fell in love with a beautiful young Christian woman and wanted to marry her. His family shunned his choice and forbade him from seeing her again. He secretly continued to date her, but the deeper he fell in love the more he wanted her to become a part of his life. He was at a loss of what to do.

When opening to channel, the Guides showed me a mental picture of a rickety wood slatted shack. I saw him inside the structure, which was, positioned way above a rugged ocean bluff. He was in the midst of a driving wind and rain was pelting away at the house. Yet with all this activity, he felt safe, out of harm's way. He looked around and realized the back door to the house was standing wide open. Although he held steadfast that the house would keep him safe from the elements, no matter what he did, he could not get the back door to stay shut.

The metaphor of the house, the high winds and the open door spoke to his internal connection to the fear-based stories that his family had passed down from one generation to the next as a way to help them to remember their roots, and their need to stick together. By holding on to the belief that conforming to behaviors shaped by fear would keep him safe, he was actually experiencing fear of loss brought on by holding to the pattern of conformity, which is just another way to say oppression.

As long as he allowed fear to rule his current life choices, he would hold himself captive to never realizing true freedom. After learning about the metaphor, the young man's question was "How do I shut the door to my fear and thereby not push my beloved away by yearning for life to be different with my family and my faith?"

The answer came with another story of another life, another experience with tribe, with faith, then another and another. Realizing that he had lived many lives in many different realities of faith-based learning, he realized that the choice was actually to be honest on all fronts about how he was feeling, and to let the chips fall where they may.

I heard from him almost a year later. He had opened himself up to speak from his heart with his parents about his choice in a life mate, and through this openness, his family learned to open their hearts as well. He eventually broke off the relationship, but through this period in his life, he had begun to let go of fear and love himself.

Again, when we yearn for life to be different or even for something or someone to come to us, we are literally pushing the creation away. Fear of not being good enough pervades our lives on many different levels, but in the context of relationship, fear of not being good enough is often manifested as yearning for a beloved to show up or the one we're with to be better. However, one thought of love knocking on our door and fear of not being good enough sets in to such an extent that we sabotage ourselves before we allow our heart to fully open.

If you find yourself in a perpetual state of yearning for outcomes that never seem to manifest or you experience near misses, or short lived, volatile romances, you may want to take a closer look at fear as the culprit. Clear the fear and your creation will shift. We are here to better understand relationship but in doing so we are to focus on what is happening within us, first, then allow the rest to be a flow.

The notes below have been synthesized from the many conversations, and group sessions I have had with others about their specific relationship issues. You may wish to scan the list and see what pops up for you. As long as we are on earth, we will never tire of learning more about relationship because that's how we learn and grow.

Points to remember:

- **Self.** Relationship is always about the self to the higher-self. Keep your focus on what's inside and you will know best and right when this same feeling shows up in your world.
- **Creation.** Remember that what ever you are experiencing in your world is what you have already created. If you don't like what's happening in your now moment, know that you can choose differently and do so. Sometimes it is just a matter of waiting for the new you to show up.
- **Focus.** Change your focus by allowing more light to flow into your heart. Practice by going into your imagination to connect your personality-self to your soul. Once you have connected as the soul having a human experience, create a bridge of light from you to your soul then out to the world at large (through feeling and imagining) to call forth what

you so desire. Focus on what you desire not the how.

- **Choice**. Know that you are not here to make choices for anyone else but you. When it comes to others, especially your children, let them know that they have all the answers inside of them, and that you know that they will make the right choice for themselves as long as they are being true to their heart. You practice this for yourself and watch your children, and those in your world, catch right on to what you are doing. Hearts will open wide the more you honor others by honoring yourself.

- **Courage**. Once you truly know what you are to do based on what you feel, be courageous and step out on faith (faith is nothing more than listening to your heart and believing it more than what is going on in your world). We are in the time of walking our talk, making heart-based choices without knowing what is on the other side. Being true to one's heart is what brings about profound change, total joy, expansiveness, and your heart's desire. Trust your intuition. It does not lie. There is no reason to.

- **Let go and allow.** As your heart's desire shows up in your world, remember to let go and allow the old patterns and beliefs to leave. Feel the difference between making a wrong choice (getting stuck in a toxic cycle) and recognize when everything is actually really right (moving up the energetic spiral).

- **Practice full disclosure.** Be honest with yourself first, then with those with whom you are in relationship with. Practicing full disclosure keeps you on track with your heart. Keep yourself honest by your continued practice. Yes, even when it is uncomfortable, it is still all play.

- **Stop the shape-shifting.** If you find yourself shape-shifting (doing or saying something to please the other or to hide your true nature), stop the behavior. Freeze-frame the feeling nature of not being true to self. Get quiet and look inward. Correct yourself by restating your intention then begin again. Showing up as your authentic self gains you freedom. Shape-shifting holds you captive in a world that is constricting and eventually you feel like you are dying.

- **Take ownership of what you desire.** It is a privilege to be in relationship with you. Anyone who does not reflect that back to you is not honoring of you, and that is all about you. You decide what feels right and reflect that back to those in your world in full expectation, anticipating that the other will reflect the love that you are back to you. If this is not happening, you are called to go back inside and ask yourself why? "Why am I allowing that? What is inside of me that is unhealed? What is going on inside of me?" are sample questions you might ask of yourself.

  If you get an emotional charge from an interaction or from something that was done to you or for you, then you know that it is about you and not the other person. In fact, everything going on in your life is about you, but check those emotional charges and find their source, then clear. This prayer was shared with my by a friend who used it for months to shift her perspective. You may find it helpful to you: "Bless him/her/them right where they are, change me." Once I started using it, I realized its power was to help me to keep my focus on me, not the other, no matter what was going on in my life. This is a great practice for reminding you that only you are in charge of your happiness.

- **Practice kindness.** And finally, be patient with yourself, practice kindness and compassion and all else will follow. You cannot share these qualities with others until you have given the gift to yourself first. Let go of the belief that you are being selfish by doing for yourself. Living life to the fullest means that you trust in your dreams and you know that the universe loves you back, and more, as much as you muster the courage to love yourself by doing what brings you joy.

- **Pay attention to what you are feeling.** Remember to discern the difference between yearning and desire. Yearning is rooted in lack. Desire is fueled by the joy of what you know to be true for you.

- **Growth.** Distinguish between growth and being stuck. "Growth" feels like a stretch even when it pangs. "Stuck" is your resistance to make a change because _____ (fill in the blank.) These myriad of reasons are always about the other person and never about the self; are usually rooted in safety and security issues, or about not wanting to change because you have become so comfortable in your own misery.

- **Flow.** Take note of pushing and being impatient. Timing is everything. You can feel that all is well while also sensing what is coming. Learn to allow life to unfold as you take your steps from day to day, moment to moment.

Intensified relationships help us to prepare for our service work.

In our world today relationships are exploding, expanding, breaking apart or coming together. No matter what the dynamic, collectively, we seem to be in a very dramatic, touchy, sensitive state of being. Why? Because the energy is pushing us to shift in consciousness. Anything and everything that is not working is being forced out. As we clear our way for experiencing deeper levels of freedom, we will find that our paths with others are more fulfilling, but only as we listen to our heart and make clear our intentions for freedom. If you are finding that your life, as played out in relationship, is in the more dramatic category of clearing, be still and ask yourself, "Is there any reflection being offered up by the other that is also inside of me?" If the answer is yes, then give thanks for the learning, and get on with the emotional clearing needed to bring you into fuller states of joy.

If you find yourself dismayed, surprised or disappointed by the other, you may wish to ask yourself, "What have I been missing, not seeing, and what do I want to be experiencing in my life now?"

If you find yourself in a perpetual state of feeling oppressed, and not expressing your joy, think again. It is not the other that is preventing you from doing so, but you. Give yourself permission to begin enjoying life again.

If your partner or your closest friends are not listening to you, not appreciating who you are, learn to speak up. Assert yourself more fully into the conversation, speak your mind about what needs to change, or walk away entirely. Only you will know that answer to what you must do to find your voice. Once you find your voice, you will command respect.

If you have allowed your rights as a human-being to be so suppressed that you have attracted another to you that abuses you emotionally, mentally or physically, then walk away. Period. Get away and then dive deep into your inner work to rediscover the love of God that you are. Take time to strengthen your light as you take the steps to surround yourself only with people who honor the truth of who you are.

Getting out of toxic relationships is very challenging because many of us do not have something different to compare what we have always known, but this is where Mother Nature comes in. Spending time in Mother Nature always helps to bring us back into balance.

I once worked with an older woman who was so depressed from having spent years in an abusive relationship that she couldn't remember what joy felt like. The Guides told her to go take a walk by the river, to sit in the sun and to look for the butterflies.

The next time I saw her, she said she had done just that, and the sun felt so very good. But, she asked, "What does this have to do with my relationship with my husband?" Once she realized that it was her right to feel joy, whether she was with her husband or sitting on a rock in the sun, something primordial clicked inside of her and she began to cry. I sensed that her tears were not of sadness (there most certainly was some of that) but relief. The rest was just a matter of taking the steps to honor the feeling now inside.

I didn't see her for almost a year after that. In our last session together, she just came to tell me how happy she was. She had left her husband and was living alone in a small house. She had taken up photography and was immersed in a group of other wildlife enthusiasts who were also celebrating Mother Nature. She told me that she never would have believed that she could feel such joy in her life, if she hadn't discovered it for herself.

I love to see the light bulb go on in my fellow brothers and sisters of the light this way, especially after hearing that they have taken the courageous steps necessary to back up their new found feeling of joy with action. It's the "taking responsibility for the self" piece that is so critical for making these kind of radical changes.

Saying this, it can be a challenge to figure out what the real lesson is before you get on with things. I encourage you to allow yourself the time to sit with the feelings that are invoked by the interactions you encounter in relationship with others, and ask for the blessing, the higher understanding, so you don't have to go on repeating a pattern again and again. Most of these learning patterns are set up to prepare you for the contribution you are here to make to humanity.

When you are ready to see the higher meaning or life lesson, even as you sit in, perhaps, a horrible life situation or have been badly mistreated, there is always a blessing to be realized when you are ready to see the learning for what life is actually teaching you. I could write volumes about those of us who are stuck in relationships trying to get out or make sense of what to do differently. But here is one example of someone who really got it—the deeper understanding of a series of painful interactions, and with that understanding, she went on to realize her higher life expression:

A young woman who identified herself as a student called me one day and asked me to open to channel. She had very few questions, and mostly wanted to better understand why she was having such a hard time with her relationships. The Guides immediately launched into her role as a major activator. They told her that her soul's calling was to do research and to teach. The nature of her work would challenge her to make tough choices, to take the unbeaten path, to be a pioneer in her field.

The Guides spoke to her that day about the importance of standing in her power, upholding a very critical line of integrity, and how important that would be for her to realize success. By doing so, people would take notice of her opinions but she wasn't there yet. Her resolve to hold her ground was still being tested. The key to achieving her long-term goal that her soul had set for her was to maintain a stance of impeccable integrity. This would be instrumental to her success.

They went on to explain that her soul had experienced very few human lifetimes. She had come from a planet where the energetic equivalent of emotion was much lighter than earth, which was why she chose earth. It made it easier for her soul to integrate higher frequencies of light into the body. She was here to bring about medical discoveries (discoveries she already inherently knew) as she was destined to work in the area of biotechnology.

They told her that the human body is laden with toxicity from humanity's growing polluted environment, which greatly compromises the liver, pancreas and kidneys. Within the next 10 to 12 years, the environmental toxicity will only grow worse. She is to be developing technologies that will alter brain wave activity. These technologies will help the body differentiate fatal toxins from positive influences to rid the body of harmful environment effects. Without her contribution and the others that she will be working with, massive amounts of people will die from the growing toxic environment and the ingestion of contaminated food.

I was so fascinated by the science of how she is to be working, and the doorways that were already opening up for her to step through, that it didn't even dawn on me that she was under duress about her immediate situation. Her total focus was on peer relationships that had gone south. As I found out much later, she was a third year medical student at a top-notch university getting straight A's. For the past two years friends who she thought of as best friends had betrayed her. Lab partners claimed credit for her work then turned her in for lying. On the surface of her awareness, her life was being tossed around by others who were accusing her of wrong-doing. The culmination of it all was that she had to appeal to the school's peer review council to defend herself from her accusers, and after all this was done, she wasn't even sure that she wanted to come back to complete her final year.

What the Guides gave her was an entirely different perspective. They explained that without the gift of these individuals who pushed her into having to make the choice to fully align with integrity rather than resort to manipulating outcomes, or acquiescing to someone else's game plan, that she had solidified her path to realize her soul's intended highest expression. The Guides went on to say that she would, indeed, complete her final year, but then would bypass becoming a practicing physician by going straight into a doctoral research program. She would then go on to do groundbreaking research. Her breakthroughs in biotechnology would come quickly, which would be followed by teaching what she knew to other scientists all over the world.

The next time I spoke with her she was half-way to successfully completing her final year. She said that after the first session, her perspective radically shifted. Instead of feeling angry and confused, she realized that she was being afforded the opportunity to rise to the occasion. She expressed a deep sense of relief and appreciation for having made it through the maze of learning that her own soul had set up in preparation of launching into her life's work. She was now focused on where to apply for a post-graduate internship, and was asking questions about best strategies for getting into her chosen doctoral research program.

I love this example because it affirms that no matter what we think we are doing, the bottom line is that everything we experience is for our highest good. The third time I heard from her, she was still experiencing a flood of gratitude for the role these individuals played in her life and totally understood the need to speak up. Later, she shared that even though she is a very petite woman, people often tell her that when she walks into a room she seems larger than life. This was just another affirmation that one's integrity speaks loudly.

Path and purpose

We're all searching for some meaning in life. It can't simply be that we are here, living, working, eating, and sleeping day in and day out without meaning or purpose. I meet many people who are frustrated because they do not understand or have misinterpreted their purpose. However, once they understand that we are here to shift the paradigm from fear to joy, the bulk of their worries fall into an entirely different perspective. Everyone seeks purpose yet we, as beings of light, inherently understand that we are here for joy, and by taking ownership of our lives as divine beings of light, we can get on with what we have come to do by helping others do the same.

Even the most downtrodden can come back from the brink of despair. For some it only takes a look or a smile in the right direction. For others it might take an act of kindness by someone who sees the beauty in the one other who is feeling so low. No matter where we have been, there is always light if we are willing to open our heart. Sometimes it is just a matter of understanding our lives from a different perspective; to realize that we are not trapped in the middle of life-circumstances, but are actually free to choose differently, if we are willing. If we are willing to let go of what is actually killing us inside. Letting go of fear liberates us to do what we have come here to do.

You'd be surprised at the number of beings who will not let go even when they are dying inside. "It's my family," they say, or "my job. It's the way I have always been. I don't know any different. What would I do? I don't know where I would go, or who would love me? They hate me now and treat me so terribly but at least I know my place. I have been depressed for over 20 years. I don't remember what happiness feels like."

For as many reasons there are just as many people who will try to convince me that they cannot change, even as they are reaching out for help. As they come seeking the help to open their heart and point them in a more loving direction, I have often been prompted to tell them a variation of the following story:

Your path was set before you even came into the body. You mapped it out, chose your players, your helpers, even your adversaries, your life partners, and your children and grand-children. You chose it all. You also chose the choices, the actual Y's in the road, and planted seeds for growing in one direction or another, and the firings, the bells, the chills and the feelings that would go off inside of you when the choice at hand presented itself. You chose your higher path, and you chose points along the way that would challenge you for the purpose of honing your life-skills in preparation for what you came here to do.

What did you come here to do? Enter life purpose. While your path is who you are, your purpose is what you do with who you are. Your purpose is the physical reflection of who you are in the deeds that you do. Seems simple doesn't it?

It actually is very simple but getting knocked around by life does confuse us. It can get pretty confusing at times. Many of us get confused in the initial life setup, or in the skills-honing phase. We get confused because when we first selected this part, in our non-physical state, it felt loving, kind, considerate and supportive. But in the physical, doing state, it felt harsh, unloving, unkind, cruel even. We became confused by what we know to be true. The confusion is made worse because we actually *experienced* our lives in our imaginings and created our choices prior to birthing into the physical world. So all these feelings are already within us. What a shock to the system to experience, in some cases, the polar opposite of unity, harmony, unconditional love of self and others.

Enter clarity. Now, in this stage of your learning, you have awakened to the game itself and you have declared your path; others are still looking at their purpose. They look at their purpose their whole life without ever taking a single step in the direction their heart has called them to take. We can sometimes look so hard at the issues around purpose that we forget that all we have to do is look back at who we are, and there it is.

If you still feel confused about what your path and purpose is, I encourage you to get quiet and ask yourself the very same questions. What is my path? What is my purpose? You can look back at your life thus far and see the trail you have left behind. Whatever has brought you pain and inner anguish to the point of running scared: hold the mirror up to that feeling, and there you are. This will bring clarity to your purpose.

As light beings, our purpose is to teach others from the strength that is gained by overcoming a life challenge. A life-challenge is anything that you have, up until now, perceived as a curse or a weakness in your life. For many in this life-cycle the life challenge is all about oppression: Overcoming abuse, being misunderstood, under appreciated, attacked, isolated, disadvantaged, etc. For others it is being given everything material yet not being loved. Find the pain, and you'll discover your purpose, and your path. Your purpose is about opening to the truth of who truly are: Love.

Once you do connect with both your purpose and your path, how do you get your message out to others? Speak from your heart; take action from the basis of what you know. That's the basic new leadership paradigm. If you haven't walked through the fire yourself, then you cannot bring your message to others. Most of us have come back to teach compassion in the face of hatred, unconditional love where there is malice, patience where there is a rush to judgment.

After hearing this dialogue, along with the details of their specific lineage of learning, most are sitting across from me with a smile, and with a voice that comes from deep within, they confirm, "Yes, I did know this all along, you know. You haven't told me anything that I don't already know."

Then, the real work begins. When I see them again, I am delightfully surprised at the breath of fresh air; the joy of being that walks up to me and says, "Do you remember me?" And then I cry. I am in awe of their transformation.

The Guides are always saying, "Honor thyself, and know that all is well." If I were to pass along any guidance that has come through over the years about the desire to connect with your path and purpose, this would be it. If you truly honor yourself by looking past your fear, then you would live a perfect life filled with joy, happiness and peace. But then again, you, like the rest of 6.6 billion others are in the game of life to learn, to grow and to wake-up. Once you are awakened, you are called to wake-up your brothers and sisters of the light. Some do this by simply being who they are — a beacon of light. But we live in a physical world; so most awakened beings quickly become new paradigm leaders who want to realize their life purpose by sharing their joy with others in service to humanity.

Being on task for realizing your life purpose requires you to break free of habitual strife.

There is no more valuable experience than direct knowing. We can begin to understand a conceptual way of creating, but without having direct experience of our lives in a way that gives us that visceral feeling, and we continue to create in what feels like a circular cycle. Habit feels like a circle, and is very difficult for most of us to break. We may understand our inner direction or intellectualize the change we are called to make, but until we have experienced the feeling nature of this change (both positive and negative) we sit in the drone of habit. The idea stays in the mind and does not travel to the deeper emotions.

Habitual ways of creating feel safe because they are familiar but our comfort, sooner or later, turns to boredom or self-destruction depending on what part of the continuum we are in. It does not matter what we think or feel about ourselves, or the judgment of any given situation. What matters more is what we do about it.

It is the rare individual that not only energetically shifts but also sets out to make positive changes in her life, and does so, to such the extent, that she breaks into an entirely new life. Up the evolutionary spiral she goes because she has learned how to surrender her fears. I would guess that about five percent of the people I have worked with are in this radical change category. Most accomplish their hopes, dreams and desires by incremental degrees and are happy to report their accomplishments. Others go around and around about why they can't or shouldn't do this or that until they get so sick of hearing themselves that they either make the one change that is least threatening to them, or find someone with whom to commiserate.

I find myself constantly telling those in this later category that this transformational work is very simple but takes, at least at first, our every waking moment to change the way we have always approached life. Many will tell you that to be human is to be complacent about life. This belief is born from fear and speaks to the mind. The heart knows no bounds. Our imagination is the most powerful tool we have. Sometimes the most painful experiences speak to our heart for the purpose of getting the mind to wake-up and to more clearly listen to the heart.

Fulfilling your life's purpose takes great courage.

Some of us who are called to create within the most refined energies that heal and transform the most hardened of hearts are some of the strongest warriors of light. These are the individuals, throughout their karmic learning, who have experienced inverted light but who have also transcended the ignorance that comes from fear-based learning. They have done so by intoning unconditional love in all aspects of their lives. These very special souls have somehow managed to avoid taking on the identity of victim or perpetrator, and have taken total responsibility for their learning. They have seen through the illusions and know what it really means to play in the third-dimension. But that does not mean that they are aloof or not a part of the game here now.

Many souls who have come through these kinds of inner-chambered experiences will tell you that there is nothing about the way the human race creates that surprises them. Their hearts are free of judgment and self-loathing that sometimes carry over from one lifetime to another, but many get caught in the trap of responsibility.

An example of this is a young woman. I'll call her Maralyn. In her day-to-day reality she is the mother of five children. She also has a large extended family, which she dearly loves. When I first met her, she was absolutely consumed by fear; the kind of terror that strikes the heart when one feels unvarnished pain. She had awakened to her ability to physically heal others years ago. Her memory of who she was and where she had come from was very much a part of her conscious awareness.

Maralyn vividly remembers talking to the angels when she was a young girl. Now a grown woman, she found herself healing others by focusing her intention on unconditional love when she felt another's pain. Over time, knowing that she had this power to heal, she became overwhelmed with the feeling of responsibility. When I met her, she told me that she cried all the time and was in constant physical pain from feeling the soul pain of humanity. She had so tuned into other's pain that she could no longer bear it. She just wanted to leave the planet or have her power to heal taken away.

Once inside the channel, the Guides explained that her goal was not to leave but to stay. They went on to tell her that she was to call forth her light as an angel in the physical body. By bringing more joy into her life that would take away the pain. If she continued to stay in fear she would only amplify not only her pain, but also the soul pain of humanity. The Guides told her that she could leave if she wanted to, but she came to the planet at this time to teach others how to heal through love.

She was here to help cure cancer, and her first task was to begin healing a loved one who was battling leukemia. By doing so, she would heal the breech in her extended family and put herself back on her path. Hearing these words, she let out a cry like a wounded animal and began to sob. Her young niece had just been hospitalized for the second time with this form of cancer, and had taken a turn for the worst. She knew that she could heal the child, and offered to do so, but her family was too fearful of what she was all about.

As she opened to bringing more joy into her life, she began to realize that the only way that she could move on in life was to let go of feeling so responsible for others. The last time I saw her she was aglow with a new excitement for life, and actively working on accepting her life purpose as a healer.

If you find yourself feeling responsible for stepping into your heart's desire, let it go. Let it all go. Only then will you begin to fulfill your life's purpose.

Knowing when to walk away

As you determine your path toward realizing your own brand of freedom, you are extricating yourself from the old ways of being, old paradigms. As you become more conscious of your ability to liberate yourself from perpetual habits, you may also pretend, for a while anyway, that you are happy in the way that you have always lived. If you are like many that I have worked with, after you have made a heart connection to your path and purpose, you may choose not to give those around you a clue about your new found discovery until you have decided what has to change.

You may play along with the old until the difference between the old life-path and the new become so apparent that you are ready to move into the higher vibrational expression of you.

If you are anything like so many others that I have worked with, the relationships that you have developed to this point in your life will be the biggest sticking point, at least at first. This very human dynamic of holding on is a reflection of a misguided sense of safety and security. It's your connection to tribe, and up until now, tribe has kept you safe, at least as a part of your story.

We each hold a vision or a mental picture inside of us of who we are and how our tribe will accept us. Some become immobilized at the point that it becomes self-evident that change is in order. We can dream our way into the new, and even feel it as we call it forth, but when it comes time to let go of out-lived circumstances and relationships, fear can grind us to a halt.

What has to happen when this occurs, is to change the inner picture of you. If you are still not taking total ownership for your life choices, you are likely to construct elaborate reasons why others are preventing you from realizing your heart's desire. It takes a lot of work to keep yourself in these kinds of patterns, but once you find the courage to admit that no one else holding you back but you, then you are half way there.

Another take on this concept of taking total responsibility for your own personal peace and happiness can be looked at another way:

Someone told me recently that when she first heard my reaction to the September 11, 2001, bombing of the World Trade Center, in New York, my words had haunted her, but made her think. When our paths crossed again, she told me that she had finally made peace with what I had shared with her and others. She decided that she finally understood my perspective. At the time, she felt it was very shocking to hear that I could have felt—and did—such exhilaration at the moment that I had connected with the energy of the event before I even had an inkling of what had actually happened. What I felt was intense movement; movement that was off the charts joyous. And then she said, "We either grow or die."

She had come to understood that my visceral reaction of

how I experienced that event as the soul in a human body. Likewise, her perspective on life, *grow or die*, rang true to the core. I believe her words offer us a literal statement. I see it all the time. Once we know what we know, there is no going back, no sitting back in the familiar and expecting to grow. It just doesn't work that way. But some of us have gotten so stuck in the old that when we really do wake-up to the new, the new is so far off center from the old that it becomes obvious that we're just going to have to walk away from it all to start anew.

Most of the people I work with come to this conclusion on their own, but then fear sets in pretty quickly. It's always quite surprising how scary this first step is for most because the prevailing thought is that there is only one source for love. Without the people they have grown so far into the familiar with, they can't fathom where more love will come from— even when they recognize that it is only a trickle in their present moment.

For most it just takes a gentle reminder that we are the love we are seeking from the others, and another gentle reminder that comes in the form of a question: "Does the love that you feel inside match what you are experiencing right now?" I have yet to hear a single person, when they first start to go down this road to awaken to their full potential, say "Yes."

In all cases, I hear the answer "No, but." My next question follows with, *What's keeping you from honoring yourself?*

This question alone opens up an entirely different line of self-inquiry and leads most to discover for themselves what they have been missing all along.

Our world is just full of illusions, most of which we create and perpetuate out of the need to be needed. Once the bubble of illusion has burst, and we begin to wake-up to how we are really living, and how we are really being treated, then we are ready to ask ourselves the following questions:

- Am I loved and appreciated for who I am?
- Do I have someone around me who understands and appreciates me for the viewpoint I bring to the world?
- Am I honored, respected and listened to when I have something to contribute?

If these three basic questions are not answered as *yes*, then at some point, you may find the need to walk away and begin anew. If you find yourself up against a wall in your relationships and/or circumstances, what are some of the *in your face* signs? Here are just a few:

- No one will talk with you about your feelings.
- Every time you open to express yourself, you are shut down or turned away.
- You feel insecure and unsafe in your surroundings.
- Your sense of creativity and ability to express yourself is unappreciated and suppressed.
- You are not able to speak through the wall of anger and protectiveness of the other(s).
- You feel unhappy and depressed by your life circumstances.
- When you suggest a change, you are shut down by the other(s).
- Fear of being provided for keeps you feeling beholden to the other.
- You are afraid for your life if you don't follow orders or the rules that others have set for you to follow.
- You are feeling unfulfilled in your work, your life, and your relationships.
- Nothing you have done to make a change has worked because you are doing so to please or to placate the other(s).
- You are living your life because of what you think you should be doing; you are living out the expectations that

others have for you.
• You feel like you are being held hostage in your own life.

Now this does not mean that if you walk away that all your problems are solved. If you do not clear the root cause before, during or after you make your choice to walk away then you will simply recreate the same dynamic all over again. But sometimes, it is best to separate to break the cycle. And not all inner calls to walk out of your life that you have been living are rooted in liberating yourself from oppression. You may be called to shift or to change your life because you are being called to fulfill your life purpose. How to tell the difference is the key. What you need to pay attention to is your inner knowing. Rather than becoming reactive to any given situation, learn to get still and go into the deeper knowing of what is guiding you. If even half of the descriptions above apply to you, then it's highly probable that you have grown accustomed to dishonoring the self. Either way, a change is in order.

Once you hear the call to go, the question at this point is *What comes next? Do you simply get up and physically, mental and emotionally walk out of your life?* In some cases, the answer is absolutely *yes.*

For some of us, we have been called to move clear across the country or the world, change careers, or marry someone different. A few have gotten stuck in fear, along the way, but most look back at how dramatically their lives have changed with gratitude. They have really gotten in touch with how they are living their lives in grace.

One of my all time favorite stories is of someone whose life path was triggered, and woke him up from a life he totally loved. That made his choice all the more confusing, but he accepted his inner visions as truth and went seeking validation.

Here is where his life and mine intersected. When I met

Thomas, he was living a very fulfilling life. He was in a loving relationship, was well liked and had a successful consulting practice. He was happy, and on the surface was very content with his life. As I did in those days, I worked with one person after another throughout the day, not knowing anything about the person sitting directly across from me other than a hand-written name on a piece of paper. In this instance, the name next on my list was Tom and the person sitting across from me was a tall dark eyed, gentle looking soul. He was so tall that his arms and legs looked like they were straddled over a doll-sized chair.

The Guides spoke of another life, a different choice waiting for him on the other side of the continent, but first he was to dive into a year of remembering ancient healing techniques that have been transmitted through a star-culture. By the use of these symbols, he would help activate corresponding symbols lying dormant in the light body. The work felt very strange and at the same time familiar to me as I witnessed the Guides activate many of these same symbols within him.

As they spoke, I watched the most beautiful geometric colors and shapes hovering above his head begin to spin and transform. Later, I learned this was the Mercaba I had seen, a series of energetic encodings that were first shared with the Egyptian kings over 24,000 years ago. But at that particular moment, I was mesmerized by the multidimensional unfolding as this light being of the highest order sat and beamed back at me the biggest, brightest smile I have ever seen.

Little did I know during that first session that he had been having visions of the very same life that the Guides repeated back to him. As our time together came to a close, I felt that I had met someone extraordinary, and I had. The last I heard from him, he had completed a year of esoteric studies in the Midwest, and was now out West and settled into the rhythm of his new life. But getting there took great courage to leave a comfortable, familiar life.

Our purpose is to make a contribution to the world by just being who we are.

Spoken like a true awakener, a recent visitor to my home commented that she was not focused on global events because she felt like she had enough on her plate just to focus on her own part of the world. It was clear to me that by focusing her attention on self that she was doing her part to create a new world consciousness. By putting her sights on becoming the happiest, brightest, most peaceful person that she can be, she is adjoining with others everywhere doing the same.

If your happiness is helping other people, then your heart is attuned to compassion in service to humanity. If your peace of mind is solving global dynamics, then you are here to build bridges of understanding. If your joy is derived from Mother Nature, then you are here to help maintain balance and harmony. If you are called to speak, teach, share, laugh or co-create in any manner, the determining factor in aligning with your highest expression is joy. We are shifting global consciousness as we create in the vibrational frequencies of joyousness. That is it. As we each realize our own unique brand of personal peace and happiness we, are contributing to the shift in global consciousness.

Joy is infectious. In the company of pain and suffering, joy serves as the catalyst to create the new paradigm of prosperity through laughter and an overall sense of well-being. I invite you to create in a way that truly brings you joy. As you do, you'll be pleasantly surprised to discover your life path and purpose.

15: SELF-INQUIRY

How, why, where and why not?

The only way to more fully trust is to go inside. As you do anything and everything that is important to remember is already there. Just ask. Help is all around you and within you. This statement has been passed down to us over the generations and has stood the test of time. Anytime we really want to know anything, or to make a choice; it's best to take a look inside. The answer is always there. So that's what this chapter is all about.

It is designed to provide you with a sampling of questions that others have asked that may apply to your life. So here we go, I trust this question and answer section will personalize your learning experience in this medium, and help you to better understand your own life through the prism of others' life experiences. The sampling that follows represents a small fraction of documented conversations. Many of which have been recorded or captured in word. The personalization has been taken out and is shared with you for the benefit of learning.

RELATIONSHIP

Pushing versus allowing

Q: You said once we are the Gods we pray to yet I have heard that pushing for what we want pushes it farther away. I feel so very young in this particular area of my life. How can I be a master teacher when I have such an Achilles heel in the relationships that I want to work?

A: Wanting or wishing for something different to occur in your life without taking action is what brings you unhappiness. It gets pretty tricky because the mind is always seeking the answer before you step, but your heart has actually already given you the answer through feeling before you are called to take a different step.

It's your inner knowing that is telling you to step out on faith. Once you connect with this feeling, the rest is simply a matter of follow-through. The heart is more of a solid navigational guide than any mind will ever be.

You can settle for less and the mind will be happy with safety and sameness. But your heart will always seek freedom: freedom of expression, freedom of thought, word and deed. Total freedom requires you to let go of any and all preconceived notions of who you are. It requires you to let go of your doubts and insecurities and totally trust that your desire will be met in the best possible way.

Yearning versus accepting

Q: I was supposed to meet the man of my dreams but it hasn't happened yet. What is going on?

A: You have already met this person and are in relationship with him but you do not recognize him as your beloved because you are judging the relationship from the perspective of your human nature. Here is an analogy for clearing old beliefs, patterns and behaviors that you may wish to consider.

You are in the grocery store looking for a jar of pickles, which are located on the top shelf. You remember that the olives are on the bottom shelf. Out of habit, you reach for the olives because that is what you always come to buy. You wonder why you cannot find the pickles but then you remember what has just transpired. You'll awaken to your desire once you get your human nature way of being out of the way, and reconnect with what you truly desire.

Timing, allowing for flow

Q: I have met the woman of my dreams, but now my

beloved says that she is not ready yet. What action am I to take? I am confused.

A: Be patient, loving and kind. Do not push the creation. Continue to profess your love as an open doorway for her to return to you, but move forward with your life. Do not wait. Waiting will push her away. Allow love to flow freely in all creations.

A metaphor for this learning pattern: You love going out into the woods, and as you do, you place a red raincoat in a certain spot in case it rains while you are out. As you go out into the woods you always find this bright red raincoat where you left it for safe keeping. In your way of thinking, you know that as you come and go, and as it is needed, you will find it there. One day, you come walking toward that favored spot, but instead of seeing the raincoat, you see a man way off in the distance wearing your coat.

The moral? As you expect things to be a certain way, they will not stay the same just because you want them to. Create as the heart calls you to, and with no attachment to the outcome. In short follow your heart, even when the other turns away. This allows for movement and what is best and right for the heart will come to you.

Self expression

Q: How do I express negative emotion in a loving way or do I even speak about the anger or fear?

A: As you love yourself, speak your truth. Speak about how you are feeling. YOU speak to how YOU are feeling. "I feel, I see, I know...." Do not point a finger at the other such as "you did this or that." Decide what has to stop. If it doesn't, decide what you are going to do. Talk it through but most importantly, follow your heart.

Breaking away from constricting relationships

Q: I have been living my life for others for 50 years, and have now decided to be free. How can I break out and do my thing when I feel so obligated to conforming to my family?

A: Freedom comes with a price to pay. The price is courage. Courage to follow your inner guidance is priceless. As you follow your inner guidance and take action, those who want to keep you where you are will push against you, but the more resolved you are to realize freedom, the easier the transition will be. Go for it!

Eros, sex and love

Q: In The Pathwork for Self Transformation, Eva Pierrakos states that the three essential components of a healthy relationship are Eros, sex and love. How do these align with the new paradigm of romantic relationships?

A: Couples first recognize one another through the fifth, sixth and seventh chakras. Then as they come together they work through the lower chakras issues together, which is quite different than traditional relationships. One hundred percent of new paradigm relationships are coming together for mutual realization of both path and purpose.

Universal love verses the romantic love

Q: What is the difference between the universal resonance of love and the resonance with a partner? Is there any? And is it possible that I mistake the healing for the healer? The love for the lover?

A: There is only love with many faces and sides to the same feeling. There are no special relationships only choices for opening, and deepening.

Awakened marriage - partnership

Q: What is marriage or romantic partnership when you are awake? And what do you see happening as our paradigm shifts and relationships change shape to accommodate expansion?

A: In the new paradigm, the choice to be free is considered a right not an exception. Freedom requires us to take responsibility for our own personal peace and happiness. This form of partnership is both path and purpose. Therefore there are those who will tell you that you cannot be free because one must submerge and one must lead. In the awakened state, it is the oneness consciousness that guides both. I love what Amma, an Indian Saint, has to say about the new paradigm partnerships. She describes marriage or romantic partners like two wings of a bird. You need both to take flight.

MIND VERSES HEART

Getting unstuck

Q: What happens if you get stuck between these two operating systems (creating with intention or life happening to you)?

A: Here's what happens: You are intending, imagining and then you are waiting for your creations to show up in your world. As you begin to shift back into that old, familiar waiting and wanting feeling, some of the following emotions that are likely to send signals to you that something is not working are:

1. Anxiety
2. Frustration
3. Anger
4. Depression
5. All of the above.

You may even begin to feel tricked by the universe because

you are "doing" everything you know to do, and the universe is not delivering. If you have been finding yourself in this state of mind, realize that you are trying to straddle two realities and it just doesn't work. Just as you would not simultaneously run two word processing programs to create one outcome, you are also called to choose one way (heart or mind) and stick with it.

PATH AND PURPOSE

Duality

Q: My question relates to people connecting with what they call the "false hierarchy". I understand the concept of *as above, so below* in the form of energy and spirit. Is there really a "false hierarchy" out to sabotage all those that are looking to bring more light into the planet? If there is, can I continue to just focus my power in the highest, and be okay in my own acknowledged safety? Or can we acknowledge this without giving any power to it, and be in complete balance if it is so?

A: Yes, and Yes. I'll answer the false hierarchy this way: We are creating a beautiful story and the story within our imagination says that all is right and possible in the way that we imagine. But the others come along who are hearing these imaginings and are saying to themselves, "She is imagining these creations, and if we do not get what she is creating then that means that we will have to do the work within our very own selves. We will begin to create our own realities as well. But we do not want to do that. We want to create what she is creating and we do not want her to get what she wants. We want to get what she is creating so we will devise a plan to begin to share our thoughts, ideas and inner stories with her so that she will do all the work for us, and we'll just take these creations for our very own selves."

And so goes the rounds of creation.

There are beings within many realms of light who are so wanting the earth to shift that they have said, "but we want it to go the way of our creative inventiveness. Therefore, we will create in a way that ensures that we will get what we so desire, but we cannot let the opposition know what this is. Our motives must be kept quiet so as not to disturb the creations of the light."

And so we go again and again. These creations are still among us and were put there by the very people who are perpetuating the creations of the light and the darkness in the skies of change. *We cannot let them win* denotes that there is something to defeat. If you determine that you must defeat something then you are looking outwardly for your very own weakness through your shield of protection. Therefore you must create from a place of light so that the dark will not come in to get you. So, you see, if you are focused on the darkness, you will draw exactly that to you. If you know that there is only light, then there is no issue.

Some will continue to play among the realms of duality and yet others will discover the truth of who they are and decide to create light because they know within them, and their outer creations, that there is only light.

Now, with this being said, discernment is what determines where you reside within this continuum of learning. Notice that I call this a continuum of learning.

Learning is what is constant to all of creation.

Learning.

Learning to let go of the darkness within you, the ignorance and the short sightedness and so on.

Learning to see the truth of who you are, and who you are not.

Learning that there is only light, there is only one source — oneness of being-ness. As you focus the flowing of source through the open vessel of oneness of being-ness, you will open to the light of God within you and whatever is on the other side of this creation does not matter.

What does matter is who shows up to create with you. That is where discernment comes in. And what matters is when they show up to play with you, that you are discerning the light of God within you. Are they reflecting back to you the truth of who you are or not? If the answer is yes, then so be it. If the answer is no, then it is time to bless and to release this energetic dynamic and be on your way.

False hierarchy by its very nature depicts something that is not. Trickery, now that's another matter. It happens all the time.

Prosperity

Q: What am I personally doing and being that's holding me back in the area of prosperity and how do I help myself with this?

A: We each bring to the table of life our own fears and you are no exception. There is a specific vibrational quality to your own life that remembers strife or turmoil. Once you remember that now is different, you will find the freedom you are seeking. Find it in your fear of change. Find it in your feeling of needing to know everything before you can make a choice. Find it in your understanding of life as it is. Then decide if those fear-based reactions to life are worth holding on to. This is a big choice for some because it brings up so much emotion. Letting go is not easy. It will change everything about how you think and feel. Honor yourself for the courage it takes to let go of fear. Then send it on its way.

This is where new opportunity comes in. Allow your heart to accept the many gifts that so freely come to you. Allow the energy of the new to create new magic in your life. Allow your heart time to adjust to the new vibration of joy in all areas of your life, not just a few. And know that as you do, your life will shift, change, and transform. All is well.

Law of cause and effect

Q: Please clarify the 5th Dimensional thought and the law of cause and effect. It almost felt to me that as we move more fully into the fifth dimensional way of being that we won't be operating under the law of cause and effect. Is part of that because 'time' shifts so manifestation, in turn, would shift?

A: No. It's because we move into a different river of consciousness. The way we manifest is different in the higher dimensional realities. Nonlinear time is more about going to the place to bring back what it is that we wish to create. It's what's already been created by the soul before we got here. The shamans call this form of retrieval going to the upper world to see what is in our destiny line.

STAR CULTURES

Light beings

Q: Is it my path to break out of my need to do good?

A: No. It's a part of who you are. It is your soul's imprint in this world.

Q: When did the light beings visit me when I was a child? I only know by feeling when my mother neglected me (age 2 or 3, age 5 and 7 when she left). Were there any other times?

A: It was during these early childhood years. They came to give you comfort. They came back when you were 14 and making a choice for love.

Q: What were the signs to help me to remember?

A: For you it's the color of crimson red. It brings you joy and reminds you of home.

How we were created

Q: I have always been under the impression that we all came from the same breath of God. I was told recently that not all beings are created on the same breath but that we are different and created in groups. Please comment.

A: We come from the same source, yet we are all different, unique in our own light, our own vibration. We were created in waves, or wave-forms of light. For this particular earthen plane, we were created for righteousness. Right service, which also means truth. Aligning with truth. Groups/Pods: These are groups of souls who have come here for the same learning, same life mission.

Star Origins

Q: What is my star family origin and my gifts? And/or are there any messages the Guides have for me?

A: You came from the planet of Sirius B. Your star culture of origin are those star beings who came during the first wave of ascension from their planet of origin in 1647 BC. You have served as an over soul for the soul groupings here for so long that you are very familiar with the system of subjugation and control on this planet. This incarnation has been a clear and decisive one in so many ways because your heart knows what is coming. It is the children that we are wishing you to focus on. They will want you to help them to adjust to the ways of old and remember the ways of new. Your gift is one of hearing those who have come to help the masses. You see what others do not wish to consider. Your awareness is keen. The infil-trators will not get far from your sight because they see what you see. Through your eyes, you are directing love for all and one of oneness. We honor you this day of days.

What voice to listen to?

Q: Am I a light being? I sometimes struggle with thoughts that I'm not a light being—that perhaps I'm just here living a strictly human life without any further purpose. Every aspect of me (heart, soul, body) all say otherwise and I am learning to listen to them closely. But even tonight on the call I had to quiet the mind's deceptive voice telling me that this call wasn't for me that I'm not a light being, that I'm not from anywhere and that everyone else is so much further along the path than I am. How destructive the mind can try to be!

A: Yes, absolutely. Every person [on that call last night] is a light being, each with a different soul imprint and light matrix. Now the second part of your comment is most telling. It's about the mind. The mind can be very tricky, because the mind does not want you, Mr. Light Being thousand-watt bulb to wake-up. The mind wants to keep you scared, doubtful, and fearful. Why? Because that is what some star cultures want from your human nature; to cultivate your mind for fear. Fear is quite a valued commodity in the other realms of light, other star systems. Become aware of these thoughts and simply send them on their way. They have no place in your life. Just by banishing fear and doubt from your life, you are doing the greatest service to humanity. The rest will come quite easy from there on.

Intergalactic Council of Twelve

Q: Some time ago you said (during one of the topics) that I am connected to the Intergalactic Council of Twelve. Do you have any insight into what this means?

A: Yes. It's the Intergalactic Council who governs this sector of the galaxy. It is the Council that decides how much energy to pulse into the planet and how much to hold steady. You work directly for the council. Just like God is not a white bearded man sitting on a cloud, the Council works through vibration, through souls here to help. Your vibration shifts the consciousness of others, and you offer aide and counsel to those who need aligning.

Colors

Q: You spoke of connecting to your color. How does one interpret the color they have? Where can you get the information on what colors mean?

A: Colors and vibration are the same. Colors depict where you are from, what soul grouping you are learning with, and what role you are playing here on the planet. It's not as simple as telling you that orange equals this and red equals that. It's very individualized according to soul path. Source? I have been asked this many times before. The Guides tell us to ask then pay attention and see what comes to you. Pay attention to feeling, the feeling that you feel inside, and to watch what you are drawn to, and how you react to color. That's the best way. There is no hierarchy in color, only sound.

Star being and Human-being Merging

Q: On [the] call you mentioned that the human race would be merging. And in this process that some of us would be leaving (those who were not ready to merge) and some would be staying (and merging). My question is am I ready to merge? Or am I one that will be leaving? Or is this yet to be determined?

A: Merging is a soul path and has only to do with aligning with unconditional love by letting go of all distortion (sadness, self-hatred, jealousy), and making peace with the body consciousness. You can discover the answer to this question by asking yourself am I ready to be free?

Dreams

Q: I had this dream where there was this being coming towards me. The being had long, long arms. It was a very strange dream and I didn't think much of it until after the call [about light beings]. Do you think my dream was related to the energy coming in? Is there energy that I might be fighting off? Or am I still holding onto some fear that is causing me to push away the being or energy?

A: Yes. We have beings of light around us all the time. Some enter into our subconscious awareness because your mind is like a fortress. No need to fight off any energy. You are in charge of your life, your light. You decide what you desire. Next time, ask the being of light if she has anything to tell you. Then listen and feel what might be.

Physical symptoms of ascension

Q: How should I interpret physical symptoms such as aches and pains, headaches and tiredness as I move through the ascension process?

A: Listen to your body. Allow yourself to rest. If you feel the body reacting, pay attention. It's more likely that you are experiencing the energy moving, shifting and making space in the body for a lighter, brighter physical vessel. It's like getting a rocket boost before launch. But at anytime that you feel that there is something inherently awry with the body, seek out the advice and counsel from an appropriate healthcare provider. To alleviate aches and pains try hot salt baths, energy healing, bodywork, acupuncture or chiropractic. Move the body.

Purpose in knowing your soul's origin

Q: What purpose does knowing my source have on my daily life? How am I to apply the information to my life?

A: Understanding where you have come from helps you to gain a deeper understanding of your life's purpose; how your soul has chosen to operate in the world and what particular challenges you might face; why you react to or avoid certain situations the way that you do; or why you might not want to even be here at all. By shifting your perspective about your true nature, you will find that you will make different choices. Knowledge is power, and to realize which star cultures play out particular roles will rock your world. Your perspective will never be the same ever again.

Soul Groups

Q: In general, why do we change soul groups?

A: We choose our soul group for learning and for helping us to accomplish our life purpose. As we connect with others to do our work, our soul group helps us to keep moving up the vibrational spiral. Once you have accomplished what you have come to learn within a particular group, you will then be guided to connect with another.

Q: More specifically why will I change soul groups so many times?

A: We move to co-create in different vibrational groups for different phase of our lives, for learning.

CHOICE AND PROBABLE FUTURE

Life Choices and Probability

Q: Once a probable future is shared it is impossible for that information not to influence a person's thoughts, actions, deeds etc. At some point those thoughts, actions, deeds go on to create exactly what the prophecy shared; a self-fulfilling prophecy. What is your take on this phenomenon, and how much of this do you see going on now with the people you work with?

A: We create our lives before we arrive on the planet. We have infinite choices to make but most enjoy making choices within a finite spectrum of life. Prophecy is spoken to those who already instinctually know who they are and what they have already chosen. Prophecy is a form of affirmation that one is headed in their already chosen direction, or not. I see people actually turn away from their highest expression. Only about 10 to 20 percent of the people that I have worked with totally shift into their highest expression shortly after receiving information about their life path.

It takes great courage to radically shift away from a life built on habitual fear. It's human nature to doubt, to worry, to step back and away from what brings us ultimate joy. I see a lot of unnecessary hardship played out because of this but in the end when those choice points come about, I hear back from many people that life played out the way it was given. Even though they first railed against the call to change, they overcame their fear and took that leap of faith.

On the other hand, I have seen others take the information and with total expectation without putting in any effort to transform. To their disappointment they return to me and ask what is up? As I go back and look, like a child waiting for Christmas, they have done nothing to spiritually grow. The prophecy is still there but it's further up the vibrational spiral just out of their reach. Once they recognize what they have done, which is sit inside the paradigm of fear and yearning, they begin living their lives by making different choices.

Free Choice

Q: As things unfold, sometimes it appears that this intricate tapestry of events is so well coordinated and so precise that "destiny and inevitability" seem more likely than free choice. What are your feelings on free choice at this point in time?

A: Absolutely free choice, but from what perspective? From the soul having the human experience, from ground zero, it may not feel like a choice at all. But from the soul's perspective, what you are experiencing is total free choice. We are much older and wiser than we give ourselves credit for.

Trust the knowing that guides you.

Discernment

Q: How do I know if I am making a higher vibrational choice?

A: Because the choice makes your heart sing. You are at peace when you have made a choice that is in alignment with your soul's purpose. These expanded feelings create higher vibrational expressions. Overlay people, places and happenings on top of these expansive feelings, and it's just a matter of feeling the difference between the nuances of mind and inner heart prompting you to keep going, keep creating. Allow for movement, and be clear about choosing joy. As you choose joy over fear, the people, places, dates, etc may change but the feeling of expansion is very easy to identify. You can feel it, and most of us know when we are fooling ourselves or ignoring our inner voice. Override your heart's desire, and you will quickly feel the difference. Remember. There is only choice. Neither right nor wrong.

Moving choices?

Q: Do my choices that are closest to my soul's desire go away or do I create new in each moment that becomes something different?

A: You are always creating in every moment. As you create in pain and suffering you cannot see or feel your heart's desire, but when you ascend to the higher vibration it is all there. The creations, in vibration, are still there but you must ascend to be able to see, hear and feel the inner connection. Let go of any sense of time or expectation. Allow your heart to lead the way your soul imagined it into creation.

INTUITION, SKILLS AND THE GRID

About inner guidance

Q: I first felt compelled to move to my new location but now I am confused. What is going on and where am I to be?

A: [This person first followed her heart and began her move to the location where she was guided. When almost there, she stopped and settled into a place not far from her final destination. Now she is unhappy and feels even more stuck than before she left her old environment.] Feel your way back into that state of being of when your heart led you to move. In this feeling of expansion, go back and let go of your fear of failure. Listen to your heart, and with a renewed sense of trust, follow your inner prompting as it is given.

What it feels like to expand

Q: I find myself at the beginning of a new transition—one that leaves me standing open and willing. I question the next step in my path and the skills that I should be learning to accomplish parts what I have come here to do. Are the intuitive cues that I have been having regarding work, movement and transition accurate reflections of the next step in my path?

A: You are describing the feeling one gets when you are being prompted to expand, to shift, to grow. These intuitive cues show up in your life, your work, and relationships to tell you that it is time for a change. It's time to grow in a different way. Once you recognize this in feeling terms, the rest is simple. Pay attention to what shows up in your work. Step back and away from what feels constricting and embrace what comes to you as an expression of joy and expansiveness.

Learning New Skills

I included this question and answer because I receive so many questions from people asking what they should do to prepare for their life transition. The answer is almost the same for all: Just be yourself. Find your joy. You have all the knowledge you need. Trust the knowing. The person who asked this question was already a remarkable young community builder.

Q: What are the skills that I should be learning to accomplish parts of my contract? And would these be important in the process leading up to the energetic shifts of 2012?

A: I wouldn't call our soul's desire a contract as much as what you have already imagined into being before you got here. In your imagination you are to be running a very large-scale operation of people who will be helping to evacuate large populations in your year of 2008. It will look and feel like chaos but it is not. It will open your heart and allow you to see you for you, and will give you many ideas of what the future will be for you and your world. There will be many who will come to you and say, but you know how to build consensus to make this happen this way, and so why do you not do this? And your answer will be that you are not here to rebuild the old but to create the new. And so you shall go! You will be adjoining with many in a new enterprise that is both honoring of your chosen profession of selfless service and your desire to travel among your people. You will be calling the shots but not pulling punches. You will be working among the people and creating the new paradigm of teamwork. You are not to worry about your feeling of abundance. You will be paid plenty in your dollars, but it will be the new bartering system that you put into place that will help so many make their way in the world as new. Give it time to take root. You will feel a bit impatient in these early stages, but give it time. It will be months not years, you see. It will fly and become quite a global enterprise. Allow, allow, allow, and know that all is well.

The grid

Q: I have a picture that I drew from something I saw. It is a picture of a sequence of squares, but they are only on the floor (it went as far as I could see), and all around (on the sides and above) was just emptiness, except for a metallic triangle that was floating above. Is this what everyone refers to as the grid?

A: Yes. It is interesting that you have out-pictured your current positioning on the grid. You are seeing it from your vantage point of looking down below into the infinity of this one called, "Universal Whole" The triangular symbol above your head is the ray of light for which you shine. Your subconscious is saying that it is okay to be above the fray, but eventually you will come to a place where you feel safe to immerse yourself into the physical expression of your vibrational frequency. It is called integration.

The web is not around you, it is you. It is the vibrational frequency of unconditional love and acceptance for all there is. As you connect more fully to the grid, without fear and trepidation, your hearing, seeing and being all that you are designed to be come more fully into your focus.

Inertia

Q: Can you share any insights [with us] regarding inertia in these times of rapid transition, and particularly how to break through it?

A: (Guides). My dear ones, we are forever wishing for you to wake-up to your divine essence and to know that you are no longer that which you are identifying with. We are not here to tell you that you may wish to remember your past regrets, hurts and slights with such valor and vim and vigor. But we are here to tell you that these are the very vibratory patternings that are causing you to feel the heaviness in the body and the mind. We are here now to instruct you as to how you may wish to release these feelings and be done with that which you are calling inertia. Inertia is an earthly term that dictates that for every action, there must be an equal reaction. This is in your mind and is not valid.

It is a belief that is rooted in your science books from the third grade during the time of Newton and Einstein or astrologers like your Galileo. They are not to be remembered now because these were earlier gateways that were necessary only to root humanity in the feeling of expansiveness.

You have surpassed this feeling long ago, yet you are feeling now that you must honor this belief as being one of truth. It is not. The actual law of the universe called inertia, in actuality is a propulsion concept and is rooted in fifth dimensionality. We are here now to release these feelings within you because you have now asked. It shall be received.

You are to close your earthly eyes as you say the words; "I release this feeling of being stuck in the physical expression of my life. I release, I release. It is done."

Say it with conviction, silently to your self, if you wish, or out loud in an expressive manner if you wish to root it deep within your conscious being. You have merely to desire that your life now be different and it shall be.

There is only one qualifier that we must articulate: As you desire, and as you receive intuitive direction in your place or center of your being, then you too shall honor that speaking and take action on your knowing. Without your action within the feeling of this knowing you shall experience more inertia and more and more until there is a feeling within you that shall say, "Enough. Enough. I shall now hear and see and feel all that I am to be. I am a divine being of Light. I am and I shall be only that, and all of that. That I Am."

As I come out of this speaking, I feel a tremendous sense of relief and expression of humor on the other side of the veil. It is as if our brethren are asking us to simply be who we are. It is as if a camel is trying to hide his huge hump on his back behind a small bush. In short, it is impossible. It is simply time for us to wake-up and to take action based on our inner knowing and know that there is no failure lurking around the corner. There is to be no fear in following the inner voice of reason. Each of us has been given enormously loving gifts of the heart. We are simply to be okay with all that is and do and be as we are stepping anew in the world as we are creating it daily, hourly, moment to moment.

16: MESSAGE TO HUMANITY FROM THE ANGELIC REALMS

The Angels' view on love and the human experience

As I mentioned at the very start of this sharing, the angels do not see humanity as separate entities, separate parts, but one single creation; many souls but definitely not separate. We are creating together as one collective consciousness. Needless to say their perspective is quite different from ours. They have a unique view of our lives in the third-dimensional realm. They speak from the mountaintop, while we are in the body experiencing the view from the valley floor. They experience reality in non-linear time (all and everywhere simultaneously) while we have put our lives into incremental boxes, closed the top to be sure that we are safe and secure only to find that we have limited our view entirely. That's what makes our relationship to them so special.

The angels and Guides are like fathers and mothers who are rooted in kindness though at times give their children a big swift energetic kick in the pants to wake them up, or to get them moving. Like any child who does not wish to be pulled away from self-destructive play, we can all attest that looking back, we are in wonder that we safely made it through childhood. It is in this spirit of learning that I find it appropriate to set aside a time for them to speak directly to you. Even though I have interwoven their messages throughout this body of knowledge, I am very blessed to share their parting words with you now.

"We have not come to wreak havoc on the human experience, but to help those who were wishing to better understand their human existence. We are not here to tell you that you must do this or that, but we are here to help you to better understand the universe of light you call love.

"Love is not what you get or give. It is the very basic element of who you are. There are many among your people who are confused, and who shift into very differing states of awareness in order to experience the feeling of oneness only to find self-hatred looming behind the facade of nice or good or right. We are here to help you to see who you are and to help you to equate your choosing with the way you are called to create. You are to create in a way that sets your heart free altogether.

"We are also here to educate you on the finer inner passageways to realizing your own brand of freedom. We do not dictate the terms of your feeling, and we do not create within the bandwidth of sorrow. We have seen the effects of this vibration on the human body, but we do not understand why you wish to create this way when there are so many other ways to reveal your heart to your very own self.

"We can never know the breadth or depth of the human emotional field because we are not in that creation cycle of cutting the self off from Source. The love that you are is still flowing through your veins until such time that you decide that you no longer wish to create in that manner, only then will you liberate yourself from your contorted creations by choosing to create differently.

"No one can help you decide to do differently. This choice is an individual one and is born only for you. You have an inalienable right to create however you so choose. The dilemma with this knowing is that many forget that, in their unconscious choosing, they have a choice, and have exercised it — even when they are calling us to come and save them from their very own selves.

"It happens every day, all day. We hear the cries, the pleas, for help without you ever realizing that there is a choice in the very moment of your despair, and there is another choice in your next moment to hear. Of course there is never a right or wrong choice to be made, merely one, then another and another.

"It is quite a simple process to decide how you wish to flow the love that you are through all your creation cycles. We will never understand why it is so difficult for you to see this point when you are in such pain. We are ready to help you better understand your choice but not to make it for you.

"As you accept the truth of who you are and begin to acknowledge your inner being as powerful — in charge of your choice — then you will begin to clear any misconceived notions of who you are. You will begin to recognize when it is time to move out of pain and confusion into the light of the God that you are.

"Allow yourself time for your choices to reveal themselves to you as you also understand truly that all is well.

"Your human game of life is a grand experience to be true, but in this experience there is wisdom to be gained, compassion to be realized, courage to be mustered. All the roles of the parts you are here on earth to play are to be played with gusto. You will find that as you awaken to the truth of who you are that many of this playing-out on a global scale will make you begin to feel like a football being bandied about to see who will throw, who will run, who will catch.

"From the perspectives of your higher understanding, everything you experience in life is all play, all joy, because you are learning individually and as a collective consciousness. There is no preconceived outcome, no goal beyond the extent of human experience. Yet we will tell you that there is an intended outcome without pushing our way into your collective outcome. Oneness, as we have talked about, is the goal of your human expression. We, as beings of light, have already realized this state of being in the non-physical state but have never, as a collective body of consciousness, realized oneness in human form.

"The human species, as a whole, has called for this state of being through the many shifts or changes in human expression. As the dense realities begin to reach a crescendo by early 2012, you will see higher understanding come into the galaxy of light known as earth plane consciousness. The breakthrough, at first, will be felt as chaos then over the following 12 to 17 years will be felt as a rebuilding and an honoring of the self will take precedence over the needs of the group.

"As human consciousness experiences great waves of sadness, the light beings will be ushering in vast waves of joy. That is why it is important, now, to create within the feeling of oneness in all that you are called to do. If you are holding onto pain and sadness, for instance, you will get swept into the wave of mass consciousness as events unfold. Under no circumstances are you to be fearful of your life being in danger. Mass consciousness will continue to play out scenarios of chaos over and over again but you are not to be dissuaded from experiencing profound joy.

And finally,

"We have shared, through this channel, and through feeling we have invoked the love that you are as you have read the many passages that told the story of your very own life. You are the hero that saves the damsel in distress. You are the one who awakens the child from slumber only to hurry her to safety. And you are the one who awakens to the singing of the birds and the whisperings of the trees. We cannot be there with you in the physical body, my child, but we are always with you in your heart. Hold us near and dear when you need to be reminded of who you are. You are a child of God. You are God united with all your brothers and sisters of light. There will come a day when we shall all be united back together again, but for now, know how very much you are loved by your creator. All is well."

— *The Angelic Realms, united in voice*

Meditation for Joy!

The angels tell us that they cannot interfere with humanity, but they are here to help when we ask. But then, they say that most do not know how to ask in the way that they can help.

Here is how: Find that place in the deepest knowing of your heart then connect with your desire through your imagination (no pushing with your mind, no yearning; just allow your heart to find its way to your own special brand of joy). Once you are swimming in the most delicious feeling of your creation, then let it go! Give it to God. Like a bird taking flight from its perch, set your heart's desire free. Know that as you let go, it is already done!

CLOSING COMMENTS

Spiritual activism in motion

I am so very humbled by the work at hand. It continues to amaze me how powerful a change can be created when all hearts align with the power and force of One. To illustrate my point, I'd like to share a recent experience. In the early part of the year, I gathered together with others who had been called to come together for healing and transformation. We didn't know exactly what was in front of us but there was an under-lying trust that whatever was to occur during our time together that it was all good.

I had put the word out, just a few weeks before; that I would be conducting a series of gatherings called Living the Miracle. Saturday, January 12th was the day set aside to explain the vision that I had received about how all that I had been led to create, especially these past seven years, was now falling into place. I was excited about the sharing, but the week before, my phone constantly rang with friends, former private session clients, a distraught relative, and frantic others seeking answers to questions or just wanting to be heard. I knew these calls were more important, in the moment, but they were also keeping me from putting my linear way of making sense of the vision on paper in preparation for the people soon to gather.

The day arrived and there we all were like a long lost family gathered together in the warmth and comfort of a familiar space. As I chattered on and on about what I had discovered it became obvious that my revelation was of no surprise to the others. Most had experienced similar visions or knowing of their own.

Something inside then said *enough*. Let the work begin. With that we were all called into the silence to ask for help and guidance for the purpose of what we had been called together to do. The Guides spoke to us about oppression and the very nature of freedom, of the holocaust, of love and forgiveness. They told us that we'd come to heal the breech of man's inhumanity to man, and by doing so were there to liberate ourselves from our own self imposed shackles. The time had finally come, they said, that we were to go out into the world and to speak our truth without fear. And so we began.

Two archangels and one ascended master presided. We were asked to listen to the names of each: Archangel Michael, Archangel Raphael, Ascended Master Nathaniel. As I spoke the names two times to provide us all the opportunity to be sure, which of the three one most resonated with. There were two among us who resonated with both Archangel Michael and Archangel Raphael, and one solely with Archangel Raphael. There were three aligned with Nathaniel and the rest with Archangel Michael.

We were then asked to receive a vision or to connect with a knowing of what blocked us; what held us back from experiencing our fullest expression of freedom before we commenced with our work. I immediately received a clear image of my hands being tied or bound together, left over right. As I looked down and studied them, I realized that I was inside a male body, dark, bearded face, very pale, emaciated. The emotional quality was one of being broken, demoralized.

After hearing from the others, I heard the word holocaust. Then I connected with what we were being asked to do. The power and force of oppression flushed through me, and with it a flood of vivid images came rushing into my awareness, so fast that the energy shook me to the core. I was suddenly watching as atrocities flashed before me. I thought I was going to throw-up from the reaction that my entire being continued to register from what was coming in. It took me a moment to find my center; to step back and away from the visceral emotion that was registering in my body. I focused my attention on remaining in the body while I re-centered myself in the higher vibrational current that was flowing through me.

Then I saw mental pictures of four among us standing back to back in a square configuration with the others facing. I sensed that the configuration of the four was to provide the strength to each as they stood together. So we began. Dachau, 1932. The four who were there were shown to me. All women but then they were two adults and two children. The essence of time was now pressing in. Get them into the configuration fast. As I pointed them out and asked the others to arrange themselves around the four, the memories and emotions flooded into my conscious awareness to varying degrees even as we began the formation. As I placed the first person shoulder to shoulder with the two that made up the adjacent sides of the square, she cried out in horror and sobbed uncontrollably. The fourth person was asked to step into the configuration to complete the square and with that she let out a wale of emotion that opened up an ocean of grief. The two others, at first, seemed a bit disoriented and confused, but I sensed their tears were coming from a deep sense of love and compassion. The pain was excruciating as the Guides continued to pulse the energy that we were transforming through my body. As I repeated their instructions to the group and followed the visual prompts, the energy began to shift from pain and suffering to sadness and remembering. The four were strong and true as they received the channeled energy exchanges from the others. As we were all asked to flow in light and color, Mark continued to channel in the vibration of healing as he played the piano just steps away.

The four were called to transform the multitudes of tortured, despondent souls while the others were asked to stand opposite the four in constantly moving configurations that prompted the one-on-one energy exchange. All were asked to channel the light of the archangels and Nathaniel and to focus on the feeling. *See the energy transforming. Look into the other's eyes; feel the love and peace inside. Touch the shoulder or the hand to transfer the energy from Nathaniel to the other. Speak the words of the angels through the voice of your own vessel.* As we moved, the music of transformation seemed to anticipate the stepped up vibration through the rhythms and tones.

As we channeled grace to one another, I saw the configuration of oppressor and oppressed, of past life connections among those helping and those receiving transform before my very eyes. Dark muted colors shifted into lighter, brighter hews of gold, and yellow; muddy, blood red bled into soft billowy pink, shadows of gray into liquid lavender. As the Guides asked us to serve as channels for freedom, for joy, for healing the hearts of all people everywhere, the crying that had transformed into sadness and peace, shifted into joyous movement and gratitude, of love and connection.

Archangel Raphael then asked us to channel grace through the power of feeling; Archangel Michael had us imagining the transformation through color; Nathaniel channeled his grace of higher knowledge by making a physical connection with others. Then it was time to create the ultimate movement to send oppression on its way. Man's inhumanity to man was asked to leave through the channel that had been opened by those of us in this configuration. *Align with joy; align your heart with freedom. Now imagine your reality of the world into creation. Dream it big, wide and truest to your heart. Create it now and know it is done. And so it is.*

The afternoon didn't stop there. Through the direction of these three Guides, each member of the group selflessly helped the other to release old hurt and pain, to allow more light, more grace, to enter into the body. One after another was asked to receive the gift of heart while the others witnessed her transformation as we were asked to channel the power of unconditional love, joyousness and freedom from the angels and the master. As each did, the others received the same gift in return.

I watched in awe and with a humble heart as the light imploded then amplified out with each acceptance of the other's gift. The power and force of grace flowed into the physical and amplified outwardly by those witnessing the other receive the magnitude of love that comes only when one opens with a total sense of trust.

The final participant was reluctant at first but with tender encouragement by those who had gone before her, onto our healing table she went. In came Jesus then the Mother Mary as she announced herself as this soul's guardian angel. The two who had been channeling the knowledge from Nathaniel were then asked to receive a gift from our sister rather than to give. With much grace, a gentle peace descended over the group. All were then asked to step back and amplify this person's field while the two holding the hands of the person on our healing table remained still. As we did, a shower of iridescent pink and lavender threaded with brilliant silver rained down upon everyone in the room.

The healing was then complete but it didn't stop there either. We were all famished, which then commenced a round of visiting in friendship and sharing that went on into the night.

The next afternoon, I heard from a friend, a shaman and sound healer. She had been driving across the country from Tucson to Denver. She called to check in and asked me what was going on? What caused the shift? During that same timeframe, she reported feeling dazed to the point of becoming disoriented. Trying to figure out what was happening, she felt her way into the grid and sensed my energy there with others. When I told her that we'd been asked to clear the energy of oppression through the eyes of those who lived during the time of the holocaust, she shuddered as she connected to the energy of what we had just experienced.

And so the mystical ways of working with the Guides continue. After yet another miraculous experience, I am thoroughly convinced that each and every one of us holds the key to creating a new a new world consciousness. We can change anything—absolutely anything—about our future as we open our heart and come together as one.

You are not unlike any other person who attended on Saturday. You hold the power to anything about your life in your heart and by doing so will change everything about your world. Every act of kindness, each loving thought toward another, counts. Just remember to accept yourself right where you are. Stop living in the past, forget beating up on yourself, and just say yes to love.

On Saturday, as the Guides showed me what each person was holding onto in order to help them release the pain, I saw that it was all self-inflicted. With each person who got up on our healing table, an enormous power was trying to make its way into the body but couldn't until the person was willing to let the other stuff go. It was not the pain caused by the deeds done by others that was the issue, but the resistance to fully accepting oneself that caused the block. Once each person accepted the gift that was so freely being given without condition, the floodgates opened. *It's alright; it's alright. We've got your back. It's alright. Let it go.* The words from the Guides are still echoing in my ears. *Let it all go.*

I encourage you to wake-up and reclaim your power now by simply making your heartfelt choice for joy, for freedom in any way you so desire. Only you will know if you have; no one else will and no one else can make that choice for you. By opening your heart, you will be welcoming enormous grace into your life and by doing so, you will be doing your part to change the world.

Definition of Terms

Activation
The activity of invoking one's heart to open for allowing more light, more grace, to enter into the body, mind and spirit.

Amplified field of grace
The affect on the body-mind continuum when one allows the energy of the cosmos to flow freely through the body and into the awareness of the soul having a human experience.

Andromeda galaxy and our sister planet
A galaxy that is spiral in formation, which resides near her sister planet and contains the identical DNA structures of the human matrix as that on earth, but without the interference of the star cultures. It's the mirror image to our earth but without the lower vibratory patterns of fear.

Angelic kingdoms
Those beings that reside in the higher realms of light whose purpose is to help humanity attain higher states of joy. These realms reside in parallel universes not unlike our own.

Archangels
Master teachers and guides; guardians and overseers of the angelic kingdoms.

Ascended masters
Beings of light who have had human incarnations and have broken through the third-dimensional density during their incarnations on earth and thereby ascended into the higher realms with their human matrix (light body) intact. These higher vibrational light beings have gained liberation from the physical. They represent the highest frequency that humanity

has achieved to date. Ascended masters amplify their collective light to humanity for the benefit of those beings who also wish to ascend.

Atamatine particles

The smallest force of light that forms consciousness.

Being(s) of light

Consciousness whose force of light is directed by divine intelligence. Where humanity is concerned, beings of light are souls who were born from the creator to one of the 32 star races. Some chose to remain with their original star tribe, and some chose to incarnate and serve as one of the 17 star tribes who first incarnated into the human species as early as 30-45,000 BC. Those who chose to remain outside the body (disincarnate) became known as helpers or guides to those who incarnated. Those who chose to incarnate into the human species and to adjoin with the human consciousness came to be known as humanity.

Body-consciousness

The aspect of the human species' consciousness, also known as the mind or the lower mind. This aspect of self is attuned to survival of the species, tribe, safety and security.

Central sun

The creator that governs this sector of the galaxy. The energetic force that moves and drives all of creation in this plane of existence.

Chakras

Seven centers of spiritual energy in the human body according to yoga philosophy. [Sanskrit cakram, wheel, circle]

Channel
A conduit or path through which electro-magnetic current can pass. A person, who serves as a channel, allows the higher vibratory patterns, which comprise consciousness, to make contact with, or to enter into or to merge with the body for gaining higher knowledge and/or communicating with non-physical beings. A way of seeing beyond the five senses; a way of seeing into the higher dimensional realms of light.

Devas
The overseers of the fairies who keep Mother Nature in balance.

Divine nature
The higher vibrational aspects of the soul, consciousness-individual or collective.

Electro-magnetic fields (also known as ley lines)
Field of energy caused by the iron core mass of the earth, and its rotational spin. This iron core emits magnetic ley lines that animals and people instinctually follow to get from point A to B. Birds following particular migratory paths year after year such as foot paths, roads, sacred sites, power spots and they are all built along ley lines. All matter emits an electro-magnetic field. The electro-magnetic fields of the human body can be sensed or felt as subtle energy.

Elohim
Non-physical beings of light that are here to help bring joy to the planet. These grand beings are actually mentioned in the Old Testament, by name, as being sent by God to serve as a reminder to humankind that we are light beings in a physical body.

Encodings
Pods or nodes of information that are imbedded in the human DNA structures. Encodings are activated by high frequencies of light, sound and color, which set off a multi-stage process of converting relatively objective sensory input into a subjectively meaningful experience.

Energetic gateways
Incremental shifts in vibration that create openings in global consciousness to allow humanity to adjust to the higher frequencies of light as the earth moves through time and space.

Energy centers
Vortexes of higher vibration caused by the earth's movement through time and space. Openings in the earth's time-continuum field. An amplification in the earth's electromagnetic field.

Entrainment
Lower frequencies of consciousness aligning and harmonizing with the higher.

Global consciousness
The consciousness of Humanity as a whole, together as one light-wave frequency.

Grid
A multi-dimensional, dynamic, ever changing, luminous field or matrix of consciousness, which interconnects everything and everyone. The grid of earth comprises seven grids, but for the sake of this body of knowledge, the author addresses the grid of humanity as one component of many aspects of the grid.

Group creation cycles
Patterns of energy shared by a group. which were formed by thought that fuels behavior.

Guides
Non-physical teachers, not to be confused with angels. Guides are helpmates or teachers who are here to help us fulfill our soul's mission on earth. Some people have a single guide (sometimes called Guardian angel) that stays with them always. Others have a group of guides that serve as an over-soul committee; guides who are here to lend us aid and comfort to help us accomplish what we have come to learn, and to do. Angels also serve as guides, but come and go depending on the particular learning or situation called forth. Guides may stick around from birth to death, or transition in and out from one phase of life to another.

Heaven (after-life)
A place we go to when we transition out of the body. Most of us imagine this place long before we get there, and at first we feel that we are home (like the home that we just left). But it's just a facade for where we really are.

Higher beings
Higher vibrational beings of light who are not of the physical but are just as real as we are.

Higher knowledge
Knowledge gained from direct knowing, direct experience beyond the five senses.

Higher state of consciousness
Frequencies of light that are accessed through direct knowing.

Human matrix
The human energy field that governs the human aspects of reality.

Human nature
The lower vibrational aspects of the human consciousness.

Humanity's creation cycles
Vibrational patterns that are formed by groups moving through the same soul-level experience.

Incarnational memories
Memories from other lifetimes, other realities, other world, other times.

Inner guidance
Listening to your heart; intuition that comes from the soul pulsing higher consciousness (higher vibrational energy) into the human energy system.

Interstellar language
Mode of communicating from one non-physical being to another through the projection of thought and feeling combined with symbols and sound.

Intergalactic star cultures
Inter-dimensional galaxies of souls who are grouped together around like traditions of learning and formations of consciousness. Star cultures comprise star races not unlike the differences found within the human race but are varied at infinitum.

Learning patterns
The soul's path that is still in play and has created a history by

how many times the soul has chosen a similar path; a line of inquiry that has created an energetic trail or history.

Lemuria

A cultural heritage of souls who bonded together around sound and healing. A time in humanity where souls achieved higher vibrational levels by striving to fully aligning with source.

Light beings

Souls who hail from star cultures, and are not human. Light beings are both non-physical and incarnate in the human body.

Light-wave frequency

A specific bandwidth of light that is created when sound is set into motion.

A wave can be characterized by its wavelength, but we can also characterize it by the frequency (how many wavelengths that pass a fixed point in a given time—think of sitting near the ocean and counting the number of waves passing in one minute) and the energy that it carries (think of a wave knocking you over in heavy surf).

Mass chaos

When humanity experiences radical movement. In our physical world mass chaos can be felt through our emotional body, and witnessed as economic, social, relational, or environmental crisis, for instance.

Mass consciousness

The majority of our human family that represents the prevailing state of consciousness.

Misguided compassion
Falling into someone else's drama.

Oneness of beingness
A state of stillness, unity, harmony, balance.

Non-linear time
A dimensional reality in space.

New paradigm leader
One who lives from the directive of the soul having a human experience.

Photon belt
A band of negatively charged ions that created a band of light, which then creates matter.

Pleiadians
Fifth dimensional beings who are here to help humanity ascend.

Quickening of light
A burst of light that occurs when the two bandwidths of light, or two rivers of consciousness become so polarized that the lower radically shifts to meet the higher. A burst of light to unite the whole.

Repatterning
Reconfiguring the human species.

Stargate
An energetic opening in time and space that is aligned with our galactic center, the core of the universe. The energy alignment requires us to reside in total stillness in order to pass through.

An inner passageway that will catapult the earth into an entirely different sector of the galaxy. The last time this stargate, the Star of David, was opened was 17,000 earth timed years ago.

Star children
Light beings whose human matrix has already been repatterned prior to birth. These children have full recall of who they are, why they are here, and what they have come to do. They are the new paradigm leaders of tomorrow.

Star cultures (Light cultures)
Nations of star beings who align with particular frequencies of light that can be described in human terms as love, truth, honor, compassion, etc.

Soul evolution
Consciousness that is moving up the vibrational spiral.

Soul fragments
Pieces or parts of the self that have been left behind, vibrationally, out of fear or trauma. Parts of the self unconsciously living parallel lives.

Soul groups
Souls who have similar missions and learning patterns.

Stellar language
The way that non-physical beings of light communicate to one another.

Third-dimensional reality
Earth that can be experienced through the five senses. The aspects of earth that are governed by the physical laws of nature.

Tectonic plates
The mass of matter that comprises the crust of the earth.

Vibration
Sound in motion.

Veil
The vibrational shift between the thrid-dimension and the higher realms.

Wave-form
Waves of energy that create a pattern; energy patterns that emanate from particular frequencies or bandwidths of light.

Resources

For more information about these simple yet power ways to heal your life, and transform the world, or to find more about how you can get involved in this global movement, see the web resources below:

Carol Fitzpatrick and the work of Arayu
Awakening to a New World Consciousness
www.carolfitzpatrick.com

Includes the following tools for transformative living and events:

- Global Conversations (inspired learning via group tele-sessions)
- Living the Miracle Series (healing circles, intuition workshops, energetic healing)
- Community Activation (soul-level global activism)
- Community Forum (creating a global village)
- Practitioner's Network (sharing what you know with others)

Planetary Awakening (Arayu Productions, LC)
www.planetaryawakening.org
- Music for healing and transformation
- Living in the Miracle Series (Music)

BOOKS